The Winona LaDuke Reader

A Collection of Essential Writings

The Winona LaDuke Reader

A Collection of Essential Writings

Foreword by Ralph Nader

Voyageur Press

Edited by Margret Aldrich
Designed by Maria Friedrich
Printed in Hong Kong

03   04   05   06   5   4   3   2

Library of Congress Cataloging-in-Publication Data

LaDuke, Winona.
  The Winona LaDuke reader : a collection of essential writings / by
foreword Ralph Nader.
       p. cm.
Includes bibliographical references and index.
  ISBN 0-89658-573-5 (pbk. : alk. paper)
  1. LaDuke, Winona—Literary collections. 2. LaDuke, Winona—Political
activity. 3. Ojibwa women—Politics and government. 4. Indigenous
peoples—Ecology—United States. 5. Indian business enterprises—
United States. 6. Indians of North America—Land tenure. 7. Indians of
North America—Government relations. I. Title.
  E99.C6 L255 2002
  973.04'97'0092—dc21
                                    2002001884

Published by Voyageur Press, Inc.
123 North Second Street, P.O. Box 338, Stillwater, MN 55082 U.S.A.
651-430-2210, fax 651-430-2211
books@voyageurpress.com
www.voyageurpress.com

Educators, fundraisers, premium and gift buyers, publicists, and marketing managers: Looking for creative products and new sales ideas? Voyageur Press books are available at special discounts when purchased in quantities, and special editions can be created to your specifications. For details contact the marketing department at 800-888-9653.

This book has been printed using soy-based inks on paper made with fiber from sustainable forests.

Contents

Contents

Native Traditions

Women's Issues

Politics and the Presidency

Fiction and Poetry

About the Author

Foreword

Foreword

This is a book mostly about the peoples of the First Nations. A book about a people who almost lost out to genocide but survived barely one hundred years ago. A book about the near death of culture and its resurgence. A book about the theft of land and the restoration of land rights. A book about the beauty of native lands and the destruction of land's use by mining goliaths and garbage giants. A book about sacred treaties and broken treaties. A book about crushed spirits and resilient spirits. A book about recovery and restoration from poverty and dispossession and exile. A book about traditions that bind and uplift, about the buffalo, industrial hemp, and self-reliance that comes from self-determination. A book about a rooted sense of place and the connectedness that comes therefrom. A book about resistance and rebirth, about women building futures, about politics and presidential campaigns, about a talented writer of fiction and poetry, about a farmer and justice fighter, a mother and a voice for indigenous people around the globe. This is a gripping book about matters of importance by Winona LaDuke. Savor, digest, reflect, and see if you can contain your moral indignation so that the fearless hope and exultation of the human spirit in these pages can capture your moral imagination—leaving you no option but to engage!

Ralph Nader
Washington, D.C.
December 2001

Native Environmentalism

The Wind that Blows over Our Ancestors: Nature's Power, Enron and Native Lands

Appeared in EARTH ISLAND JOURNAL, *Fall 2001.*

"These mountains are very important to . . . my people. On these mountains along the Columbia River is about one of the only places left more or less untouched for some of our Native foods and medicines. All of our upper valley . . . have all become farmlands. So what we have left are these mountains."
—Chief Johnny Jackson of the Cascade Klickitat

It is here, on some high bluffs that overlook the Columbia River that our ancestors lie resting in the arms of their mother, looking up towards the heavens. Here golden eagles nest and medicinal plants work their way up the soil towards the sky. It is also here that the Enron Corporation seeks to build its 15,000-acre windfarm. It is a strange and twisted tale in which ardent environmentalists and the Yakama Indian Nation have found themselves opposing an alternative energy bid.

In the days before the dams, 16 million fish would thrash their way up the Nch'I'Wana (the Big River) to spawn. The giant Dalles Dam on the Columbia put Celilo Falls under water. These falls were the epicenter of the Nch'I'Wana Native community's cultural and spiritual practice. Today, among other modern depredations, is the blight of the Hanford Nuclear reservation, with its radioactive leaks that find their way to the river. And now there is a new assault on all that remains of the river valley—windmills.

Winds rolling over the Columbia Hills average a constant 20 miles per hour. Over the past seven years, various incarnations of a huge wind project have appeared in the minds of developers as they look at the Columbia Hills. In 1994, the Kenetech Windpower Company approached Klickitat County and secured leases from private landowners to roughly 15,000 acres for a windpower site. The plan was appealed by the Yakama Nation and the Columbia Gorge Audubon Society and Kenetech's project stalled. The company's stock tumbled from $30 a share to $1 a share in the span of 12 months. In 1996, Kenetech filed for Chapter 11 bankruptcy.

Enter Enron, a broker of capital in the energy market with an innate ability to sense opportunity. Enron picked up Kenetech's assets—which included the Klickitat County Board of Adjusters' conditional use permits for a 345-turbine wind project in the Columbia Gorge. The proposed 15,000-acre industrial windfarm with its rows of 200-foot-high turbines was no small project. The entire project would produce, on average, 30 to 50 megawatts. At full capacity, the system could generate 115 megawatts. Kenetech's environmental impact assessment (EIA) indicated that up to 382 acres of land would be directly impacted by roads and turbine placement and that up to 10,000 loads of gravel would be required to build the site.

THE YAKAMA

The Yakama Nation does not oppose wind energy. In fact, the Yakama have expressed an interest in wind development in several locations within their nation. The problem is that the Columbia Gorge site is one of the most revered areas in Yakama and Klickitat territory. The Yakama's oral history supports this traditional use of the area from time immemorial.

The Yakama Nation and the reservation are comprised of a number of separate indigenous peoples, a consequence of the forced relocations and military policies of the U.S. government. Included in those peoples are the Klickitat, who have their own traditional chiefs.

One of those leaders is Johnny Jackson, a slight and soft-spoken man whose wisps of hair and wiry frame belie the potency of his words. Jackson recalls the words of his ancestor Ta-wa-tash, who had a vision "that two men would come down the river from the east. One was a greedy man and one was a good man, but Ta-wa-tash did not know which was which. So he did not trust either of them and would not speak to them. My ancestor saw in his vision that when the men came they could corrupt the land. He said there was going to be trouble here. And then the war came, and Governor Stevens brought his army, and the Klickitat people fought back, and the Cascade people fought with them, and the land was divided for the new people."

Those men were Lewis and Clark. The war, known as the Klickitat War, was fought in the Columbia Hills. The 1855 treaty ending the war removed the Klickitat and the Cascade people from the land.

"The Klickitat War was right back of them mountains in the valley of the Klickitat," Johnny remembers. "Hard to make them understand that our people are buried there. They took them up to the mountains so they'd be closer to the heavens. That's got a lot to do with the sacredness of that mountain."

The Klickitat, like many other Native people, have specific teachings about these ancestors, ones that they plan on keeping. "Within our teachings, we say that we don't disturb the people when they are in the ground. Because the Creator says that 'when you arrive to me, I want you to answer to me with everything I give you,' and that's why this land is so important and sacred with our elders." The area is also host to other religious sites, including places for fasting and for harvesting of traditional and medicinal plants.

The Klickitat and Yakama people are not alone in their opposition to the wind facility. The Audubon Society considers the Columbia River Flyway one of the most important raptor areas in the Northwest. The project's Environmental Impact Statement (EIS) documents 34 Special Status Species, seven Washington Department of Fish and Wildlife Priority Habitats and numerous high-quality native plant communities within the project area. The concrete will obliterate most of the plant and animal communities in the area and the windfarm will literally shred the raptors.

ENRON'S END RUN

Now meet the adversary: Enron. Not actually much of a power producer, Enron's profits are in the financing of energy and the brokering of resources.

Enron has done pretty well for itself. In 2000 alone, Enron's wholesale trading and services business reported a pre-tax income of $777 million, nearly three times that of the previous year. Total net income of the corporation jumped an amazing 32 percent in 2000 with revenues of $101 billion, up 150 percent. These increases have been reflected in the stock exchange: Enron's stock has increased 175 percent over the last two years.

The company is rumored to be North America's most powerful energy broker. "Enron is at the top of a group of corporations that has the ear of George W. Bush," says Craig McDonald, Executive Director of Texans for Public Justice. The Center for Public Integrity reports that Enron was Dubya's leading patron in Austin, donating more than $500,000 to the governor. Enron also supplied its corporate jets for Bush's presidential campaign and gave $250,000 to underwrite the Republican Party's national convention.

ENRON GOES NATIVE

Sensing the potential of Indian country and feeling the need to shore up some of its relationships (particularity around the issues of rights and access to oil and gas lines), Enron put together an "Indian desk." Jerry Pardilla, a Penobscott and director of the National Tribal Environmental Council, was lured away from the NTEC to head the Indian group at Enron.

Pardilla saw the potential of a collaboration with Enron to help tribes "build their energy infrastructure and creating means for tribes to build their economies." Pardilla points not only to the energy resources held by many tribes, but also notes that many tribes are large purchasers of residential energy.

Enron's interest in the Native American desk, however, seems to have been short-lived. The desk was dissolved less than a year after its creation.

Enron's interest in the indigenous communities has sparked interest in a number of quarters, including at environmental groups like Friends of the Earth (FOE) and Project Underground. Both became concerned with Enron's behavior in the Bolivian-Brazilian Cuibià project. In 1999, FOE used a shareholders resolution to ask Enron to report on the environmental and human rights implications in its worldwide operations. The resolution gained nearly a nine percent "yes" vote and secured a meeting between FOE and Enron officials. In late 2000, Progressive Assets Management, on behalf of the Solidago Foundation, asked to join FOE's campaign and expanded the resolution to include Enron's impacts on "biodiversity and indigenous peoples."

"We recognized that we had Enron in our portfolio and began to find that they couldn't pass our social screen. That began the process of formulating a shareholder action," explains David Rosenmiller, executive director of the Solidago Foundation. A bit more research found that others had also been disturbed by Enron's apparent lack of interest in "biodiversity, indigenous and human rights." By the spring, Solidago was joined by Domini Social Investments, FOE, Trillium Assets Management (on behalf of the Oneida Nation) and the General Pension Board of the United Methodist Church in the expanded corporate resolution. Solidago's concerns expanded as they continued their work with the Indigenous Environmental Network (IEN), a national Native organization with Johnny Jackson on the board. "Because of IEN's involvement, we decided that we should take a lead on filing a shareholders' resolution. We were concerned, as a grantmaker, that Enron was doing damage to a community that we worked in."

Bullitt Foundation Director (and Earth Day pioneer) Denis Hayes speaks for many environmentalists in the region. "I can't believe that with all the windpower in this region, we can't find ways to put up projects that benefit both the tribes and the economy," Hayes says. To most, however, the project remains a sore reminder of all that has been lost—and the critical importance of what still remains. Johnny Jackson views the situation through the eyes of the ancestors, today's youth and the generations still ahead.

"When something is in the ground there, they put into the soil no headstones, markers, concrete, etcetera so they can see heaven," Jackson says. "We're not against windpower, if you have it in the right area. We just want to have it in the right place. There's Horse Heaven and Mabton; the wind blows just as strong there. Let them put it there."

The Blackfeet Wind: Apatew

Appeared in E/THE ENVIRONMENTAL MAGAZINE,
July/August 2001.

The wind whips through the passes of the Rocky Mountain front blowing swiftly and endlessly across the Blackfeet, or *Pikuni*, reservation in northern Montana. The land rises from the austere prairie to the towering mountain range today comprising much of Glacier National Park—lands within the treaty area of the Blackfoot Confederacy. Borders, landownership, neighbors, and government policies may change, but one thing is certain: the wind will blow through the passes, and through Pikuni territory.

The Siyeh Development Corporation is under the direction of Dennis Fitzpatrick, a Blackfeet tribal member, who today leads the development of the tribal wind energy project. A present pilot project powers Browning municipal facilities at the heart of the reservation. New projects will power more homes and hopefully put the Blackfeet squarely into the alternative energy market. "The wind project of Siyeh represents a project which is in keeping with Blackfeet culture, and is a resource which will provide for future generations of Blackfeet," Fitzpatrick explains. By the fall of next year, the Blackfeet hope to produce enough power to supply 6,000 homes.

This fall, SeaWest Wind Power, a San Diego based company with a track record of producing 544 megawatts of electricity in Wyoming, California, the United Kingdom and Spain, joined with the Siyeh Development Corporation to put up a new power project. The project will consist of 15 wind turbines, and construction is slated to begin in May of 2001. The turbines will provide thirty construction jobs and four or five permanent jobs in the Browning area, as well as an estimated $250,000 per year to the tribal government once the project is producing, hopefully by October of 2001.

The wind projects of Siyeh are aptly placed: the Blackfeet reservation is considered to have some of the greatest wind energy potential in the United States. The Great Plains is considered potentially the Saudi Arabia of wind energy, with enough potential power to provide up to one third of present U.S. electrical consumption needs. According to the American Wind Energy Association, Montana itself has enough wind potential to produce 116,000 megawatts of electricity; North Dakota enough energy from Class 4 and higher winds to supply 36 percent of the electricity needs of the lower 48 states.

Wind energy is now the fastest-growing renewable energy source, with 35 percent more wind generation capacity in 1998 than in 1997, or enough to power more than a million households in the U.S. alone. At the current rate for installation of wind energy, the World Energy Council projects that wind power could provide energy for between 60 and 158 million people globally, even at U.S. consumption levels.

In keeping with Blackfeet and other Native traditions, wind energy is also a renewable resource, and a source of clean, nonpolluting electricity. In 1990, California's wind power plants offset the emission of more than 2.5 billion pounds of CO_2 and 15 million pounds of other pollutants that would have otherwise been produced. (It would take a forest of 90 million to 175 million trees to provide the same air quality.) "Gaining electricity from the winds here on the reservation has been talked about for many years," Tribal Chairman Earl Old Person said. "We are gratified that this idea has finally become a reality." It is a small start, but a beginning, and it is a future that has endless possibilities. Governments, borders, and people may change, but the wind will always blow through Blackfeet territory.

Dioxin, Incinerators and Breast Milk

Appeared in OJIBWE AKIING, *May 31, 2000.*

Violet Yeaten, an Inupiat, is an environmental specialist for her remote village of Port Graham in Alaska. For her, just eating is now increasingly dangerous, as pollutants from the United States and elsewhere end up in her ecosystem, and subsequently her body. Some "80% of our people's diet is made up of our traditional foods. On an average, our people eat between 12 and 15 fish meals per week. When we eat the whole fish, we consume all the concentrated chemicals."

Just east of her, Inuit communities in the newly created Canadian province of Nunavut find they are similarly challenged. A recent report notes, "Although there are no significant sources of dioxin in Nunavut or within 500 kilometers of its boundaries, dioxin concentrations in Inuit mothers' milk are twice the levels observed in southern Quebec." That's the kicker: Mother's milk is sort of the sacred essence of motherhood, yet today, this milk— and even the placentas themselves—are becoming increasingly contaminated with pollutants, compromising the health of families and those yet to come.

The toxic substances found in the Arctic are known as Persistent Organic Pollutants, or POPs, and represent a dangerous combination of pesticides and unwanted byproducts of production such as dioxin and industrial chemicals. The chemicals are long lived and have a tendency to migrate towards colder regions in the north through air and water currents. The chemicals accumulate in the body's fat tissues, and become concentrated higher in the food chain. The chemicals are of special risk to children, whose delicate systems are in the primary stages of development.

Ironically, it is the emissions from two almost adjacent incinerators that have found their way directly to the Arctic. With the help of new, sophisticated tracking mechanisms, it has been discovered that it is indeed the residues of our own garbage in the breast milk of these women.

Using a sophisticated model developed by the federal government, a research team studied sources. Researchers from the North American Commission for Environmental Cooperation, or NACEC, studied some 44,000 sources of dioxin in North America. The researchers tracked them into the pristine ecosystem of Nunavat. Nunavut, an almost entirely Inuit region of Canada, is considered an ideal test ground, since there are no significant sources of dioxin in the territory, nor within 300 miles of its boundaries.

Of particular interest, in the top ten sources of dioxin found in the Arctic, was that coming from an Xcel Energy–owned incinerator at Red Wing, Minnesota, with a similar incinerator just south at French Island in LaCrosse, Wisconsin.

Overall, U.S. facilities, primarily medical waste and garbage incinerators, were found in the NACEC study to contribute between 70 and 82 percent of all dioxin deposited at the eight test locations in Nunavut. Canadian facilities, by comparison, contributed 11 to 25 percent, and Mexican sources, largely from backyard burning of trash, contributed between 5 and 11 percent.

There are a number of initiatives underway to reduce the toxic emissions released in both Canada and the U.S., including new EPA regulations, which should reduce dioxin emissions by 90 percent from municipal waste incinerators and 95 percent from medical incinerators. At some incinerators, however, like the incinerator at French Island, there has been a bit of dodging of the more stringent regulations. Until October of this past year, the EPA allowed the French Island Incinerator at LaCrosse to be on sort of an honor system of reporting how much dioxin-producing garbage it was burning. Then, a tip off by Midwest Environmental Advocates pushed the government to take a closer look. That look caused the EPA to redesignate the incinerator as a large incinerator—meaning that it should comply with more stringent emissions rules by December of 2000.

Not surprisingly, the federal government has not enforced the law and Xcel has not brought its incinerator into compliance. In response, Midwest Environmental Advocates has put the company on notice that it will sue them if they continue to violate the law. The Ho Chunk Nation has also weighed in on this issue. On April 3, the Ho Chunk Legislature passed a resolution calling on the Environmental Protection Agency to require Xcel's facility to close until it reduces its toxic emissions.

This past December, other moves were also underway. A delegation of Native people from North America traveled to Johannesburg, South Africa, seeking to address the international transfers of toxins through a United Nations Global Treaty. Over 120 countries, including the United States, began final negotiations on a global and legally binding treaty for the elimination of toxic substances. The final signing of the treaty is scheduled for May of this year in Stockholm, Sweden.

The Native representatives included Violet Yeatin, Evon Peter, Charlotte Caldwell, and Tom Goldtooth from the Indigenous Environmental Network. All went to discuss the more than 100,000 chemicals that have been introduced globally into the environment since the 1940s, and the disproportionate impacts of these contaminants in Native communities engaged in subsistence cultures. The United Nations Environmental Program mandated the world's governments to create a treaty banning the worst of the pollutants, and today that treaty focuses on twelve of the most deadly chemicals, including PCBs, DDT, and other pesticides. Dioxin is one additional byproduct of industry, which, since 1985, has been considered by the EPA the most potent carcinogen ever tested in a laboratory.

Evon Peter of Arctic Village, Alaska was one of the delegates saying, "Our land is a sinkhole for these contaminants." The short- and long-term solution is known. "Elimination is the only solution to stop the northern flow of these chemicals, which are disrupting the delicate balance of nature here in the Arctic," explains Pam Miller, director of Alaska Community Action on Toxics, based in Anchorage.

Over 250 tribes have approved an NCAI resolution supporting the elimination of the so-called POPs, and over forty tribal governments have passed resolutions and subsequently strong treaty negotiations calling for the elimination of POPs. The treaty signing is considered by most activists, including Pam Miller, as an unprecedented opportunity to stop the northward flow of chemicals.

There was, after intense negotiations, quite a set of agreements by those parties participating. Included in the final wording was the goal of elimination of POPs as a centerpiece, utilizing strong precautionary language in various forms in the preamble, objectives, and elsewhere, obliging developed countries to provide financial support for less developed countries in POPs elimination, and stressing pollution elimination as well as other essential components. This treaty must now be approved by the U.S. Congress, hopefully prior to the May meeting in Stockholm.

Meanwhile, back in the Great Lakes region, we have our own quandary. Fish from Lake Michigan show levels of dioxin more than 100,000 times higher than the surrounding water, plants and sediment. However, two thirds of the dioxin exposure to the public comes from eating milk, cheese, and beef, a result of cows eating contaminated food crops. The pulp and paper industry ranks as the leading source of dioxin exposure to the public—a direct consequence of the use of chlorine bleaching in their processes. Second after that is waste incineration—ironically, Minnesota burns three million tons a year, more than any state except New York. Those waste incinerators are spewing out dioxin that ends up in pastures and on food crops, which eventually end up in our own bellies.

Back to the problems of Xcel and the incinerators at Red Wing and French Island in LaCrosse. So now with the wonders of modern technology, we find that we can spew poison to the remotest regions of the globe, and can actually test the breast milk of women in Nunavut and find our own garbage. What about the women in

LaCrosse, Red Wing, or Minneapolis? Thus far, we've not taken much interest in such sophisticated testing, but considering all the dairies, cheese, and food that is produced in the St. Croix River Valley, one might take a wee interest in our own contamination.

There are, of course, solutions. Elimination is at the front end of the proposals. That would mean that proposals to build more incinerators should be canned—in fact, since 1985, over 300 separate proposals to build incinerators have been defeated or put on hold. There are a few myths that are beginning to unravel, which likely contribute to the lack of ambition in building the incinerators. For instance, incinerators do not make waste disappear—they reduce it to ash and atmospheric emissions, both of which are still incredibly dangerous. In fact, up to 40% of the waste is still around. Nor will the incinerators solve our landfill problems. As far as medical waste (actually the highest source of dioxin), only 10% or less of a typical hospital's waste stream is potentially infectious, according to Washington-based Essential Action. And that can be sterilized with heat or microwaves. In the end, the production of dioxin from the incineration of the waste may be causing more health problems than the waste itself.

On the other hand, there is the slightly more challenging, and less based on denial, set of solutions—those would be recycling, re-using, and eliminating many of the things we send flying to the dump and to the incinerator.

Far away, in Johannesburg, in the halls of Congress, and in Sweden, there will be work underway to negotiate this Treaty on Persistent Organic Pollutants. I am hopeful it is positive work. Here at home, our own incinerators need a clean up. That would be our work.

Nuclear Waste ... and Native Land

Appeared in EARTH ISLAND JOURNAL, *Spring 2000.*

What weighs thirty tons, has as much radiation as 200 Hiroshima bombs, and is projected to pass within a half-mile of your home? The answer: A canister of high-level radioactive waste, traveling from one of 109 aging U.S. nuclear power plants to Yucca Mountain, Nevada—the proposed "final resting place" for America's most deadly garbage.

It is to this mountain, at the heart of the Western Shoshone Nation—a place of deep spiritual significance to Shoshone and Paiute peoples—that the federal government hopes to send 98 percent of the U.S.'s radioactive waste generated during the entire Nuclear Age.

Despite heated criticism by Native and environmental forces, Yucca Mountain remains the only site under government study for the permanent disposal of high-level nuclear waste. The Department of Energy (DOE) has already dumped $3 billion into the projected $35 billion project. Last August, the DOE released its draft Environmental Impact Statement (EIS) for a proposed Nuclear Waste Repository at Yucca Mountain. This marks another step toward opening the dump by the projected completion date of 2010.

More than 200 grassroots groups—Native and non-native—have joined forces to challenge the EIS because it largely sidesteps the issue of transport. High-level waste designated for Yucca Mountain will be moving on U.S. highways and train routes by the front yards of more than 50 million Americans. Transportation of this waste poses a huge public health risk. DOE studies project a rate of one accident per 343 shipments. That translates into, at the very minimum, 268 accidents over the next 30 years, as up to 90,000 shipments of nuclear waste make their way to Yucca Mountain.

The Shoshone are also asking people to support Native land rights issues raised by the EIS. What is continually glossed over by decision-makers—and ignored in the EIS—is the fact that Yucca Mountain lies within Newe Sogobia, land guaranteed to the Western Shoshone Nation by U.S. treaty. The Shoshone want the DOE off their land, and their mountain restored to them.

Upholding the treaty can be an important political and legal tool to stop the dump, but the Shoshone face extreme geographic and political isolation. Without sufficient public support, they fear their voices will not be heard. A statement by Rep. Lindsey Graham (R-SC) added a note of racism to the refrain of low-level logic. According to Graham, "God made Yucca Mountain for the express purpose of storing high level nuclear waste. There's nothing within 100 miles of the place."

The DOE study admits that the steel canisters inside Yucca Mountain will eventually leak. Nonetheless, the DOE plans to store more than 70,000 tons of spent nuclear fuel in miles of tunnels 1,000 feet underground. At least one of the more than 10,000 storage canisters is expected to fail within the next thousand years. After 10,000 years, the *New York Times* reports, all the canisters may degrade.

What may be worse is that an earthquake at Yucca Mountain could cause groundwater to surge into the storage area, forcing dangerous amounts of plutonium into the atmosphere and contaminating the water supply. This is not an unlikely scenario, given that the area is a seismic minefield. Over the last 20 years, more than 621 earthquakes have been recorded in the area, at a magnitude of 2.5 or higher. This may be why the nuclear industry has opposed setting any groundwater radiation standards for the facility, saying it could threaten the entire project.

The Nuclear Waste Policy Act of 1992 (NWPA) requires that

radiation standards for the facility must be set by the Environmental Protection Agency (EPA). The EPA has proposed a 15-millirem-per-year exposure limit for people living near the site, but environmental groups say this is inadequate for the protection of human health.

Shoshone groups are adamant that any additional radiation risk to their community is unacceptable. The Shoshone Nation—site of the U.S. Nevada nuclear testing facility—is already the most-bombed nation on Earth. The Shoshone suffer from widespread cancer, leukemia and other diseases because of fallout from more than 600 atomic explosions in their territory. To add to this risk is outlandish injustice.

In the meantime, pending congressional legislation would rewrite the NWPA to strip the EPA of all authority to set radiation standards at Yucca Mountain. Rewriting the NWPA has been attempted—and defeated—for the past five years. These proposed rewrites would pretty much "throw radiation standards out," says Michael Marriot of the Nuclear Information Resource Service in Washington, D.C. With the stroke of a pen, such legislation would miraculously overcome most of the public health hurdles to the Yucca Mountain project.

Over the past few years, the members of the Nuclear Energy Institute (i.e., your electric utilities) have given about $12.8 million to their congressional delegations to encourage pro-nuclear law that would put an end to their nuclear waste dilemma.

The latest revision of the NWPA allows onsite storage of nuclear waste outside power plants until Yucca Mountain or an "interim" dump site is ready. If the nuclear industry has its way, that "interim dump" may be built in Utah, on Skull Valley Goshute reservation land. The bill also provides for the federal government (meaning taxpayers) to take ownership of the waste and accept liability for it. What this means is that the utility companies will be abdicating responsibility for waste they created over the past 30 years.

Under the Wild Rice Moon

Appeared in the MINNEAPOLIS STAR TRIBUNE,
September 19, 1999.

PONSFORD, MINN.—It is the wild rice moon in the North
Country, and the lakes teem with harvest and a way of life.

"Ever since I was bitty, I've been ricing," says Spud Fineday
of Ice Cracking Lake. Spud, with his wife, Tater, this year started
ricing at Cabin Point, and then moved to Big Flat Lake, lakes within
the borders of the Tamarac National Wildlife Refuge.

"Sometimes we can knock four to five hundred pounds a day,"
he says, explaining that he alternates the jobs of "poling and
knocking" with Tater, a.k.a. Vanessa Fineday.

The Finedays, like many other Anishinaabeg from White Earth
and other reservations in the region, continue to rice to feed
their families, to "buy school clothes and fix cars," and get ready
for the ever-returning winter. The wild rice harvest of the
Anishinaabeg not only feeds the body; it feeds the soul, continuing a tradition that is generations old for these people of the lakes
and rivers of the North.

The ricing tradition that Spud Fineday has practiced since
childhood is a community event, a cultural event that ties the
community in all its generations to all that is essentially
Anishinaabeg, Ojibwe.

As the story is told, Nanaboozhoo, the cultural hero of the
Anishinaabeg, was introduced to rice by fortune and a duck.

"One evening Nanaboozhoo returned from hunting, but he
had no game. . . . As he came toward his fire, he saw a duck sitting on the edge of his kettle of boiling water. After the duck
flew away, Nanaboozhoo looked into the kettle and found wild

rice floating upon the water, but he did not know what it was. He ate his supper from the kettle, and it was the best soup he had ever tasted.

"Later, he followed in the direction the duck had taken, and came to a lake full of *manoomin*. He saw all kinds of ducks and geese and mudhens, and all the other water birds eating the grain. After that, when Nanaboozhoo did not kill a deer, he knew where to find food to eat. . . ."

Manoomin, or wild rice, is a gift given to the Anishinaabeg from the creator, and is a centerpiece of the nutrition and sustenance for our community. The word *manoomin* contains a reference to the creator, who is known as *Gichi Manidoo*. In the earliest of teachings of Anishinaabeg history, there is a reference to wild rice known as the food that grows upon the water, the food the ancestors were told to find so we would know when to end our migration to the west.

It is this profound and historic relationship that is remembered in the wild rice harvest on the White Earth and other reservations—a food that is uniquely ours, and a food that is used in our daily lives, our ceremonies and in our thanksgiving feasts. It is that same wild rice that, ironically, exemplifies the worldwide debate on issues of biodiversity, culture and globalization.

The crispness of early fall touches my face as we paddle through the rice on Blackbird Lake. Four eagles fly overhead, and a flock of geese moves gracefully across the sky. Through the rice, I can see officers of the law, ensconced in their work. They are ricing. Eugene Clark, a.k.a. Beebzo (Ogema mayor and Becker County deputy sheriff), and John MacArthur, a Mahnomen County sheriff, are Anishinaabeg, and they are police officers. Today they are continuing the harvesting tradition. As they move swiftly through the rice bed, MacArthur is knocking and Clark is poling.

Both men began ricing as teenagers. "We're out here to eat, not to make money," they tell me. They are ricing for their families. On this day, they bring in a couple of hundred pounds of green rice.

Ronnie Chilton is working at the Native Harvest (White Earth Land Recovery Project) rice mill. He too has a long connection to ricing. "I've riced my whole life, most of the time with my dad." He considers ricing a part of his family's tradition as well, and wishes he were on a lake, even as I am interviewing him.

It's said that there are fewer rice buyers this year on the reservation, although Beebzo maintains that "there were more people at the rice permit drawing [for Tamarac Lakes] than vote in most elections." There are also lots of ricers. By two weeks into ricing season, Native Harvest bought from 30 or 40 ricers.

There is always a debate about the rice crop—this year is deemed by many to be better than the last few. However, Big Rice Lake, in the northwest corner of the reservation, is seen as sort of the Shangri-La of rice—the paradise for ricers. A perceived reduction in the crop on that lake causes opinions to fly. The reasons are speculative: high water levels, agricultural herbicide runoff, the usual suspects.

"It used to be you would get lost in the rice on that lake," Russell Warren, a 20-year rice processor, tells me. "They used to have to put flags up at the landings, so you could find your way back. It's the fertilizer, and the runoff, that ruins the crop."

As with farmers anywhere, there's much discussion as to the status of the crop, the international markets and their subsequent impact on local production and the preservation (or lack of preservation) by state officials of the water quality around the rice crop. There may well be a diminished interest in the Native-harvested rice, as the big food companies—Stouffer's, Uncle Ben's, Gourmet House and the others—drive a paddy wild rice market, the vast majority of it out of state.

MIRROR OF CHANGE

This fall, the state's Agriculture Department discusses a probable 10 percent decline of the farmers in this northwest region, attributed to the economy, the weather and yet another bad year. I am struck by how the transformation of agriculture from family farms to large corporate farms is mirrored in the wild rice industry. Consumer and biodiversity scholars maintain that the recent enactment of multilateral trade agreements (i.e., GATT) means that, for the first time, multinational corporations are within reach of controlling the planet's genetic wealth. Indeed, this is reflected in food production, processing and marketing, where today corporate agribusiness manufactures and markets over 95 percent of the food in the United States. We increasingly rely upon a smaller group of sources for food.

The concentrated control over not only food production but the seeds themselves has become a significant controversy, as local varieties disappear and farmers lose control over their seeds. Patents are bought and sold, and the actual life itself becomes a market commodity. Many of the seed companies have been acquired by multinational chemical corporations. According to the most recent issue of *Consumer Reports* magazine, Monsanto, for example, has spent nearly $8 billion since 1996, purchasing seed companies. Dupont is buying Pioneer Hi-Bred. According to the Worldwatch Institute, these combined purchases make Dupont and Monsanto, respectively, the world's largest and second-largest seed companies.

A similar concentration is underway in the wild rice industry. Minnesota's paddy wild rice production began aggressively in 1968, representing roughly 20 percent of the state's crop by the harvest of that year. Paddy rice production increased the available quantities of wild rice, and by 1973 had increased the yield to some 4 million pounds. The increase in production, and interest by the larger corporations (i.e., Uncle Ben's, Green Giant and General Foods), in many ways skewed perceptions of wild rice and altered the market for traditional wild rice. In 1977 the Minnesota Legislature designated wild rice as the official state grain.

That was perhaps the kiss of death for the lake wild rice crop. With an outpouring from state coffers, the University of Minnesota began aggressively to develop a domesticated version of wild rice. By the early 1980s, cultivated wild rice had outstripped the indigenous varieties in production. Ironically, Minnesota lost control over wild rice production to California, which by 1983 produced more than 8.3 million pounds, compared with Minnesota's 5 million pounds. By 1986, more than 95 percent of the wild rice harvested was paddy grown, the vast majority produced in northern California. When the glut of wild rice hit the market in 1986, the price plummeted, not only affecting the newly emerging domesticated market but devastating the Native wild rice economy.

Now, ricer Joe LaGarde, the White Earth Tribal Council and other Indians are concerned not only with economics but also with biology. "Man thinks he can improve on something that's been developing over thousands of years. Eventually, he might end up with nothing," LaGarde says. He's concerned about the genetic strains of paddy rice and their possible impact on the lake rice crop. Every ricer knows that the rice is distinct between lakes.

"There's sand-bottom rice (usually shorter grains), muddy-bottom rice, all of that," Joe explains. "We're concerned about the possible [crossbreeding] of these 'hybrid cultivated varieties' with our lake rice." The White Earth Tribal Council even wrote a letter to the University of Minnesota asking it to "quit messing with the rice," Joe says.

He is worried, and remembers a childhood spent ricing at Mitchell Dam on the Refuge, camping for a week or so. He'd like to keep that memory a part of a living culture, not a relic of the pre-industrialized agriculture age.

Meanwhile, the wild rice market now serves consumers who demand a big black grain, rice that boils up exactly at the same pace as white rice. That market is huge. Jerry Schochenmaier is the general manager of Indian Harvest Wild Rice Co., in Bemidji, Minnesota. An affable fellow, Schochenmaier is a major promoter of wild rice, and is interested in the preservation of the wild harvesting of the rice, and the Native community.

Interestingly enough, Indian Harvest, which is the nation's largest wild rice processor, is pretty much an operation with few "Indians," although some lake rice is in its program. The plants and operations, for the most part, are in California, where this year Schochenmaier expects to process around 75 percent of the national crop. Indian Harvest reflects the national trends and market in wild rice, which remains focused on the cultivated varieties.

Schochenmaier has been in the wild rice business since the fall of 1997. In 1989, Indian Harvest processed some 1 million pounds. By 1994, production was up to 6 million pounds, increasing to a projected 13 million pounds this year. "The rice mill was originally designed to be in Bemidji"—the footings for the building are still at Bemidji's industrial park—"but California was identified as the place to produce rice if you were going into the business," he says.

The rice found in the major markets is quite different from the rice most of us see in northern Minnesota. Commercially processed wild rice, for Uncle Ben's, Gourmet House, Pillsbury, Stouffer's, General Mills, ConAgra and the other big companies, is processed black and scarified, so as "to get its cook time to match that of white rice," explains Schochenmaier. That way, those who seek to create "gourmet" meals can ensure that their meals are brought to the table in a timely manner.

While international taste buds and global corporations have one idea of what wild rice is, their market-driven impacts have been felt on the lakes of Becker County and throughout the North Country.

RETURN IN THE RAIN

A pickup pulls up at the rice mill. Eugene Davis and Tony Warren bring in around 300 pounds of rice from South Chippewa Lake. They are tired, wet from the recurring morning rain, but they are happy.

"This is the only job we can make $50 an hour at up here," 19-year-old Eugene Davis tells me. "I like it when it rains out there. It's nice, you can't hear anything but the rain."

It is that peace which brings the ricers back. It is also the memories. I ask Eugene Davis what he thinks about the fact that probably five or ten generations of his family have been on that same lake. "I like knowing that they were on the same lake. It makes me feel good," he responds, and smiles.

Receiving the rice are Ronnie Chilton, Pat Wichern, Pete Jackson and a few other men who gather under some tarps at the offices of the White Earth Land Recovery Program on Round Lake. The sweet smell of parching rice wafts through the dusty air, ancient machines shift and creak as the husks blow off, and the rice slowly moves through a long chain of events. The air is filled with dust from the rice. Ronnie, Pat, and Pete look a bit like Anishinaabeg chimney sweeps, covered in rice hulls, but smiling beneath all of it.

The equipment is ancient, and much of it handmade—a 1940s Red Clipper fanning mill, a handmade thrasher, a 1980s set of George Stinson (a Deer River celebrity) parching drums, a '50s-vintage gravity table.

The men fiddle with the machines, fine-tune the gravity table, and then the rice comes out—colors of dark green, tan and brown. They are local producers, and this is the perfection of the small batch, and the simple joy of this life. Ronnie, Pete and Pat grin through the dust. They are doing their job. This rice, like that of their ancestors, is going to feed families and feed spirits.

To Pat, Ronnie, Spud, Tater and the rest of the ricers of White Earth, this season, the Ojibwe Wild Ricing Moon—*Manoominigiizis*—is the season of a harvest, a ceremony and a way of life.

"I grew up doing that," reflects Spud Fineday. "You get to visit people you haven't seen for a whole year, because just about everyone goes ricing."

Far away a combine is harvesting wild rice in California, and consumers are eating a very different rice. The Anishinaabeg would not trade for the rice, or the combine. In the end, this rice tastes like a lake, and that taste cannot be replicated.

Return of the Sturgeon:
Namewag Bi-azhegiiwewaad

Appeared in NEWS FROM INDIAN COUNTRY, *August 31, 1999.*

Randy Zortman is the head of fisheries for the White Earth Band of Chippewa, and has, with a loyal team of recruits, made history. Make that remade history. On Memorial Day weekend, when thousands of Americans were returning from Canadian lakes—boats and fish in tow—Randy and Matt Heisler did as well. They had fish, lots of them.

Some 50,000 sturgeon fry came to the White Earth fish hatchery on Ice Cracking Lake, designated this fall for White Earth and Round Lakes. "We stopped at the customs office in Baudette," Randy recalls. "They asked us if we had any fish with us, and Matt Heisler said, 'Yeah, around 50,000.' They pulled us over but we had all the paperwork and permits."

It is with that casual air that Randy makes history. For it is, by most reckonings, the first time in about fifty years that sturgeon may grace these waters, and that is an amazing thing in itself.

Here is the traditional story, as told by Ron Geyshick:

"It was springtime, so a family went out to net sturgeon at a small waterfall near Darky Lake. Just after they arrived one of the young girls reached her puberty. So her grandmother made a little wigwam not far away from the camp where the girl was to stay for eight days. After four days and four nights, everything turned quiet. The smell of the fires was gone. The girl wondered what was going on down there, but she was afraid to break her solitude by leaving the tent. For two days she waited, then she sneaked quietly down to the camp to investigate.

All the fires were dead and no one was around. It looked like they had all left in a big hurry. Then the girl heard a scratching noise come from inside of her grandmother's tent. When she had parted the deer-hide flap to look inside, she saw in the shadows that the woman was turning into a great fish.

Her grandmother said, "I am so glad you came. I have been waiting for you. See this red stripe on my belly? These sturgeon we have been eating are a different kind than we used to get here. And from now on, this is where our family will be staying inside Darky Lake. So please, help carry me down to the water now. Then go back to our village. Someday, you will come and live here too."

The girl gently lifted her grandmother, who was heavy now, over the rocks to the river. As the old woman touched the water, she turned into a fish, and swam away. The girl paddled back alone to her village.

From her spirit, we learned never to eat a sturgeon with a red stripe on its belly. Sturgeon are people, very much like us. You must be careful which ones you eat, and make offerings and feasts when you catch them. They're one of our Indian foods.

When the sturgeon run is the time we have our spring feasts and ceremonies, the time when our boys and girls do their fasting. Everything must be done in the right way."

Name is the word for sturgeon in Ojibwe. Pronounced "namay," the sturgeon is almost a mythological creature in terms of its significance to the Anishinaabeg. It is a relative, one of the clans of the Anishinaabeg (in the same family as the other fish and turtle clan), and an animal which has been a source of sustenance for the Anishininaabeg for generations.

Sturgeon are also old. At the time the Rocky Mountains began to rise, and the dinosaurs were in their glory, the lake sturgeon was swimming the waters. That was around 136 million years ago, in what is called the Upper Cretaceous period. A very long time before us two leggeds moved into the scene, that is for sure.

The lake sturgeon, or *Acipenser fulvescens*, is one of twenty-seven sturgeon species world wide, and extends its range from the St. Lawrence River in the east, to Hudson Bay in the north, west to the North Saskatchewan River in Alberta, south to the Tennessee River in Alabama. This population is one of the only populations of sturgeon in the Tennessee River in Alabama.

It is also one of the only populations of sturgeon in the world that is not endangered, at least in the overall scheme—while those in the Caspian, Baltic, and other seas of Europe have been almost obliterated. They are, however, diminished substantially in numbers in this region, and absent from the White Earth reservation area.

"It was that Frank Laquier, he was from Mahnomen. He was the one who killed that sturgeon. He lived up there in White Earth Lake," remembers elder Paul Bellecourt. "He killed it at White Earth Lake, there where they got a sandbar. The sandbar, it runs to shore. And the sturgeon was stuck on that sandbar. That Frank Laquier, he took a pitchfork. That's what he did. Then he let the news out about it. It weighed over 175 pounds that sturgeon did. That was in the '40s." It was that sturgeon which ended up in the Coast to Coast store in downtown Detroit Lakes.

Sturgeon are a critical part of Anishinaabeg culture and the ecosystem of this region. They teach us much in their very existence. They can outweigh humans, and they outlast us, with a lifespan of about 150 years. Males do not mature until they reach 13–15 years of age, and females 22–24 years of age.

Males then spawn typically once every two years, and females spawn once every four to five years, all of which accounts for how they may not be able to keep up with overexploitation. Fish up to 176 pounds and measuring seven feet three inches have been found on the White Earth reservation, the last of that size recorded in 1926.

Tim Holzkamm is a sort of keeper of sturgeon lore and historic fisheries data. As the crow flies, he lives about five miles from my house, but it was actually the bands of Anishinaabeg from Rainy River who referred me to him. Holzkamm has done a great deal of expert testimony and research for them on historic fisheries.

The era of the great fish was almost ended in this region, according to Holzkamm, an ethnohistorian and Bad Medicine Lake resident, a result of overfishing and a host of other activities. "We have a record of sturgeon harvest from Rainy River which goes back to 1835," Holzkamm explains. "Very few fisheries' records go back that far. One of the things that shows is a fairly stable period of sustainable harvest by Anishinaabeg until the advent of white commercial fishing, and resource exploitation— i.e. dams on the Rainy River, the incredible pollution from the pulp mill."

DNR Fisheries director Gary Huberty echoes Holzkamm in his thinking about this area. "Dams, that's the problem. In other words, the major reason the sturgeon went down the tubes was the dams, because they are a real wide ranging fish species and they need all that habitat and range."

Holzkamm recorded much of the decline of the sturgeon in a series of papers and as an expert witness in a number of legal cases in Canada. According to this research, sturgeon harvest in Rainy River's traditional Anishinaabeg-managed harvest between 1823 and 1884 averaged 275,000 pounds annually and was an essential part of the nutritional base of the Anishinaabeg community.

With the advent of the commercial harvest and the drive for increasing amounts of isinglass (a distilling agent) in 1886, the sturgeon harvest exceeded one million pounds and caused a collapse of the commercial harvest and, subsequently, the population. By 1925, the fish had declined to about one percent of their original population, something like the decimation of the buffalo.

Holzkamm thinks that, "It was not until the 1970s that the sturgeon started to have a chance to recover. With the Clean Water Act, and its subsequent enforcement, rivers formerly choked with logs, silt and pollution began to recover, and with them, the sturgeon themselves began to recover."

The sturgeon of this area have started to spring back, also, because of the work of some Anishinaabeg in Canada, the Rainy River First Nations, the Minnesota DNR and other agencies.

The Rainy River First Nations, a group of seven bands of Anishinaabeg situated on the Rainy River system, (near Fort Frances, Ontario) established a sturgeon hatchery in 1993, one of the last strongholds of the sturgeon. Joe Hunter is the Hatchery Manager at the Rainy River Hatchery, and has been since the bands began it. "Our elders said that we should be doing what we could for those fish, to restore and enhance the population."

As well, the band thought this might be a way to restore some of the traditional economy of the region. That hatchery has utilized wild fish from the Rainy River (the fish are returned after one spawning season), and has developed the only sturgeon hatchery in Canada, and a viable population of fingerlings to begin restoration into the entire watershed. The largest fish this year was a female, weighing around 77 pounds, from which came around 16 pounds of eggs, most of them eventually ending up at White Earth.

My family was fortunate enough to attend the Rainy River Fish Fry this year, an annual thanksgiving feast and welcome, attended by some 1,000-plus fans of the sturgeon, the Rainy River, and the Anishinaabeg.

Even luckier was our visit to the hatchery, where it just happened that Joe Hunter, his colleague Lorraine Cupp, and a Hungarian sturgeon reproduction specialist named Tomas Gulyas were making sure that all of the big fish were in the mood to spawn.

Joe and Lorraine's outfit had captured about 50 or so of the big sturgeon (weighing in at around 50 pounds each) for this very important breeding season. Little small hands of Ashley and John Martin from Rice Lake, and Waseyabin and Ajuawak Kapashesit from Round Lake reached in and petted the immense fish.

I must say that they almost allowed you to pet them, something like a cat. "The sturgeon are pretty docile fish," explained Joe Hunter, who is also fondly known as the Sturgeon General of Canada. "They aren't predator fish like northerns and walleyes." He tells me, "They pretty much have had no one bother them, so they don't bother anyone either."

Dr. Tomas Gulyas, a Hungarian Fish Reproduction Biologist, came in to "midwife" the big breeding at Rainy River. Gulyas, the world's most renowned expert in sturgeon reproduction, works for the International Union for the Conservation of Nature, (ICUN), is a United Nations affiliate, and spends most of his time trying to protect and restore sturgeon populations, these gentle giants, worldwide.

"They are very close to extinction in the Danube, in the Black Sea," he explains. "They usually call me in when there's only a few fish left."

Loss of habitat is one of the main causes of the extinction of the fish—big dams, pollution, all of that takes a toll. Then there is greed. Gulyas considers that to be one of the biggest problems. If one sturgeon produces a good chunk of caviar, and some of that caviar can be worth up to $3,000 in the delicacy market, "poachers kill a lot of the fish." They are almost gone in much of the world.

That is perhaps why Gulyas, Randy Zortman, Sturgeon General Joe Hunter, and those Shenabs from Rice Lake are so excited about these fish. This is the strongest, most viable population in the world.

"Gulyas couldn't comprehend coming here and working with a population that wasn't threatened. Here, he could relax a little more," Hunter surmises.

The sturgeon of White Earth were not so lucky. They were all gone until a couple of years ago, when the White Earth Land Recovery ceremonially restored the first four fish to Round Lake, fish which came from Rainy River. It was that same year that the Minnesota DNR started sturgeon restoration in the area.

From the DNR's perspective, Gary Huberty points out, "We

have a desire to restore rivers, fishing and fisheries, and the two just kind of meshed well together. The sturgeon stocking was started in Detroit Lake two years ago—50 in October of 1997, 25 stocked last year, and another proposed 50 stocked this fall."

All of those sturgeon came from the Rainy River system as well. Then the WELRP joined up with the White Earth fisheries department to begin bringing the sturgeon home to the reservation. Although there are some initial concerns about the health of the new baby fish, there is a commitment to insure that the sturgeon return, and a group are to be released this fall.

It is a lucky thing for White Earth that Rainy River is a part of the same watershed, the Red River watershed. Randy Zortman was somewhat surprised himself at his fortune. This was "ten years coming . . . a long wait. I didn't think we were ever going to do it, because I wasn't sure if there was a strain that was the same. After they went extinct on the reservation, where do you find the same strain and the genetics that you can stock?"

Holzkamm noted that the DNR sort of overlooked the Anishinaabeg initially. Instead of working with Rainy River, the DNR went on their own, but, over time, hopefully that will all get worked out. "They were just leaving the White Earth and Rainy River totally out of it."

As Holzkamm surmises, "Its time to recognize that the tribes' efforts are serious, and deserve involvement. There should be co-management. Especially considering things like the Mille Lacs decision. We are lucky that they are coming back to White Earth. The fish themselves never knew that invisible border of the U.S., Canada, or any of the counties" (or any of the other jurisdictions). Maybe the fish will help a diverse set of people work together to make something right.

The ability of the sturgeon to move a great distance, and disregard jurisdictions, is perhaps one of the best reasons for the multitude of agencies, landholders, the Native community, and the general public to work together. Take the DNR-planted sturgeon for instance.

Gary Huberty expressed some surprise in the distance those

sturgeon moved in a short period of time. "There's a sturgeon that was tagged in the Ottertail River in the Fergus Falls Management area, somewhere downstream from Fergus Falls, that ended up found (caught and released) in Lake Winnipeg.

"I have a record here of at least four or five who have been captured and released in Manitoba, and others that have been captured and released all along the way. One I think even is in the Cheyenne River." Both the DNR and the White Earth band look forward to working together on this issue, largely because it requires that level of collaboration.

"River connectivity is the term which describes both the range of the sturgeon, and the needs of the species, and others, for a range of habitat at different periods in their lives. The main problem with achieving this river connectivity will be dams, the first of which—one in downtown Fargo—was recently altered to accommodate the fish, with hopefully more to come.

"Right in the Detroit Lakes area, the sturgeon stocking was a hope to spur some local grassroots effort and interest in all of this," Gary explains.

The fact is that all the fish species do better when they can move up and down the river. The more spawning habitat walleye, sturgeon, etc. have available to them—and all types of habitat, including wintering areas and other needs—the healthier the population.

In the end, it is a lot of terrain to cover, and probably a lot of years. Gary and I laugh about that fish fry we might be able to have forty years from now. Sturgeon restoration is a long way, and will require a lot of cooperation.

That is one of the great lessons of the return of the sturgeon. Then there is the humility of time, and thinking past yourself. As I watched those big fish swim in tanks at the Rainy River hatchery, I thought about how most of them were at least twenty years my senior, and reflected that it would be thirty to fifty years before we would see many sturgeon on White Earth.

I realized that this whole effort was not about my generation. It is about Ashley and Jon Martin's generation, about Wasey and Ajuawak, and all those descendants.

Those are the ones who will come to know the fish again, the fish who are our relatives. That's exactly what those old Anishinaabeg were thinking about, all of those treaty signers seven generations ago.

Holzkamm recalls his research into historic Anishinaabeg fisheries. "If you look at the records of negotiations, minutes, etc., the chiefs were always very positive about the fact that the things they were negotiating for were not for themselves, but their children, their grandchildren, the 'children yet to be born'—that's what they called them in the treaties."

So it is with the work of Joe Hunter, Randy Zortman, Matt Heisler and all those fish biologists at White Earth, Gary Huberty from the Department of Natural Resources, Dr. Gulyas, and others—it is about those generations to come. The fish help us remember all of those relations, and in their own way, help us recover ourselves.

Elder and Spiritual leader Joe Bush offered a prayer to the returning fish at the White Earth fish hatchery the day after Memorial Day. He, too, was pleased with how all the people worked together to bring back a long lost relative.

"I feel good about them that they survive and really multiply in our lakes up here—that's coming back, that's what I hope.

"They've been extinct, but they were abundant before—I used to see a lot of them in the rivers and lakes up by Ely and Tower and those places; I had never seen one on White Earth. It's good. Good to have them back."

Building with Reservations

Delivered at the ASSOCIATION OF COLLEGIATE SCHOOLS OF ARCHITECTURE NATIONAL CONFERENCE, *Minneapolis, Minnesota, March 1999.*

"I don't really believe in sustainable logging at all. I know we have practiced traditional logging where we take what we need. We take care of it, but now they destroy it all. We are part of that Old Growth forest. We are the natural inhabitants as well as the owl. We live there with our ancestors. We take what we need as well as the trees but we always give thanks. We take the bark for clothing, for shelter—ones that we use for sweat lodges, those are our brothers and sisters. So we are spiritually connected. Everything is sacred to us. It has to do with our mentality. Anything that is destroyed out there, it affects us."

—Loretta Pascal, Lil'Wat, 1st Nation
from the 1994 Indigenous People's Forest Summit

I like to introduce myself in my language, which is Anishinaabe. I'm from the Bear Clan of the Mississippi band, from a reservation in northern Minnesota. I'm from the northwoods where there are seven large Ojibwe reservations; my reservation is about 4.5 hours northwest from here. I always greet people in my language because I believe that cultural diversity is as beautiful as biodiversity, and that is reflected in language. My language is one of the four native languages *not* projected to be extinct by the year 2050 in the U.S., which is a frustrating thought for any people. But it is reflective, I think, of some of the challenges you face in architecture as well. The challenge against cultural monocropping, or we may call it architectural mono-cropping, where everything becomes a big Wal-Mart or a big mall. I'd like to see a little diversity when I look out across the landscape.

I'm always honored to be asked to speak, and I'm particularly honored to be asked to speak to architectural educators. I don't usually talk to people like you. I usually talk at hearings, court trials or to a lot of small children. Yesterday I went to speak at a hearing that had a little to do with landscape architecture. There's a huge struggle going on here in the city of Minneapolis over a place called Hwy 55. There's a proposal to take Hwy 55 and make it bigger and fancier so people can save about three minutes to get to the airport. The consequence is the destruction of a sacred area of the Mendota Dakota people. The sacred area is a spring, and this is part of their creation story. And what is so ironic is that in the Hwy 55 planning they preserved a military base, Fort Snelling, but did not consider the preservation of a sacred site. I spent a half an hour of the hearing describing that there was a mandate under Federal and State law that the interest of the state would be served in preserving the site. The irony does not escape me when one culture has to go to another culture to have them judge what is sacred and what is not, and if their policies and institutions will honor that. That is quite often what I do in my work; I end up in that kind of situation. I know that you are the people who design these projects, and maybe in my talking to you, you'll hear a little about what we go through in our community and that will help you in your thinking. I am fully aware of how little an American education teaches you about Native people.

While I was introduced as an activist, I consider myself more a concerned parent. To be a mother in this day and age, you have to be concerned with a wide array of issues. It is not so much just how much sugar is in my son's cereal, but how many PCBs are in his tissue at this point in time. And that is, in fact, a direct consequence of public policy. It is a consequence of what we eat and the decisions we make in this society. For instance, we are a fishing community. You may be surprised to know that almost every lake in northern Minnesota has a Fish Consumption Advisory for it. You can only eat one walleye per week or month if you are a woman of childbearing age in many of those lakes because of PCBs or mercury. This is why I need to take this interest in wider public policy if I want to retain my cultural integrity; if we want to be what the Creator intended us to be. Because the Creator did not say, "Go forth Ojibwes and go to Safeway." The Creator said, "Those are fish; you eat those fish that feed not only your belly but your soul." That is the challenge I find myself in.

If I were to describe the architecture of my community, I would describe it both as an architecture of poverty and an architecture of what is sacred. That is what coexists in my community. We do not have, as you can imagine, big high-rises. We have a two-story tribal office building. The casino in the reservation does look like the Taj Majal, but I don't know who built it. We have mostly the architecture of poverty. First of all, much of our housing is overcrowded or substandard by the government's own standards. This is true of any reservation in this country. Most of the architecture, the houses in which my community lives, is made by HUD—they are HUD housing projects. They took all the trees out and made these housing projects and painted them in these loathsome pastel colors. It looks like a box of mints. It is all so unimaginable—any Indian reservation you go to in this country, you see the same thing. But this is where our people live.

That is the sad thing in our communities, because indigenous people are a community of great architectural wealth consisting of a great diversity that is based on the land. In the north you have sod houses with whale bones; there are the long houses; and pueblo adobe architecture in the southwest, as well as the underground house systems. We have wigwams. I haven't seen anyone improve on the tepee—you can have a fire inside it, and you can move it. In my community, I see this diversity. But there is this sorrow—I have to say a sorrow—that exists when you are stripped of the cultural integrity of your house, of your architecture, and given something that does not resonate. Sure, it provides a shelter, but as you all know, a house is more than a shelter: It is a home, it is something that reflects you. So that is the architecture of poverty that exists in my community.

And then you have the architecture that is sacred. Next to some of those houses, you'll see a sweat lodge, or you'll see a *miichwaap*, which is like a tepee, but it is used for smoking meat. The most beautiful thing to me is when I consider the fact that a lodge that is used for one of our ceremonies is based on the mirror of a star constellation; it reflects where the poles are located. That, in its essence, is sacred architecture. I think that that is the most beautiful thing in our community.

Let me talk now about what I do in our community, and how it perhaps relates to what you do. I direct an organization called the White Earth Land Recovery Project on a local level, and I also work at a national level. My own organization was formed as a grassroots citizen's organization that was formed by our own initiative to work on issues of land, culture and environment. We're not a part of tribal government; we're independent. What happened in our community happens in many other communities. I am talking about the fact that our tribal government was corrupt and was beset with controlling those limited resources that came into our communities. For those who had tribal jobs, if you opened your mouth, you would lose your job. You would lose your house. I can tell you this now, but it is not as if corruption in politics is something that is unknown to white people. You have a little experience with that as well, I understand. So in 1996, my whole tribal government went to jail, and those of you who are from Minnesota know this. The whole White Earth government went to jail for corruption charges, twenty-three separate indictments and convictions each. A couple of them just got out. That's what happens when you're a white-collar criminal, I guess. You get out pretty easy. If you steal a reservation, you get out pretty fast. If you steal a car, you're in longer. Our community knows both.

But we waited for tribal government to take care of it. I was always waiting for tribal government to take care of our land issue, or work on our culture, or work on the preservation of that which our community held so important. And they did not . . . they did not. They were preoccupied with their own selves. So we formed our organization. We looked around and said, "We're all adults. Who's responsible for this community? Is tribal government responsible for this community? Is federal government responsible for this community?" I should let you know, I'm legally a ward of the federal government. That's the ironic situation in which we find ourselves. We're legally wards of the federal government, which isn't competent enough to handle its own affairs. But we waited for the government agencies to take care of the situation, and found that they did not. We did not want to sit around and become aggravated at their inaction, frustrated or angry, living absent the dignity that every community deserves. We said, let's go try to do something ourselves, and we struggled with the issues of land, culture and environment.

Our project was formed after a long and protracted land-rights struggle. A lot of you are involved in development, and the relationship between land issues and indigenous people is an ongoing issue on this continent. And why is that? Because most of this land was procured illegally. And you and I can make nice about it. In Minnesota, they say we made nice about it a long time ago. They say, "You Indians should get over it." Well that's really nice to say when you are holding all the assets. Why are Indian people the poorest people in this country—in every economic or social statistic at the bottom or the top of where you don't want to be? Is that because we're stupid? No. It's because we have structural poverty enforced by intergenerational appropriation of our wealth. That's the reality.

So today in our community we find that 90 percent of reservation land is held by non-Indian interests. Inside *my* reservation. We're not asking for two-thirds of Minnesota. We're asking for what I consider to be a reasonable request: recovery of land within a reservation. A reservation reserved by treaty, reserved by law: 837,000 acres of land. The courts ruled first that our land was taken illegally. In many ways, our land was taken as tax-forfeiture. The State of Minnesota took a third of our reservation for taxes, which is totally illegal under the law. But greed is what dictated it. Some of the foundations of Minneapolis's fortunes came from our reservation. The courts ruled that our land was taken illegally, but in 1986, in a second court decision, they ruled that although our land was taken illegally, the statute of limitations had expired. That we should have asked or filed suit for our land within seven years of the original time of taking. That puts us in a bad situation. You have a community like ours, where my great-grandma could not read or write English, legally a ward of the federal government, and you're supposed to go out and procure an attorney. Having not done so, basically, we're out of luck.

So if you are me, you look at that situation and you say: The court said your land was taken illegally, and then the court said, we're not going to return it. I look around and say, what am I going to pass on to my children; this same situation of structural poverty? Or will I try to change it somehow? What could I do to change it? We looked at the process and came up with some options. Our first suggestion is that over the next fifty years we would like to see the return of public land holdings within our reservation to our community. This comprises about a third of the reservation. Return those land holdings to our community. I think that's a reasonable request. It doesn't involve the displacement of a single non-Indian landholder.

The second proposal is acquisition based on a willing-seller/willing-buyer basis of lands from non-Indian landholders inside the reservation. I think that that is a reasonable proposal as well. The fact is, as most of you probably know, the rural area is dwindling in population. White people are moving out. That is the reality in any state. And which population is growing in that area? Indians. Our birth rate is three times that of non-Indians. The average age of an Indian person is sixteen years of age, and the average age of a non-Indian person is fifty-one years of age. Those of you who are into public policy and planning can take those statistics and project them out over the next twenty years. What you have is a situation that needs some kind of resolution;

otherwise you will have large concentrations of Indian people living in housing projects, surrounded by non-Indian landholders. So our proposal is this long-term recovery of land. We've acquired about 1,300 acres so far, on which we operate agricultural projects. We've started an organic raspberry farm and we have a 5,100 tap-maple sugar bush operated with horses. I don't like those tubes, those PVC pipes. The Creator didn't give us PVC pipes. Some other land was also acquired for agriculture and cemeteries.

The loss of our land was largely tied to the issues of environment and culture, specifically to the timber industry. In 1889, 11 million board feet of timber was taken off my reservation; the next year, 15 million; and the next year, 18 million. By 1897, an excess of 76 million board feet of timber had been taken off my reservation. That timber built a lot of Minneapolis. That is where the Pillsbury fortune came from; that is where the Weyerhaeuser fortune came from. There is a direct relationship between this wealth and our poverty. These resources were appropriated to form large corporations and to build what are viewed as "the most beautiful" houses. I have seen some of those houses and they are beautiful.

My land is also beautiful. It is beautiful with trees. It is more beautiful with trees than with clear-cuts. That is the truth in our community. Our community is a forest culture. The Anishinaabe people are a forest culture. We're not a Prairie culture or a Plains culture. The Creator did not put us out there; the Creator put us in the forest. And what you find is that to actually be a forest culture, you have to have a forest in which to live. So I spend a lot of my time fighting clear-cutting (Potlatch Mill Expansion—that's our big one right now). I spend my time illustrating that forests are worth more standing than cut.

I also spend time working on culture—restoration of our cultural practices and their relationship to the forest, whether it is our song, our relation to the sugarbush, our language and our stories. A couple of years ago some architects from Minneapolis helped us to design a roundhouse for our ceremonies. Many of our ceremonial structures are round because that is part of our teachings. Before we cut the logs, however, we had a ceremony. And when we took those logs, we took them with horses. Then we had a guy come in with a portable sawmill. This saves a lot of wood because it is technically more efficient. I tell you this story to demonstrate how one recovers sacred architecture itself. To me, it is not only the form. It is the practice. That is a central part of our teachings—the relationship between where the wood comes from, how you take the wood, and how you build from there.

My national work is a mirror of my work in my own community. I work with grassroots Native organizations nationally, working on issues from trying to stop a clear-cut, to trying to stop a mine, to trying to stop a dam project. I also work internationally. The ironic situation is that for people who are "landed" people, like indigenous people, who have so little land left, this very land is of immense interest to industrial society. We have two-thirds of the uranium, which is used for nuclear power plants, on Indian reservations. One third of it is used for coal. The single largest hydroelectric project in North America is on our lands, the James Bay II project in Northern Canada. We have about 50 million board feet of timber. I spend a lot of time fighting with county commissioners because they look at my reservation and refer to it as timber resources; I call it a forest. It's a very different way of thinking. I do not look out there and see timber resources; I see a forest. That does not mean that I'm opposed to logging. It does mean that I'm opposed to lazy logging, which is what I call clear-cutting. You can selectively cut in a beautiful manner, and leave a forest standing.

For those of you who have never seen the Menominee reservation in northern Wisconsin, it is an excellent example of selective cutting. They have the same amount of trees standing today as they did 150 years ago; the same amount of diversity, in terms of age and canopy and size. And they've cut that reservation the equivalent of three times over. They employ about 400 people in their logging industry. That's sustainable logging. I'm not opposed to that.

But these issues that I find myself working with are issues that are totally and intimately related to your work. That is the reality. The fact is that if you have these natural resources, someone always wants them. Society has not yet figured out how to say, "I'm going to restrain myself." That is not yet a part of this culture. Instead one of the challenges we have is that society has this entitlement complex. If we can buy it, we should have it, no matter what the price is. I have spent almost all of my adult life fighting bad projects, largely energy projects. Why can't they just leave it? Just because the coal exists, do they have to strip mine it? Just because the water flows, does that mean they have to dam it? Just because the trees are there, does that mean they have to cut them? At what point do we restrain ourselves in this society so that something is left because it has value on its own?

This society consumes a third of the world's resources and has a small percentage of the world's population. It has the largest energy market in the world. The U.S. consumes seven times more wood products per capita than any other industrialized society. Sometimes when you ask people to consume less, to not use it and toss it, there's this puzzled look like, "That sounds painful. That sounds like I'm not going to really get what I want, and I have a right to it." That's what we have to deconstruct.

It is from our communities that much of this consumption comes. It is almost impossible for us to retain our cultural practices, our cultural diversity, our sacred sites, as long as this level of consumption continues. We must wake up every day and fight a mine. My friend Gail Small in Northern Cheyenne has been fighting mines for twenty-five years. Can you imagine what kind of stress that causes; one bad project after another?

Your industry—the construction industry—consumes about a third of the wood that's out there right now. There's a lot of waste. We don't have to build everything with frame houses. There are plenty of alternatives, but almost everything that is constructed right now is constructed with wood. You have to change that. You have to seek out more innovative sources. Use recycled sources, for example, so you do not have to continue consuming virgin timber in your industry.

I have a friend, Loretta Pascal, who's from the northwest coast. She's a grandma. One day she says to me—she spent a long time fighting clear-cutting—"Our people hang the umbilical cords of our children in those trees. Those trees are our relatives." But corporations like McMillan Bloedell look at those trees and say: Pulp. Lumber. The question she asked me is the question we must ask ourselves: "What makes their rights supersede mine? Why is it that a big corporation has a right that supersedes my inter-generational right to just live here?"

So, the challenge that I pass on to you is to try to figure out how to transform your industry so that the Loretta Pascals, the Ajuawak Kapashesits, my little boy, can have a forest. You must try to transform the wood consumption and the energy consumption in your industry. You and I know that whether it is the use of passive solar or just simple conservation, about a third of the power that is consumed can be conserved. Our community desperately needs for that to happen.

I think that the time has come for this society to reconnect with some of the things that I think are missing. You are in an occupation that uses the most sacred resources, and that fulfills one of the most sacred needs of people. And it is, in my estimation, one of the challenges of your profession to return to that sacred process, so that what you produce is not only beautiful to look at, on the surface, but has, as much as possible, some beauty from its origin . . . all the way through it. You might call it ethical. I call it sacred.

There should be beauty in "process," whether it is harvesting with intelligence, whether it is the use of recycled materials, or whether it is observing energy efficiency. I learned one thing in the northwest that really astonished me: Today, many scientists are studying what they call "culturally modified trees." The Haidas, the people known for making the big totem poles and these astonishing big cedar houses, have been doing this for years.

Of course, these houses hardly exist in the northwest because anthropologists hauled entire villages away to museums. When the Haidas want to see their grandmas' houses, they have to go over to Washington, D.C. or Boston and visit the museum. To return to my point, however, those houses are made of planks. The Haidas grew trees in a certain way, working with them for 150 years, so that they could take a plank off a tree and leave the tree standing. They continue this practice today. That is something to aspire to. *That* is real sustainable building. And that is what some cultures did, the cultures that the American education system teaches you were quite primitive. Those people did something that Weyerhaeuser can't do. None of these corporations have any idea how to do this. These people did. They built entire villages while leaving their forests standing. So I leave you with that thought.

Like Tributaries to a River

Appeared in SIERRA, *November/December 1996.*

Bimaadiziwin o'ow nibi
Jiigibiig nindana kiimin
Jiigibiig ningaganoonaanaan Gizhe Manidoo
Jiigibiig Ninbabaamadizimin
Nin Miki go-imin wisiniwin minikwewin nibi kaang
Nin dinawamaaganag ayaawag nibi kaang
Gi-bizhigwaadenimoa Gizhe Manidoo maji-mashkii
atooyegnibikaang Ji-ganawendamang nibi gigi minigoomin
omaa gidakiiminaan

Water is life.
We are the people who live by the water.
Pray by these waters.
Travel by these waters.
Eat and drink from these waters.
We are related to those who live in the water.
To poison the waters is to show disrespect for creation.
To honor and protect the waters is our responsibility
as people of the land.
—Winona LaDuke
Translated from the Anishinaabe by Marlene Stately

We live off the beaten track, out of the mainstream, in small villages on a vast expanse of prairie, in dry desert lands, or in thick woods. We drive old cars, live in old houses and mobile homes. Our families are important to us, and there are usually some small children and relatives around, no matter what else is going on. We seldom carry briefcases, and we rarely wear suits. You're more likely to find us meeting in the local community center or in someone's home than in a convention center or at $1,000-a-plate fund-raisers. We are the common face of Native environmentalism.

We organize in small groups, with names like Native Americans for a Clean Environment, Diné CARE (Citizens Against Ruining our Environment), Anishinaabe Niijii, and the Gwich'in Steering Committee. We have faced down huge waste dumps, multinational mining and lumber companies, and the U.S. Office of the Nuclear Waste Negotiator. We are underfunded at best, and more often without funding at all; yet individuals throughout the Native nations keep fighting to protect our lands for future generations.

We have close to 200 grassroots Native organizations in North America resisting the environmental destruction of our homelands. Most of these groups are small, perhaps five to ten volunteers working out of their homes. Many operate in remote areas without phones or cars. There are another 500 or so environmental organizations in the environmental justice movement and collective networks coalescing around regional and international agendas, groups such as California Indians for Cultural and Environmental Protection, Southwest Network for Environmental Economic Justice, Indigenous Environmental Network.

Despite our meager resources, we are winning many hard-fought victories on the local level:

• In 1991, Diné CARE defeated Waste Tech's plans to build a "recycling center"—actually a toxic-waste incinerator—near Dilkon, Arizona, in the western portion of the Navajo Reservation. A year later, it was working on tribal forestry issues. The Navajo Nation's own logging company proposed clear-cutting the Chuksa Mountains. In a battle waged over several years, and costing at least one life (activist Leroy Jackson, called the Chico Mendez of the Navajo, died under suspicious circumstances during the struggle), Diné CARE finally succeeded in halting the clear-cutting.

• The Gwich'in in Alaska have fought—successfully, so far—to keep oil-drilling from invading their homeland and dispersing the Porcupine caribou herd.

• The Good Road and Natural Resource Coalitions, both Lakota groups, mobilized Pine Ridge and Rosebud reservation residents to stop plans for toxic-waste dumps on their reservations in South Dakota.

• Native Action, a grassroots organization in Montana, protected the sacred Sweet Grass Hills from desecration. The Canadian company Pegasus Gold operates the Zortman-Landusky mine complex near the Fort Belknap Reservation; one mine has lopped off the top of one of the mountains most sacred to tribes in the region. Native Action won an extension on a moratorium on gold mining in the sacred hills that was to have expired in August 1995.

• Following a ten-year battle against mega-dams on James Bay, the Cree people built a sophisticated international coalition that succeeded in securing a moratorium from Hydro Quebec on a project called James Bay II.

• The White Earth Land Recovery Project on the White Earth Reservation in Minnesota has restored over 1,000 acres of land within the reservation, defeated several ecologically and culturally destructive development proposals, and begun to restore the traditional land-based economy that depended on local products like maple syrup and wild rice.

After centuries of attempts to remove us from our land, we are still here. We are not about to go away.

Native environmental groups have a commitment and tenacity that springs from place. "This is where my grandmother's and children's umbilical cords are buried. . . . That is where the great giant lay down to sleep. . . . That is the last place our people

stopped in our migration here to this village." Our relationship
to land and water is continuously reaffirmed through prayer, deed,
and our way of life. Our identity as human beings is founded on
creation stories tying us to the earth, and to a way of being,
minobimaatisiiwin, "the good life." Our intergenerational residence in place reaffirms that relationship and knowledge. The
earth is our Mother; it is from her we gain our life.

Native peoples have courageously resisted the destruction of
the natural world at the hands of colonial, and later, industrial
society, since this destruction attacks their very identity. This
resistance has continued from generation to generation, and provides the strong core of today's Native environmentalism. This is
why 500 or more federally recognized reservations and Indian
communities still exist, why one-half of our lands are still forested, much in old growth, and why we continue the work of
generations past by opposing dams like the Kinzua Dam in Pennsylvania and those on the Columbia River, clear-cutting, nuclear-
waste dumping, and other threats to our lives and land.

To understand Native environmentalism, it's a good idea to
redraw your mental geography of Native America. Over 700 Native communities dot the continent. In the United States, Native
America covers 4 percent of the land; Native people are the sec-
ond-largest collective landholders after the federal government.

To the north, in Canada, the situation is different. Reservations, or "reserves," are generally smaller in size (Canada's Indian
Act was incredibly stingy). But the northern communities do retain vast areas by treaty or agreements for hunting and trapping.
North of the 50th Parallel, 85 percent of the population is Native.

With this new map in mind, consider that:

• Most environmental struggles over the boreal forest in Canada
involve Native peoples. The Brazilian rainforest is being cut down
at the rate of one acre every 9 seconds; one acre of Canada's forests disappears every 11 seconds. Approximately the same number of Native people live in each.

• According to Worldwatch Institute, 317 reservations in the United States are threatened by environmental hazards, from toxic-waste dumping to clear-cutting to radioactive waste. Two-thirds of all "domestic" uranium resources are on Indian lands, as is one-third of all western low-sulfur coal. Sixteen proposals to dump nuclear waste have targeted reservations, and over 100 proposals have been made in recent years to dump toxic wastes in Indian communities. Few reservations have escaped environmental degradation.

• The Association on American Indian Affairs lists 77 sacred sites nationally that have been disturbed or desecrated through resource extraction and development activities.

• Eighty million acres of Alaskan offshore oil lease sales lie in water surrounding Native coastal villages.

• Over 1,000 uranium mines sit abandoned on Diné land, leaking radioactive contaminants into the air and water. On the same reservation is the largest coal strip mine in the world, operated by Peabody Coal Company. Diné teenagers have a cancer rate 17 times the national average.

• The Western Shoshone in Nevada are the most bombed nation in the world, with more than 700 atomic explosions over the past 45 years. Now the federal government is studying Yucca Mountain, sacred to the Shoshone, as a dumpsite for high-level nuclear wastes.

• Faced with encroaching development and state building codes that ruled their traditional "chickees" substandard housing, the 300-member Seminole Nation in Florida is fighting for its survival, through litigation and a possible land acquisition with support from a private foundation.

"I have fished here forever, through my ancestors," says Margaret Flint-Knife Saluskin, a Yakama fisherwoman. She stands by an ancestral fishing scaffold at Lyle Point on the Columbia River in Oregon—where the Yakama are fighting plans for a huge housing development. "This is where the fish come to give up their spirits. It is a sacred place. I will not come to fish for my family next to tennis courts and the swimming pools of luxury home developments."

In the Northwest, virtually every river is home to a people, each as distinct as a species of salmon. The Clatsop are from north of the Columbia; the Tillamook, Siletz, Yaquina, Alsea, Siuslaw, Umpqua, Hanis, Miluk, Colville, Tututni, Shasta, Costa, and Chetco: all people living at the mouths of salmon rivers. One hundred and seven stocks of salmon have already become extinct in the Pacific region, and 89 others are at high risk. The stories of the people and the fish are not so different; environmental destruction threatens the existence of both.

Susanna Santos, an artist and fisherwoman turned Greenpeace campaigner, is from the Tygh band of the Lower Deschutes River. The Tygh today include a scant five families, trying to survive as a people as they struggle to keep up their traditional way of life and their relationship to the salmon.

"That's why I came back to fish," says Santos. "I wanted to dance the salmon, know the salmon, say good-bye to the salmon. Now I am looking at the completion of destruction, from the Exxon Valdez, the Trojan Nuclear Power Plant, Hanford, logging, and those dams."

"Seventeen fish came down the river last year. None this. The people are the salmon and the salmon are the people. How do you quantify that?"

In 1992, the Environmental Protection Agency set allowable levels of dioxin discharge from paper mills in the Northwest; this standard was based on a human consumption level of 6.5 grams of fish a day, the national average. Agency officials knew that Native Americans, Asian Americans, and other low-income people in the area consumed up to 150 grams of fish a day—creating a cancer risk of 8,600 per million. The risk allowable by statute is one per million.

In January 1990, the Yakama Indian Nation enacted a resolution calling for an end to the use of the chlorine bleaching process by the pulp-and-paper industry. In testimony before the Oregon Environmental Quality Commission, Harry Smiskin of the Tribal Council of the Confederated Tribes of the Yakama Indian Nation said, "The Yakama Indian Nation is not interested in discussing with you or anyone how much TCDD or any of the other hundreds of toxic chemicals can be dumped into the Columbia River by the pulp-and-paper industry. The Yakama Indian Nation does not want to debate mixing zones for toxic pollution, nor do we want to debate whether a mile, two miles, or the entire Columbia River is water-quality-limited, and what that means for beneficial uses. Those topics wrongly assume that it is okay to dump pollution into the river that can impact the health of our fish and the health of our people."

I live on a reservation in northern Minnesota called White Earth, where I work on land, culture, and environmental issues through an organization called the White Earth Land Recovery Project. We, the Anishinaabeg, are a forest people, meaning that our creation stories, instructions, and culture, our way of life are entirely based in the forest, from our medicine plants to our food sources, from forest animals to our birchbark baskets.

Yet virtually my entire reservation was clear-cut at the turn of the century, providing the foundations for major lumber companies, including Weyerhaeuser, and setting in motion a process of destruction that has continued for nine decades in our community.

"I cried and prayed our trees would not be taken from us, for they are as much ours as is this reservation," said Wabunoquod, an Anishinaabe on the White Earth Reservation in 1874.

In 1889 and 1890, Minnesota led the United States in lumber production, with the state's northwest as the leading timber source. Two decades later, 90 percent of our land was in non-

Indian hands, and our people were riddled with diseases, with many leaving to become refugees in the cities. Today, our forests are just beginning to recover. But the process of recovery is far from complete: three-fourths of all tribal members remain off-reservation, and 90 percent of reservation lands still remain in non-Indian hands.

When Potlatch, a major lumber corporation, announced that it would double and triple the size of its pulp-and-paper mills in our region, we resisted. Potlatch—and Blandin, and International Paper, and other companies—not only destroy our trees, they destroy the foundation of our culture.

All this is to say that Native communities are not in a position to compromise, because who we are is our land, our trees, and our lakes. This is central to our local and collective work. This is also why the conflicts remain in Native America between corporate interests and our traditional ways, and between segments of our community who embrace the values of industrial society and those who continue to embrace traditional values. There is no comfortable compromise in these situations, and corporations that look at a project and a bottom line often find themselves with a snapping turtle as an adversary—a creature reluctant to let go. Native communities can bring up a broad set of issues when opposing a project: tribal jurisdiction, federal trust responsibility, treaty rights, preservation of cultural and religious freedoms, the economic benefit or harm to a village or community, and gravesite protection.

While there is great potential for these strategies, there has been a very awkward courtship between Native environmental groups and larger environmental organizations. For instance, the Nature Conservancy came to my reservation, bought 400 acres of land, and gave it to the state of Minnesota. The Sierra Club has openly opposed transfers of public land to tribes on occasion. In addition, animal-rights groups have opposed traditional harvesters of seal, beaver, fish, and whales. These conflicts make it cumbersome to try to build alliances, as most Native groups view the larger, more politically powerful environmental groups with suspicion after meeting them on opposing sides in lawsuits or proposed legislation. The truth is that an "alliance" does not mean that Native communities must embrace all facets of an environmental group's agenda, or vice versa. The important thing is to build trust. Mainstream environmentalists would do well to build relationships and alliances with Native groups—but first they must be willing to listen to our point of view.

Over the past 20 years, Native organizations and communities have crafted a diverse and comprehensive strategy for defending their ways of living and charting a course for the future. This blueprint has taken some organizations and nations to various United Nations forums and into a decade-long process to secure an international declaration on the rights of indigenous peoples, as well as to codify traditional laws and practices, join in litigation in the white man's courts, and restore traditional economic packages.

This past summer the Indigenous Environmental Network held its sixth annual Protecting Mother Earth Gathering at the Cherokee Nation in North Carolina. Founded in 1990 at the Diné village of Dilkon, Arizona, the Network has helped often isolated and widely scattered Native groups find common ground on issues and philosophies, such as the reaffirmation of traditional and natural laws, recognition of environmentally sound lifestyles and livelihoods, and the promotion of indigenous voices in the environmental movement.

In 1995, grassroots activists, traditional elders, and organizers from the Albuquerque-based Native Lands Institute developed an "Indigenous Environment Statement of Principles," written for working in the Native community, to help integrate the alienated terminology of technological society (risk assessment, resource management, mitigation) with traditional values. This document calls for using Native language and culture in assessing the environment, rather than the terms of the dominant culture.

Native environmental activists in northern Wisconsin who have worked for decades on fishing, mining, logging, and other issues in northern Anishinaabeg territory are proposing a Seventh Generation Amendment to the United States (and tribal) Constitution that would embody the principle of the Haudenosaunee (Iroquois) Six Nations Confederation (and our own Anishinaabe) that "every deliberation we make must be in consideration of the impact on the seventh generation from now."

Across the continent, on the shores of small tributaries, in the shadows of sacred mountains, on the vast expanse of the prairies, or in the safety of the woods, prayers are being repeated, as they have been for thousands of years, and common people with uncommon courage and the whispers of their ancestors in their ears continue their struggles to protect the land and water and trees on which their very existence is based. And like small tributaries joining together to form a mighty river, their force and power grows. This river will not be dammed.

Honor the Earth Tour Journal

Appeared in INDIGENOUS WOMAN, *Volume II, Number III, 1995.*

The Honor the Earth Tour traveled to over twenty cities and Native communities, reaching over 40,000 people and in the process raising money, awareness, and political support for Native people on the front line working for their survival. The tour targeted three essential components of the Endangered Peoples, Endangered Species Campaign:

• The defense of homelands and ecosystems

• The protection of sacred sites

• The building of sustainable communities

The tour supported the commitment of local groups and individuals to honor the earth and to increase visibility and people's awareness for their issues. The work to protect endangered peoples and species is key to the survival of all of us. The tour sought to leverage the financial and political resources necessary for Native people to carry out that work.

WAABIGONI-GIIZIS
MAADAGINZO (MAY 1)
GAAWAABAABAANIKAG
White Earth Reservation

Slowly I look around my house one last time. I water the plants, touch my photographs, feel the keys of my piano, then move towards the door. The car starts. My children are safely tucked away at my neighbor's—Merrie Butcher. Earl Hoagland, a board member and an Indian doctor, has agreed to accompany me. He patiently waits outside having a smoke. One last time I go back into the house to see what I may have forgotten.

A quick trip to Minneapolis, a short flight to Madison, and then check into a downtown hotel. It's midday before I meet up with Amy Ray and Emily Saliers (the Indigo Girls), Geoff Trump (manager), and our tour coordinator, Mark Tilsen of Direct Events. We all shuffle our feet, a little nervous, excited, unsure, but happy.

At the Oscar Meyer Theatre, Earl and I find our way backstage through a maze of dark hallways. There are about twenty-five people there. The Indigo Girls band has five musicians: Amy Ray, Emily Saliers, Sara Lee, Jane Scarpantoni, and Jerry Mortella. Management and production numbers ten, most of whom are known only by nicknames like Tuffy, Scooter, or Belvedere. It is a large group and very few have ever worked with Indians.

With Earl's soothing words and my instinctual herding abilities, we gather in a circle at the back of the stage. Earl has placed all his sacred items out for the blessing ceremony. He speaks to me quietly, asking me to explain a few of our customs. Awkwardly, I do so. Then he begins to pray, blessing us as smoke from the smudge envelopes each person in the circle. I am relieved, reassured and thankful for his prayers and blessings.

A press conference announces the tour. Walt Bresette, an Ojibwe, speaks of Exxon's and Rio Algom's proposal to open a copper sulfide mine on the Mole Lake Reservation. The mine would occupy a surface area of 866 acres, and would disrupt a large area of Wisconsin. It would generate an estimated 60 million tons of toxic sulfuric waste. The mine site lies on territory ceded by the Anishinaabe Nation to the U.S. government in 1842. Treaties guarantee Anishinaabe access to wild rice, fish, and some wild game on the ceded lands—an integral part of Ojibwe culture. The mine would devastate the Wolf River watershed and the region's wild rice beds.

2,500 people come to see the Indigo Girls and Ulali—a Native singing group out of New York City. The two groups resonate off each other beautifully. The entire concert, with music, slide show, and speeches (Walt and I say a few words), forms a powerful image of the Native community and our friends defining the struggle for the future. The audience stands for the entire Indigo Girls set. They sway with the music in pure adoration.

WABIGONIGIIZIS
ZHAANGASWI (MAY 9)
GAKAABIKAANG
Minneapolis, Northrup Auditorium

A blur of reporters, fans, friends. Ulali and the Indigo Girls create a magic that is uniquely their own. The Native drum of our slide show seems to roll into the Indigo Girls' opening set, moving through songs like *Least Complicated, Ghost,* Amy's gender busting cover of Dire Straits' *Romeo and Juliet* and *Galileo.* The audience is on their feet throughout the show.

WAABIGONI-GIIZIS MIDAASWI
ASBI-BEZHIG (MAY 11)
White Earth

I have never seen so many reporters at White Earth in my whole life. You either have to take over the tribal council or get the Indigo Girls to come to the reservation to attract this kind of attention.

Traditional drums open the afternoon. Earl Hoagland prays. The Indigo Girls take the stage in a tribal school gym filled with 1st through 12th grade students and folks from the community. A few non-Indians from Detroit Lakes and the surrounding prairie have ventured into the heart of the White Earth reservation to join in on the event. Kids squirm and giggle. Emily tries to explain complicated lyrics to 2nd grade kids, "Galileo was a nice guy who had new and different ideas that the church didn't like. And that was not good," she said.

After the concert, tours of the band's bus were given by six-year-old Waseyabin. Peace pops and Ben & Jerry's ice cream bars are handed out. We all pile into the bus and head out for some horseback riding near Itasca State Park.

WAABIGONI-GIIZIS MIDAASWI
ASHI-NIIZH (MAY 12)
ONIGAMIINSING
Duluth

This past February in Duluth, on a lonely hill overlooking town, Diane Olsen, a 32-year-old mother of four children was found frozen with a bullet in her head. She was a White Earth enrollee. Two men are charged with her murder. I tell her story to the audience. Backstage I visit with people from a women's shelter.

Camille LaCapa, the artist who drew the tour poster and manager of WOJB radio, comes to interview Amy and Emily. I am pleased for Indian radio stations.

The show is nearly sold out. The audience stands for most of the show, dancing through the encore. A lot of people enjoyed themselves and the music was great. I cannot stop thinking of Diane Olsen.

WAABIGONI-GIIZIS MIDAASWI
ASHI-NISWI (MAY 13)
Winnipeg

All we ask is to be allowed to govern ourselves. Why are we who are Innu, so badly off, when after all this is our land and we have been living here for thousands of years? Why is it so hard for us to survive in our own territory? We only need to look at the development of Nitassinan to see what's killing the land: military testing, hydroelectric dams, logging. And the roads being built for these purposes, they, too, are killing the land. We demand only to be able to live on and off our land. . . .

I know what Nitassinan was like before the military testing began, and I've seen what the practice bombing runs have done to it. I've gone twice myself to inspect the damage done in the company of women and children . . . I am very proud that it is the women who are there to defend the land, that they are standing up to do something, and I hope that all women will stand together to continue the fight to defend the territory.

—Elizabeth Penashue,
Innu elder from Sheshashit, "Labrador," Nistassinin.

We hit customs about seven in the morning. Drowsy, we stumble from the buses, clad in sweat suits and pajamas. Custom agents peer at us over forms, nod, grunt, and send us on our way. Why is it that the Canadian government won't leave the Innu alone? That is the question I cannot help asking. Canada touts a human rights image internationally, yet remains as resource crazy as Brazil. One acre of Brazilian rain forest is cut every nine seconds, compared to one acre of Canadian forest every eleven seconds. Both forests have about the same number of Indians. The Innu had a successful decade long battle to defeat the siting of a NATO base in their territory. The Canadian government, however, will not relinquish its hopes. Instead of a formal NATO base, the government proposes to have 18,000 "test flights" with live ammunition flown over Nitassinan (Innu territory) annually.

The Canadian government has money for bombers; but not for aboriginal schoolteachers. In Winnipeg, fifteen teachers are slated to be laid off by fall. The Innu should not have to fight forever.

Backstage is a little strange. The walls feel like a prison. Rattling sounds inside the walls and empty rooms scare the children. Young women with dreads and pierced noses "volunteer" to help out. They chastise our eating habits and the crew's beer and pizza. Patchouli oil wafts through the air. Our only Canadian audience, in true form, is polite and seated. I always suspected it is a leftover British "manners" thing. A great show.

WABIGONIGIIZIS MIDAASWI
ASHI-NIIWIN (MAY 14)
Fargo

It is unprecedented for an Indian woman to have an audience of 2,200 in Fargo. At least one half of lake shore on the White Earth Reservation is owned by people from Fargo, yet I am sure they do not know this. Sixty percent of the White Earth Reservation is held privately, about one half by absentee landlords. They are *Wiiji gamigishka wiig*—my neighbors.

The last Indian woman I saw in the pages of the *Fargo Forum* was Martina Greywind. She spent several weeks on the front page of the paper in 1992. Greywind was a homeless Dakota woman pregnant with her seventh child when she was thrust into the national spotlight. She had been arrested twelve times in eleven months for sniffing spray paint. On February 7, her life took a dramatic turn.

After being charged with endangering the life of her fetus by her chronic drug use, an anonymous donor offered to pay for an abortion. The Lambs of Christ sprang to the rescue, promising her $12,000 if she would carry the pregnancy to term. She was used as a political pawn, played by one side against the other.

Greywind chose an abortion. The endangerment charges were dropped and Greywind underwent drug abuse treatment at the North Dakota State Hospital.

Abandoned to the streets, she was arrested in March, again in April and three times in May. I do not know where she is today.

By mid-afternoon fans start lining up for open seating at the Fargo Civic Center. The place starts to fill up. With only a few seats left, the tour donates tickets to the Native American Center located in Fargo, a women's shelter, and the Fargo Women's Health

Clinic—the only clinic in North Dakota which provides abortions.

There is a big story in the Forum about the Indigo Girls, and the mesh of our different and committed politics. Native rights, pro-choice, and a gay performer. Whoa . . . Fargo isn't used to this.

It is a great feeling to play in Fargo. Bob Shimek from the White Earth Land Recovery Project introduces the show.

Vern Cheechoo, a Cree folk and country singer, from Moose Factory, Ontario (Dark Light Records) opens the show. I take the stage for ten minutes. A lone heckler is quieted and one of Fargo's neighbors talks about the land which divides us and brings us together. We board the bus and awake in Rapid City, South Dakota.

WAABIGONI-GIIZIS MIDAASWI
ASHI-LNGODWAASWI (MAY 16)
BWAAN AKIING
Pine Ridge

We drive down to Pine Ridge in a couple of Suburbans—these roads can't take a tour bus. Oglala Lakota College has a ninety-five percent graduation rate and was the first four-year college on any reservation. Eighty percent of all graduates are women. We lunch with staff and students.

Little Wound School greets us. About 1,000 kids fill the gym for an assembly featuring the school band, Jackie Bird, and the Indigo Girls. Non-Indian kids from Rapid City sit in the middle of the auditorium surrounded by Pine Ridge. We share some common music territory and a lot of ice cream.

We are guests of the KILI radio show with Cecilia Fire Thunder. She makes us feel at home.

We travel to Wounded Knee, site of the 1890 massacre and the 1973 occupation. We are all deeply moved.

WAABIGONI-GIIZIS MIDAASWI
ASHI-NIIZHWAASWI (MAY 17)
Bozeman, Montana

"The Sweet Grass Hills contain their own revelation—they're the foundation of our survival. The Sweet Grass Hills are sacred as a source of life, and it is the spirit of life within them that people worship."

—Curly Bear Wagner

Dominating the landscape, the Sweet Grass Hills tower above the high plains of Montana. They are sacred lands and have been honored for centuries by the Cheyenne, Blackfeet, Gros Ventre, Salish, Kootenai, Assiniboine, and the Cree in the vision quest and ceremonies.

The Sweet Grass Hills are threatened by gold mining companies. In 1993, prompted by the strong, united opposition of Indian Tribes and local non-Native communities, the Secretary of the Interior temporarily withdrew the sacred Sweet Grass Hills from mining claims. In August 1995, the temporary mining moratorium will expire.

Native Action, a grassroots project from the Northern Cheyenne reservation comes to make an appeal for the Sweet Grass Hills. Gail Small calls on the Bureau of Land Management (BLM) and Congress to protect the sacred site. There is no such thing as multiple use of a sacred site.

The Bozeman show and the two following ones generated about 6,000 postcards for the Sweet Grass Hills.

WAABIGONI-GIIZIS MIDAASWI
ASHI-LSHWAASWI-NFISHTANA (MAY 18-20)
Jackson Hole, Park City, Denver

Jackson Hole
Drunk people in the audience yell at me, "Save the wilderness, save the buffalo." "We are all Indians."

A man shot one of thirty wolves released into Yellowstone Park. "I thought I was just shooting a big dog or a coyote," he says in explanation. "I didn't know I was shooting an endangered animal." Nice logic.

Rich town, lots of things Indian, few Indians.

My six-year-old disappears from backstage. We tear apart the place looking for her. We find her in the crowd of 2,200 in the third row, smiling, and dancing away with three nice young women.

Denver

Lots of Indians, Feds, and Indigo Girls fans and friends join us for a reception. Creek poet Joy Harjo and her band Poetic Justice open the show.

Indian Country—Southwest

Taos Pueblo is struggling to get back a chunk of land (800 acres) they need for ceremonies. We have a gracious meeting with the War Chief and visit with the buffalo herd. We sent about 1,500 postcards to the Governor of New Mexico to support the return of the Taos "Bottleneck area."

We meet with Diné CARE and discuss land and environment issues on the Navajo Nation. Then we travel over to the Hopi Civic Center for a show. Four hundred kids listen and dance away in a whirling sort of style, peculiar to 2nd graders and Dead Heads.

The Hopi Foundation takes us through Hotevilla, fifty houses have solar panels on them. We see some restored clan houses. We walk through town in three groups, looking out over gardens and vistas. I am struck by the irony of the situation. While the Hopi live simply and plant their gardens in this arid land, the coal companies drain over a million acre feet of water each year to slurry coal by pipeline from Black Mesa to the Arizona/California border.

Water, so precious, so wasted.

WABIGONIGIIZIS NIISHTANA
ASHI-NAANAN, ASHI-LNGOSWAASWI MINAWA,
ASHI-NIIZHWAASWI (MAY 25-27)
Shows blur—Phoenix, San Diego, Santa Monica

Old friends show up—lots of fun. Barbara Williams, an actress I was chained to for five hours, comes to visit. We had locked the gate to a phone book factory that uses clear-cut trees.

"They're still cutting," she whispers. "We've made some headway, but they are still cutting."

WABIGONIGIIZIS NIIZHTANA
ASHI-ZHANGASWI (MAY 29)
Anchorage, Alaska

For the past fifty years, anything America has wanted has been taken from Alaska (gold, oil, fish, and trees). Alaska produces a good chunk of oil, America's huge factory trawlers using driftnets mine the ocean for fish, in many cases throwing away up to sixty percent of the catch. Lumber companies eye what's left of the forests, like the Tongass and the delicate strip of Prince William Sound for clear-cutting.

We hold a press conference at the University of Alaska with Gwich'in, Athabascan, and Eyak Native activists. The calving grounds of the Porcupine Caribou herd at the Arctic National Wildlife Refuge (ANWR) is on the chopping block for the federal deficit. The Alaskan Congressional delegation wants to rename ANWR the Arctic National Oil Reserve—"Newt Speak."

We are blasted in the *Anchorage Daily News* for our outspoken Native and environmental politics.

We travel to Prince William Sound. It has been six years since the Exxon Valdez spilled 11 million gallons of crude oil into the pristine waters and beaches of Prince William Sound. Now the 1,200 miles of coastline once coated with oil are suffering another large-scale environmental catastrophe—clear-cut logging of ancient, old growth rain forests.

According to projections, more than fifty percent of Prince Williams Sound's rain forest will be clear-cut by the year 2000. Currently 50,000 acres have already been clear-cut in the Chugach National Forest.

ODE'MINI-GIIZIS (JUNE 2)
Cordova

The state and federal bureaucrats who administer the Exxon Valdez oil spill settlement sit at a long table in the elementary school gym. The crowd gathered to testify includes the usual players from across the environmental spectrum—commercial fishermen, activists, Native corporation officials, business owners. The federal government's top official in Alaska, a prim and crisp-looking lawyer named Deborah Williams, calls out names and keeps the testimony moving.

Such hearings have become largely routine in the six years since the Exxon Valdez spill but there was nothing typical about the entourage seated near the front of the room.

Nine or ten people speak. A fisherman urges Board Chair, Williams, to consider evidence that twenty percent of oil spilled in the ocean sinks to the bottom. A Native elder describes finding weirdly deformed seals with unhealthy livers, a condition he suspects was caused by the spill. Then Williams looks toward the out-of-towners.

"Would the Indigo Girls like to go next?" she asks. The Indigo Girls do want to go next. The pair of Grammy-winning rock-n-roll stars from Georgia had come a long way and rearranged their schedule several times so they could tell Williams and her colleagues what they think about clear-cutting in the Sound and why they want the oil-spill trustees to make a deal with Eyak Corporation to stop logging in the nearby Orca Narrows.

Amy goes first. She explains that her band is on a tour of the United States to raise money for Native environmental issues. She wears a T-shirt, hiking boots, and a pair of ragged jeans and pushes her brown bangs out of her eyes.

"I believe you can't have a culture without a piece of land to subsist on," she tells state Fish & Game Commissioner Frank Rue and the others.

Emily Saliers, today wears bib overalls. She writes gentle ballads and sings with a sweet rich soprano, and speaks next. "I encourage the council to please resolve your negotiations with the Eyak Corporation. There are Native people who are willing to sell out for money. There are also corporations that are willing to take advantage of that."

We play a show at Cordova High School to 500 fishermen's wives, families, and community people. Emily's words haunt me still, "We believe in people, not corporations."

Sleepy, we rise early the next morning and shuttle onto planes to Portland for the tour's finale.

ODE'MINI-GIIZIS (JUNE 3)
Portland

We honor four Native women who exemplify the struggles for justice, the environment, and future generations. Indigenous Women's Network founder and activist Janet McCloud, Pulyallup fisherwoman and grandmother to forty grandchildren; Myra So Happy (Yakama); Margaret Flint Knife Saluskin (Yakama), mother of six children and grandmother to one; and Mililani Trask, Kia-Aina-Head of State of the Hawaiian Nation.

"This is where fish come to give up their spirits. It is sacred. I will not come to fish for my family, for my elders, for my people, next to tennis courts and the swimming pools of a luxury home development." Margaret Saluskin embodies the spirit in her words.

I am humbled by their presence, deeds, and lives.

An Honor the Earth Festival was held at Portland Meadows. The stage was donated by the Grateful Dead, food and work donated by community. Amy and Emily commit to doing the tour again and call on others to take up the political torch. We will still be here.

GAAWAABAABIGANIKAAG:
Ode'mini-giizis (June 11)

My children are asleep downstairs, house quiet. A loon calls, echoing across the lake. I touch the keys to my piano, as if to recall harmony I heard and remembered. I heard our drums at the pow-wow this weekend, I danced my way home. 40,000 people, 22 shows, 13 states, and 29 days later, I am home.

Keewayndah.

Traditional Ecological Knowledge
and Environmental Futures

Appeared in the COLORADO JOURNAL OF INTERNATIONAL
ENVIRONMENTAL LAW AND POLICY, *Vol. 5:127, 1994.*

Traditional ecological knowledge is the culturally and spiritually based way in which indigenous peoples relate to their
ecosystems. This knowledge is founded on spiritual-cultural instructions from "time immemorial" and on generations of careful
observation within an ecosystem of continuous residence. I believe that this knowledge represents the clearest empirically based
system for resource management and ecosystem protection in
North America, and I will argue that native societies' knowledge
surpasses the scientific and social knowledge of the dominant
society in its ability to provide information and a management
style for environmental planning. Frankly, these native societies
have existed as the only example of sustainable living in North
America for more than 300 years.

This essay discusses the foundation of traditional ecological
knowledge and traditional legal systems, the implications of colonialism on these systems, and the challenges faced by the
environmental movement and native peoples in building a common appreciation for what is common ground—Anishinaabeg
Akiing—the people's land.

> *I had a fish net out in a lake and at first I was getting quite a*
> *few fish in it. But there was an otter in the lake and he was*
> *eating the fish in the net. After a while, fish stopped coming*
> *into the net. They knew there was a predator there. So similarly*

*game know about the presence of hunters as well. The Cree say,
"all creatures are watching you. They know everything you are
doing. Animals are aware of your activities." In the past, animals
talked to people. In a sense, there is still communication between
animals and hunters. You can predict where the black bear is
likely to den. Even though the black bear zigzigs before retreating
into his den to hibernate, tries to shake you off his trail, you can
still predict where he is likely to go to. When he approaches his
den entrance, he makes tracks backwards, loses his tracks in
the bush, and makes a long detour before coming into the den.
The hunter tries to think what the bear is thinking. Their minds
touch. The hunter and the bear have parallel knowledge, and
they share that knowledge. So in a sense they communicate.[1]*

To be secure that one will be able to harvest enough involves
more than skill; it also involves careful observation of the ecosystem and careful behavior determined by social values and cultural practices.

"Minobimaatisiiwin,"[2] or the "good life," is the basic objec-
tive of the Anishinaabeg and Cree[3] people who have historically,
and to this day, occupied a great portion of the north-central region of the North American continent. An alternative interpretation of the word is "continuous rebirth." This is how we traditionally understand the world and how indigenous societies have
come to live within natural law. Two tenets are essential to this
paradigm: cyclical thinking and reciprocal relations and responsibilities to the Earth and creation. Cyclical thinking, common to
most indigenous or land-based cultures and value systems, is an
understanding that the world (time, and all parts of the natural
order—including the moon, the tides, women, lives, seasons, or
age) flows in cycles. Within this understanding is a clear sense
of birth and rebirth and a knowledge that what one does today
will affect one in the future, on the return. A second concept,
reciprocal relations, defines responsibilities and ways of relating
between humans and the ecosystem. Simply stated, the resources of the economic system, whether they be wild rice or

deer, are recognized as animate and, as such, gifts from the Creator. Within that context, one could not take life without a reciprocal offering, usually tobacco or some other recognition of the Anishinaabeg's reliance on the Creator. There must always be this reciprocity. Additionally, assumed in the "code of ethics" is an understanding that "you take only what you need, and you leave the rest."

   Implicit in the concept of Minobimaatisiiwin is a continuous inhabitation of place, an intimate understanding of the relationship between humans and the ecosystem, and the need to maintain that balance. These values and basic tenets of culture made it possible for the Cree, Ojibway, and many other indigenous peoples to maintain economic, political, religious, and other institutions for generations in a manner that would today be characterized as sustainable.[4]

I. A MODEL

By its very nature, "development"—or, concomitantly, an "economic system" based on these ascribed Indigenous values—must be decentralized, self-reliant, and very closely based on the carrying capacity of that ecosystem. By example, the nature of northern indigenous economies has been a diversified mix of hunting, harvesting, and gardening, all utilizing a balance of human intervention or care, in accordance with these religious and cultural systems' reliance upon the wealth and generosity of nature. Because by their very nature indigenous cultures are not in an adversarial relationship with nature, this reliance is recognized as correct and positive.

> *A hunter always speaks as if the animals are in control of the hunt. The success of the hunt depends on the animals: the hunter is successful if the animal decides to make himself available. The hunters have no power over the game, animals have the last say as to whether they will be caught.*[5]

The Anishinaabeg or Ojibway nation, for example, encompasses people and land within four Canadian provinces and five U.S. states. This nation has a shared common culture, history, governance, language, and land base—the five indicators, according to international law[6] of the existence of a nation of people. This nation historically and correctly functions within a decentralized economic and political system, with much of the governance left to local bands (like villages or counties) through clan and extended family systems. The vast natural wealth of this region and the resource management systems of the Anishinaabeg have enabled people to prosper for many generations. In one study of Anishinaabeg harvesting technologies and systems, a scientist noted:

> Economically, these family territories in the Timiskaming band were regulated in a very wise and interesting manner. The game was kept account of very closely, proprietors knowing about how abundant each kind of animal was. Hence they could regulate the killing so as not to deplete the stock. Beaver was made the object of the most careful "farming," an account being kept of the numbers of occupants old and young to each "cabin."[7]

The killing of game was regulated by each family. . . .[8]

The Anishinaabeg employed a resource management system that used techniques for sustained yield. Such systems show a high degree of unification of conception and execution (possible because the "scientist" is the "resource manager"). There has only been limited imitation of this system by the scientific community.[9]

This system has allowed traditional land-based economies to prosper. Conceptually, the system provides for both domestic production and production for exchange or export. Hence, whether the resource is wild rice or white fish, the extended family as a production unit harvests within a social and resource management code that insures sustained yield. Traditional management practices have often been dismissed by North American settlers as useless in the current circumstances of more significant populations. However, it is important to note that previous North American indigenous populations were substantially higher than they are now. This indicates that these management practices were applied in greater population densities, an argument which is useful in countering the perceptions that all Native American practices have occurred with very low populations. I believe there is a more substantial question meriting discussion: Can North American society craft the social fabric to secure a traditional management practice, based on consensual understanding and a collective process?

II. COLONIALISM AND UNDERDEVELOPMENT

The governance of this land by traditional ecological knowledge has been adversely affected by genocide, colonialism, and subsequent circumstances that need to be considered in the current dialogue on North American resource management, the role of the environmental movement, and indigenous peoples. The holocaust of America is unmatched on a world scale, and its aftermath caused the disruption necessary to unseat many of our indigenous economic and governmental systems. There can be no accurate estimate of the number of people killed since the invasion, but one estimate provides for 112,554,000 indigenous people in the western hemisphere in 1492 and an estimated 28,554,000 in 1980. Needless to say, this is a significant depopulation.[10] This intentional and unintentional genocide facilitated a subsequent process of colonialism, which served to establish a new set of relations between indigenous nations and colonial or "settler" nations in the Americas.

Three basic concepts govern relations between colonial "settlers" and indigenous nations. Colonialism has been extended through a set of "center periphery relations" in which the center has expanded through: (1) the cultural practice spreading Christianity and, later, Western science and other forms of Western thought; (2) the socioeconomic practice of capitalism; and (3) the military-political practice of colonialism.[11]

These practices have resulted in the establishment of a set of relations between indigenous economies and peoples and the North American colonial economy that are characterized by dependency and underdevelopment. Underdevelopment—or, more accurately, "underdeveloping," because it is an ongoing practice—is the process by which the economy both loses wealth and undergoes the structural transformation which accentuates and institutionalizes this process.[12] This process, underway for at least the past 200 years, is characterized by the appropriation of land and resources from indigenous nations for the purpose of "developing" the U.S. and Canadian economies and, subsequently, the "underdeveloping" of indigenous economies. The resulting loss of wealth (closely related to loss of control over traditional territories) has created a situation in which most indigenous nations are forced to live in circumstances of material poverty. It is no coincidence that Native Americans and Native Hawaiians (as well as First Nations in Canada) are the poorest people both in the United States and on the continent as a whole. As a consequence, indigenous peoples are subjected to an array of socioeconomic and health problems that are a direct consequence of poverty.[13]

In this process of colonialism, and later marginalization, indigenous nations become peripheral to the colonial economy and eventually are involved in a set of relations characterized by dependency. As Latin American scholar Theotonio Dos Santos notes: "By dependence we mean a situation in which the economy of certain countries is conditioned by the development and expansion of another economy to which the former is subjected."[14] These circumstances—and indeed, the forced underdevelopment of sustainable indigenous economic systems for the purpose of colonial exploitation of land and resources—are an essential backdrop for any discussion of existing environmental circumstances in the North American community and of any discussion of sustainable development in a North American context. Perhaps most alarming is the understanding that even today this process continues, because a vast portion of the remaining natural resources on the North American continent are still under native lands or, as in the case of the disposal of toxic wastes on Indian reservations, the residual structures of colonialism make native communities focal points for dumping the excrement of industrial society.

III. INDIGENOUS NATIONS TODAY

On a worldwide scale, there are more than 5,000 nations and just over 170 states. "Nations" are defined under international law as those in possession of a common language, land base, history, culture and territory, while "states" are usually recognized and seated at the United Nations.[15] North America similarly contains a series of nations, known as "First Nations" in Canada and, with few exceptions, denigrated in the United States by the term "tribes." Demographically, indigenous nations represent the majority population north of the 55th Parallel in Canada (the 50th Parallel in the eastern provinces) and occupy approximately two-thirds of the Canadian landmass.

Although the United States has ten times the population it had during colonial times, Indian people do not represent the majority, except in a few areas, particularly the "Four Corners" region of the United States (so named because four states—Arizona, Utah, New Mexico, and Colorado—all meet at one point) where Ute, Apache, Navajo, and Pueblo people reside. However, inside our reservations, which occupy approximately four percent of our original land base in the United States, Indian people remain the majority population.

In our territories and our communities a mix of old and new coexist, sometimes in relative harmony and at other times in a violent disruption of the traditional way of life. In terms of economic and land tenure systems, the material basis for relating to the ecosystem, most indigenous communities are a melange of colonial and traditional structures and systems. Although U.S. or Canadian laws may restrict and allocate resources and land on reservations (or aboriginal territory), the indigenous practice of "usufruct rights" is often still maintained and, with it, traditional economic and regulatory institutions like the trapline, "rice boss," and family hunting, grazing (for peoples who have livestock), or harvesting territories.

These subsistence lifestyles continue to provide a significant source of wealth for domestic economies on the reservation, whether for nutritional consumption or for household use, as in the case of firewood. They also, in many cases, provide the essential ingredients of foreign exchange; wild rice, furs, woven rugs, and silverwork. These native economic and land tenure systems, which are specific to each region, are largely invisible to U.S. and Canadian government agencies' economic analysts who consistently point to native "unemployment" with no recognition of the traditional economy. The Bureau of Indian Affairs labor statistics are categorized by sector, as is most employment data available from the U.S. Census Bureau.

In many northern communities, over half of local food and a significant amount of income is garnered from this traditional economic system. In other cases, for instance on the Northern Cheyenne Reservation in Montana, over ninety percent of the land is held by Cheyenne and is used primarily for ranching. Although they do not represent formal "wage work" in the industrial system, these land-based economies are essential to native communities. The lack of recognition for indigenous economic systems, although it has a long history in the North American colonial view of native peoples, is particularly frustrating in terms of the current debate over development options.

Resource extraction plans or energy mega projects proposed for indigenous lands do not consider the current significance of these economic systems nor their value for the future, as demonstrating what remains of sustainable ways of living in North America. A direct consequence is that environmentally destructive development programs ensue, many times foreclosing the opportunity to continue the lower-scale, intergenerational economic practices that had been underway in the native community.

IV. INDIGENOUS ENVIRONMENTAL ISSUES

The conflict between two paradigms—industrial thinking and indigenous thinking—becomes central to the North American and, indeed to the worldwide, environmental and economic crisis. As native communities struggle to survive, issues of sovereignty and control over natural resources become central to North American resource politics and the challenge for North Americans of conscience. Consider these facts:

• More than 50 million indigenous peoples inhabit the world's remaining rain forests.

• More than 1 million indigenous people will be relocated to allow for the development of hydroelectric dam projects in the next decade.

• The United States has detonated all its nuclear weapons in the lands of indigenous people, more than 600 of those tests within land legally belonging to the Shoshone nation.

• One-half of all uranium resources within the borders of the United States lay under native reservations. In 1974, Indians produced 100 percent of all federally controlled uranium.[16]

• One-third of all low-sulfur coal in the western United States is on Indian land, with four of the ten largest coal strip mines in these same areas.[17]

• Over 40 billion board feet of timber stands on Indian reservations—trees now coveted by U.S. timber interests.[18]

• Fifteen of the eighteen recipients of phase one nuclear waste research grants, so-called Monitored Retrievable Nuclear Storage sites, are Indian communities.

• The largest hydroelectric project on the continent, the James Bay Project, is on Cree and Inuit lands in northern Canada.[19]

For many indigenous peoples, the reality is as sociologist Ivan Illich has suggested: development practices are in fact a war on subsistence.

Notes

[1] Fikret Berkes, "Environmental Philosophy of the Chisasibi Cree People of James Bay" Brock University, in *Traditional Knowledge and Renewable Resource Management in Northern Regions* (Occasional Paper No. 23), at 7, 10 (Milton M.R. Freeman & Ludwig N. Carbyn, eds. 1988).

[2] "Minobimaatisiiwin" can be literally translated as the "good life"—"mino" means "good" and Bimatisiiwin" means "life" in the language of the Anishinaabeg people.

[3] Anishinaabeg, which means "the people," are also called the Ojibway or Chippewa, and are an Algonkin-speaking people who reside in the Great Lakes region. The Cree or Eeyou, which can be translated as "the people" in their language, are close relatives of the Anishinaabeg.

[4] For discussion, see generally, Colin Scott, "Knowledge Discussion Among Cree Hunters: Metaphors and Literal Understanding," LXXV *Journal De Societe Anthropologic*, 1989, at 193, 193–208.

[5] Berkes, supra note 1, at 10.

[6] Jason W. Clay, "What's a Nation?," *Mother Jones*, Nov.–Dec. 1990, at 28.

[7] Frank G. Speck, "The Family Hunting Band as the Basis of Algonkian Social Organization," 17 *American Anthropologist*, 289, 296 (1915).

[8] See generally, ibid. at 289–305.

[9] Peter J. Usher, "Property Rights: The Basis of Wildlife Management," in *National and Regional Interests in the North* 389, 408–09 (1984).

[10] Robert Venables, "The Cost of Columbus: Was There a Holocaust?" *Northeast Indian Q.*, Fall 1990, at 29, 30 n.7.

[11] John Galtung, "Self Reliance: Concepts, Practice and Rationale," in *Self Reliance: A Strategy for Development* 19, 20 (Johan Galtung et al. eds., Bogle-L'Ouverture Publications, Ltd. 1980).

[12] Samir Amin, *Unequal Development: An Essay on the Social Formations of Peripheral Capitalism* 201–3 (Brian Pearce, trans., Monthly Review Press 1976).

[13] *American Indian Policy Review Comm., Final Report Submitted to Congress May 17, 1977* (Comm. Print 1977).

[14] Theotonio Dos Santos, "The Structure of Dependence," in Readings in

U.S. Imperialism 225, 226 n. 1 (K.T. Fann & Donald C. Hodges eds., Porter Sargent 1971).

[15] Clay, supra note 6.

[16] Winona LaDuke, "Native America: The Economics of Radioactive Colonialism," *Review of Radical Political Economics*, Fall 1983, at 9, 10.

[17] Ibid.

[18] Interview with Marshall Cutsforth, Bureau of Indian Affairs Office of Trust Responsibility (August 10, 1993).

[19] See Boyce Richardson, *Strangers Devour the Land* (1976).

I Heard the Owl Call My Name:
Indian Forests, the Endangered Species
Act, and Endangered Cultures

Fall 1993

*"In the meantime, we would like to see Navajo Forest Products
Industry and the BIA comply with the laws of the United States,
including the National Environmental Policy Act, the National
Historic Preservation Act, and the Endangered Species Act. If
we can do no better than the beligaana's minimal respect for the
land, we should at least comply at that minimal level. . . ."*

—Diné CARE, October 22, 1993
Statement to Navajo Nation Council

Leroy Jackson, a Diné (Navajo) man who had dedicated much
of his life to protecting the Chuska Mountain forests, died
mysteriously this fall. His body was found in his van after he
disappeared during a business trip in northern New Mexico.

For the past three years, Jackson, with Diné CARE, a grassroots
environmental group, had worked diligently to confront logging
interests in the Chuska Mountains, hoping to turn the Navajo
Forest Products Industry towards more sustainable forestry practices, particularly in significant sacred and cultural areas such as
the Chuskas—the Male Deity of Diné religion. In 1991, he began
a crusade to save local forests from overcutting, and spearheaded
efforts by Diné Citizens Against Ruining our Environment (Diné
CARE) to negotiate with the Diné Nation's forestry enterprise to
manage the Chuska forests more responsibly. When negotiations

failed, he reluctantly accepted the prospect of legal conflict, and challenged the tribe to begin complying with national environmental standards for forestry. Later that month, in fact, Jackson was scheduled to fly to Washington D.C. to argue against the BIA policy which would have exempted the Diné Tribal Council from logging prohibitions to protect the Mexican Spotted Owl.

Jackson's death brings many Native forestry issues to light, particularly the internal battle within many reservations between economic pressures and traditional cultural practices and values. On the Diné reservation, as elsewhere in North America, these struggles will play out with increasing intensity as the value of Indian timber in a shrinking supply market adds new pressures to the ecology and cultural fabric of Indian Country.

Between the U.S. and Canada, there are many trees, and a good portion are on Native land, or, in Canada, on lands to which Native people possess unextinguished Aboriginal Title. All of them appear to be up for grabs. The Clinton Administration announced this summer in the Forest Plan (July 1), "federal assistance to bring to market backlogged timber sales from Indian reservations," or what some Native activists have called the Clinton Administration's "equal opportunity logging policy." Or alternately, as Terry Virdon, Assistant Director of BIA Forestry notes, "the Clinton Administration, and federal government have always looked to the tribal timber as 'their reserves.' They basically say, 'we'll carry on business as usual, and have those for later. . . .'" Finally, the Free Trade Agreement guarantees an easy supply of "foreign timber" offered up as an alternative to clear-cutting American forests. On U.S. reservations alone stands some 56 billion board feet of Indian timber ("timber" and "woodland")—comprising some 15 million acres, or a little less than one third of all reservation holdings today.

This is a battle—make no mistake. It is about deforestation and cultural transformation. Throughout Indian country, lines will be drawn, and ecosystems may be transformed. And, tribal sovereignty will play centrally in the conflict—as tribes decide to exercise their rights to cut their forests and, for instance, circumvent the Endangered Species Act protection of spotted owls (a proposal forwarded by both northwest and southwestern Nations) to cut their old growth. Or Native Nations may decide to utilize their tribal sovereignty and build a sustainable forestry program based on whole cultural and ecosystem management. The choices are clearly ours.

DEFORESTATION: THE LAY OF THE LAND IN NORTH AMERICA, NOT JUST THE AMAZON

The destruction of the world's forests is taking place at an unprecedented rate. Although forests still cover one fifth of the earth's land surface, fifty acres are destroyed every minute. An area one-fifth the size of Saskatchewan is deforested every year. Only 5% of American forests remain now. While depletion of tropical rainforests continues, Northern Canadian rainforests are also on the verge of extinction. Scientists report that temperate rainforests on the west coast may disappear even earlier than those in the Southern hemisphere—possibly around the year 2010 if current practices continue.

FRONTLINES IN THE NATIVE FOREST CONFLICT:
Clayoquot Sound, Lil'Wat Territory, and Gitsan Wetsuetan Territory, British Columbia:
In that province, approximately 1,000 square miles of forest are logged each year. In 16 years all the commercial coastal old growth forests will be gone except for a small amount protected by "parks." On December 10, after a decade of bitter battle, the provincial government entered into an interim agreement giving control of Clayoquot Sound back to the Nuu-Chah-Nulth people. The Nuu-Chah-Nulth have stated unequivocally that they oppose clear-cutting.

Cree Territory, Saskatchewan:
In 1986, the Saskatchewan government turned over 50,000 square miles of the province—land occupied by Cree and Dene people—to Weyerhaeuser. This is an area the size of Great Britain.

IMAGES OF THE NORTH AND THE SOUTH: A COMPARISON BETWEEN BRAZIL AND CANADA		
Category	Brazil	Canada
Size (square kilometers)	8.5 million	9.9 million
Percentage covered by forest	45%	45%
Hectares cleared	1,382,000 (1990)	1,021,619 (1988)
Number of seconds to clear one acre	9 seconds	12 seconds
Amount of productive forest land now barren or not restocked	12%	10.3%
Estimated number of Native people in forest	200,000	170,000

Lubicon Cree Territory, Alberta:
In 1986, the Alberta Government gave the Daishowa Corporation a 12,000 square mile cutting lease to Lubicon Cree territory in Northern Alberta, and supplemented their $600 million pulp mill with federal and provincial money, as well as building the roads, rail lines and infrastructure for the mill.

"Until about ten years ago, the questions of land, band membership mineral rights, and rights generally were essentially academic. Our area was relatively isolated and inaccessible by road. We had little contact with outsiders, including government officials. We were left pretty much alone. We were allowed to continue our lives, raise our families and pursue our traditional

way of life without much interference. But ten years ago, the provincial government started construction of an all-weather road into our area. The road was completed about five years ago. Faced with the prospect of an influx of outsiders into our traditional area, we tried to file a caveat with the Provincial government, the effect of which would have been to formally serve notice to all outsiders of our unextinguished, aboriginal claim to the area."

—Bernard Ominiaayak, Chief of Lubicon

The new pulp mill will be the largest hardwood pulp mill in Canada, employing 600 people, and will consume 4 million trees a year. The timber lease to supply the new pulp mill completely covers the entire Lubicon Land area.

The Daishowa timber lease sits astride oil leases opened by the Alberta provincial government in violation of treaty and land claims agreements with the Lubicon Cree band. In 1990, when Daishowa subcontractors attempted to establish a logging base, the logging camp was set on fire. No further logging took place in 1990 and 1991. In 1991, Bernard Ominiaayak went to Japan to seek public support against Daishowa's activities. After pressure by environmentalists and a Canadian boycott of Daishowa, the company succumbed to pressure and did not log in the 1991 and 1992 cutting period. The Lubicon want to have their land rights secured, and to stop the logging, and are asking for continued support for the boycott and their actions.

Enola Hills, Columbia River:
For the past few years, Columbia River fishing people, and other Native people from the region have worked to stop logging at Enola Hills, a sacred area, which the U.S. Forest Service sought to clear-cut. A part of larger issues of Native Religious Freedom, this past spring the Forest Service backed down on cutting proposals.

Northern Minnesota:
Six timber rich reservations lie within the borders of this state, as do three proposed huge pulp and paper mill expansions. Recent state proposals, including a generic environmental impact statement on timber harvesting seem to cast a covetous eye on 5 billion (plus) board feet of Indian timber up north.

"When I heard our pine had been sold, I cried and prayed it would not be wrested from us. For it is as much ours as is this reservation. . . ."
—Wabunoquod, Mississippi Band Headsman, White Earth Reservation

Eyak Forests, Alaska:
Eyak territory is the site of a struggle between the ANCSA created Eyak Corporation and traditional leadership, over what remains of their forests. The Eyak Rainforest Preservation Fund was established two years ago to represent the Eyak Tribe's efforts to preserve the pristine ecosystem of the Prince William Sound, as well as their cultural heritage as tied to the land. Their territory sits aside Prince William Sound, which four years ago was the site of the 25 million gallon Exxon Valdez spill, devastating 1,200 miles of coastline. Today, the ecosystem faces the spectre of clear-cutting. Already 12,000 acres of the Eyak forests are gone, and during the next two years, the Eyak Corporation proposes to clear-cut another 90,000 acres. This clear-cutting will affect literally hundreds of traditional Eyak sacred sites including burial grounds, village sites, and subsistence fish camps. As Traditional Chief and elder Marie Smith Jones explains, "It was the bodies of our ancestors that fertilized these trees and their spirit and strength lives on in the forest. This is why the land is sacred. It provided for us and protected us and we want to keep it that way. The forest is sacred."

Diné Forests:

Navajo Forest Products Industry (NFPI) was formed in 1958, on the advice of BIA consultants and by 1963 was operating the largest lumber mill in the Southwest, serviced by a forest that had a lower than average commercial forest base for the region. The corporation (NFPI) borrowed heavily for plant renovation although the lumber market was diminishing, and by the early 1990s had become mired with debt. When requested for a stumpage fee repayment plan, NFPI proposed two steps: 1) to ask the Navajo nation for lower stumpage fees, and have that be enacted retroactively to cover past timber sales and, 2) ask the tribe for forgiveness on whatever debt remained after the stumpage fees were lowered. The newly coined term for this type of "forgiveness" is "racial royalty."

The environmental impact has been significant. "Condition Reports," prepared by Diné forestry personnel in the late 1980s indicate a number of problems. Including, not the least, that there was no replanting from 1880 to 1975 on the reservation. In 1981, it was estimated that it would take 160 years of concerted regeneration to return the forests to a situation of sustainable yield.

Leroy Jackson, and Diné CARE, have for several years been working to alter Navajo forestry harvesting practices, particularly in the Chuska Mountains, the male diety of Navajo cosmology and home to many "grandfather" a.k.a. "old growth" trees. Diné CARE, like other segments of the traditional Diné community recognize that the "Female Mountain" of the Diné—Black Mesa—is already being desecrated by strip-mining, and are concerned that this desecration of the "Male Mountain" will cause further imbalance in their way of life. Diné CARE and Jackson have made some enemies. Last summer, angry loggers hanged an effigy of Jackson, blaming him and his organization for layoffs at NFPI. However, Chairman of the Board of NFPI, George Arthur, states that "mismanagement rather than environmentalists" led to the layoff of 85 of 400 workers at the tribally owned facility.

Diné CARE has proposed a new integrated forestry management plan, based on sustainable and culturally sensitive practices, and also based on reforestation. Lori Goodman, Diné CARE organizer puts their recent history in context of a larger picture. "Leroy was killed fighting pro-logging policies of the BIA. There's been 113 years of impact on Diné forests. People have been killed defending Native forests, and he was one. . . ."

TRIBAL SOVEREIGNTY AND CULTURAL SURVIVAL:
I HEARD THE OWL CALL MY NAME

The battle continues and it is not a pretty sight. The Bureau of Indian Affairs, on behalf of some southwestern tribes (Diné Nation, Mescalero, White Mountain, and San Carlos Apaches, and the Hualapai), seeks to follow suit with the Northwestern tribes and secure an exemption from the Endangered Species Act in reference to the Mexican Spotted Owl Habitat. In an August 1 letter to the Fish and Wildlife Service, three southwest regional directors of the BIA (Sid Mills, Wilson Barber and Walter Mills) argued that, "In this case, not only are issues of sovereignty, self governance and economic development involved, but cultural and religious issues are also entwined, as well, since the owl is held in low esteem by the Navajo, Apache and many Pueblo people. . . ."

Diné CARE's September response to the letter argues that BIA forestry practices are based on "industrial models," which do not reflect traditional culture and represent only pro-development segments of the Native community, and a later October letter to the Navajo Nation Council urges that NFPI should come into compliance with federal law, arguing that, "Sovereignty comes from within, [yet] policies reflect the European/American lack of respect for the environment." Diné CARE continues, noting, "If we can do no better than the beligaana's minimal respect for the land, we should at least comply with that minimal level. . . ." Diné CARE responds to all the recommendations forwarded in the letter, concluding with the BIA assertion that the owls are held in low esteem.

The owl is an integral part of our culture. It is true that the owl has negative connotations in Navajo philosophy, but it is not "negative" in the sense of low esteem, as the letter asserts. Negative and positive, the aggressive and the passive, the male and female are complementary parts of the whole. Without one part, the whole is incomplete. The owl is a messenger. Its presence in the woods is certainly no cause for fear or negative feelings. . . . As animals of the woods, they are part of the connected web of life. And they are vital parts of our cultural and ritual life. . . .

Some would ask if we are selling out our relatives to make Clinton's Quota.

FORESTRY FOR THE SEVENTH GENERATION

There are sustainable forestry models, and they are Native. For instance, it is said that the Haida people of the Northwest coast could fashion their plank houses from living trees. Haida foresters were able to cut a plank from a living tree, and leave the tree standing and alive.

In the 1990s, the only "green certified" forest in North America is on the Menominee reservation. It sticks out as a dark mass in an otherwise mostly clear-cut region of northern Wisconsin. For the past 135 years, the Menominee have worked carefully to manage their forests. Early timber estimates indicate that around 1.5 billion board feet stood on the reservation. Since that first estimate (1865) around 2 billion board feet has been cut off the reservation. The most recent inventory of trees indicates that there's still 1.5 billion board feet of timber suitable for logging—the same volume of trees after 135 years of harvesting the same land.

The Menominee Forestry Program has carefully crafted a program based on sustainable and intensive management. The system involves both computer assessments and inventories (of, for instance, the some 109 different regions of the reservation), and an eye to cultural and spiritual needs of the Menominee. As a result, over 220,000 acres are currently under management and serve as the resource base for the Menominee Tribal Enterprises Sawmill, employing almost half of all those working on the reservation. This long-term management plan has survived for well over a century and is viewed in North America as "a model for the seventh generation."

Grand Portage reservation, nestled at the tip of Lake Superior, has a similar story. All 56,000 acres of the reservation is wooded and supports a chipping mill and pallet mill, which allows the tribe to capture the "value added" for their forests.

"In 1985, the BIA wanted to upgrade the forest management plan. They picked Grand Portage and came up with their forest management planning staff from the central office, and when they got here, we wanted to do something completely different than what they wanted to do," Rick Novinsky, Tribal Forester explains. "We wanted to look at things in a wholistic way—timber, recreation, waterlife, wildlife, resources—and manage each one with the others in mind. We ended up doing that plan, and it turned out to be the first integrated forest resource management plan approved by the BIA."

The Forestry program set aside land into distinct designations—recreation, wildlife, and forestry—and has mapped a program based on the reality that there are more moose than people in the county. When approached by timber interests to expand their mill capacity and double shifts, the Grand Portage Tribal Council basically shrugged, pointing out that they already had almost full employment on the reservation, and upping the capacity of the mill would only require them to import a non-Indian labor force. Rick Novinsky underscores their strategy. "The tribe should determine their agenda for the forests and their mill. It shouldn't be driven by outside forests. These are, after all, our trees and our land. . . ."

There is, indeed, much that may be learned from our own experience and much at stake.

There are also larger discussions, in which Native people need to be heard. For instance, "demand" for forest products is driven by consumption, or, more appropriately, "overconsumption." The U.S. consumes seven times as much wood products per capita as any other country. Is that a good use of our forests? And, a good portion of North American wood goes off the continent as a raw product, meaning that neither Indians, nor any other timber-dependent community usually capture much "value added" for that wood—those supplementary jobs go elsewhere. Finally, there is the issue of "sacrifice areas." While some "American forests" may be protected under the Clinton Plan, is it fair that either tribes should be pressured to cut, or that areas like Lubicon Cree territory or Northern Saskatchewan should be clear-cut to supply American sawmills?

For over a hundred years, our people have fought to protect our forests, recognizing in them medicinal plants, animal relations, and the knowledge of generations of ancestors. There are many who will argue that we are those forests. Over time, some of the nuances have changed, yet the questions and challenges remain the same. We need now to face those challenges in our own communities with the honesty and courage our ancestors have had. Perhaps a Central American Indigenous leader summarized it best, in saying, "The difference between a white man and an Indian is this: A white man wants to leave money to his children. An Indian wants to leave forests. . . ." Leroy Jackson would probably agree.

Drowning the North
for Minnesota Electricity

Appeared in THE CIRCLE, *December 1991.*

Worried about the destruction of the Amazon rain forest? Concerned about global warming, the greenhouse effect and other climatic changes? A $70 billion mega-project on the shores of Ontario and Quebec's James Bay and Manitoba's Hudson Bay promises to bring it all home to U.S. consumers. The series of new dams, water diversions, and hydroelectric projects at issue will, according to the National Audubon Society, "make James Bay and some of Hudson's Bay uninhabitable for much of the wildlife now dependent on it." Audubon senior staff scientist Jan Beyea reports the society is "convinced that in 50 years [this entire] ecosystem will be lost."

For the indigenous people of the Sub-arctic, the plan represents an ecological nightmare of yet unknown proportions. Widespread mercury contamination, the by-product of methane gas—which also contributes to the greenhouse effect—and significant destabilization of land/water systems in the north are already problems resulting from the existing James Bay area dam complex, constructed during the 1970s, and the Manitoba Northern Flood projects. The new projects, including James Bay II, will destroy four major river systems in northern Quebec: the Great Whale, Lower Broadback, Nottaway, and Rupert. It will also flood Lake Bienville. Further, James Bay II will impact some 356,000 square miles, an area the size of Maine, Vermont, and New York State combined.

In Manitoba things are almost as bad. Since the early 1970s, seven gigantic dams with power turbines the size of houses have been put into place on the Nelson and Churchill River systems; and now spin out 2,600 megawatts of power. The Kettle Rapids plant (1,300 MW), the Long Spruce project (1,000 MW) are the first of a series on the Nelson River. In total, another eleven generating stations are proposed, which could produce an additional 6,000 megawatts.

Between them, the Churchill and Nelson River combined drain one of the largest watersheds in North America, extending from the Rockies in the west to the Mississippi and Lake Superior drainage basins to the south and east. The engineers proposed joining the flow, diverting one of the rivers into the other so that there would be enormous volumes of water to keep huge turbines spinning. By 1976, the engineers had achieved their dream. A control dam at Missi Falls on the Churchill River (400 miles from the mouth), had cut the flow from an average of 1,050 cubic meters per second to an average of 150, and turned all the water back through the 180-km long Southern Indian Lake.

Fifteen years later, Manitoba Hydro says, "the benefits are believed to supersede the environmental costs."

The Cree people who live there would disagree. Manitoba Hydro's dams have devastated their ecosystem. These dams are in permafrost—meaning they flood an area which is perpetually frozen. When they put the projects in, Manitoba Hydro (the provincial electric corporation) thought the shoreline would re-establish. It hasn't yet—almost 20 years later.

The problem is that the water temperature is always higher than the temperature of the land, causing essentially a constant melting away of shoreline. According to Dr. Robert Newberry of Winnipeg's Freshwater Institute, the annual rate of shoreline "retreat" is 40 to 50 meters. It may be 80 years before there is a 90 percent recovery of shoreline stability, and complete stabilization is possibly 300 years away.

The silting chokes the reservoirs, may eventually make the

dams inoperable, and right now has caused widespread mercury contamination and devastation of wildlife: 98 percent of waterfowl has disappeared from South Indian Lake (one site), and one out of six people in the impacted Nelson River area suffer mercury contamination.

ENVIRONMENTAL DEVASTATION BECOMES GENOCIDE

The hydroelectric flooding made refugees of thousands of Cree people, and has wrought havoc on their communities. In the early 1970s, at least 75 percent of food and the majority of income came from the land (trapping and commercial fisheries). Today that is not possible. Very little food comes from the land; people are forced to buy store-bought food (at prices up to ten times that paid in the south). At Moose Lake, for instance, two-thirds of their land was flooded, and 634 people were moved into a housing project. "After the flooding, 90 percent of the adults are estimated to have substance abuse problems," Jim Tobacco, chief of Moose Lake Band, says. "There's a very hostile attitude in the community. Our young people are always beating up each other. My people don't know who the hell they are. They live month to month on welfare. Our way of life and resources have been destroyed. We were promised benefits from the hydro-project. Today, we are poor and Manitoba Hydro is rich."

Elsewhere suicide epidemics plague the communities that have been flooded. "There's just a feeling that they're being exploited, they're being used," says Allan Ross, Chief at Norway House, another flooded community. His small village had 15 suicide attempts a month during the 1980s, and at Cross Lake, 20 suicide attempts occurred per month during an 8-month period—ten times the provincial average. A clear message through all of it is that to get to the land, you must kill the people. For that reason Cree and Inuit people living on James and Hudson Bays have unified in their opposition and are calling for a moratorium on all dam construction in the region.

THE MINNESOTA CONTRACT

Minnesota is complicit in the devastation of James Bay. The Manitoba Hydro dams on the Nelson and Churchill Rivers were constructed primarily for export contract—an economic development program based on colonizing the north. The two largest agreements are with Ontario and Minnesota utilities—namely Northern States Power and the United Power Association.

Export sales are projected to triple (worth at least $320 million annually in contracts), of which NSP has a big part. The firm commitment to import 500 MW from 1992 on, and other contract will provide much of the needed capital to move along the controversial Conawapa—a powerhouse—a 1,390 MW facility with a price tag of $55 billion. This fall Manitoba will petition Canada's National Energy Board for a permit to export the power from these dams to the Northern States Power and U.P.A. consumers for at least 700 MW worth over the next two decades.

Ironically, it's all unnecessary. The Minnesota Department of Public Service and most knowledgeable parties agree that at least half of all electricity could be conserved. George Crocker, longtime Safe Energy advocate concurs, and adds that the rate system "should be restructured to reward the efficient use of electricity rather than reward consumption." Crocker suggests telling "industry and regulators that *before* these contracts are approved they should make some changes."

It's not enough to oppose nukes and coal in Minnesota. Hydroelectric power can be just as devastating. We need to make sure we don't support someone else's genocide in our name.

Foreword to *Strangers Devour the Land*

Appeared in STRANGERS DEVOUR THE LAND *by Boyce Richardson,*
1991.

As I sit at my desk I can almost see the shore of James Bay— ten miles downstream from the island of Moose Factory in the Moose River. Almost Arctic Ocean beachfront, some would say, yet I'm coming to think of it as a Hydro viewpoint. As a matter of fact, if all the plans go ahead I may no longer live on an island but on a peninsula of the mainland overlooking a huge freshwater reservoir, where presently I've become accustomed to the saltwater of James Bay, which at the base of Hudson's Bay is the largest bay and estuary system on the continent. Dams upstream from this small village promise to lower water levels and change the ecosystem permanently. And amazing as it may sound, a powerful group of engineers has a proposal to place a dike over the mouth of James Bay to create a vast reservoir of fresh water to sell to cities in the southwestern U.S.

There are many things Cree people have taken for granted over countless generations: that the rivers will always flow, the sun and moon will alternate, and there will be six seasons of the year—yes, six. That is how time is counted here in the North, in seasons based on the migrations of caribou, geese, sturgeons, and other relations, and on the ebb and flow of ice and water. The Cree also have assumed that there will always be food from the land, so long as the Eeu, the Cree, do not abuse their part of the relationship to the animals and the land. Now, the rivers do not always flow, the animals are not always there, and strange as it may seem, there are no longer six seasons in some parts of this land. Hydro-Quebec has made sure of that.

In *Strangers Devour the Land* Boyce Richardson provides an intimate look into the people and communities of James Bay, particularly the Cree of the east coast of James Bay, those most heavily affected by the first stage of the Hydro-Quebec project. This book, originally published at the onset of James Bay I, is the testimony of people and the land. Richardson brings the reader to the hunting territories, the traplines, and the powerful rivers that are the lives of these people. The book is a moving chronicle of the resistance of people to the dams, the story of James Bay I, and how Hydro-Quebec came to begin the largest single hydroelectric project in North America.

This is also a story about all of us, about how industrial society is consuming the lifeblood of this continent. Unfortunately, we must now tell not only the story of James Bay I, the project which devoured the traplines and hunting territories of many of the people written about in this book, but we must tell of the proposal of James Bay II.

As people contemplate the destruction of the Amazon rainforest, global warming, "the greenhouse effect," and other climatic changes, this $60 billion mega-project brings it all home to U.S. and Canadian consumers. The new dams, water diversions, and hydroelectric projects at issue will, according to the National Audubon Society, "make James Bay and some of Hudson's Bay uninhabitable for much of the wildlife now dependent upon it." Audubon senior staff scientist Jan Beyea reports that the Society is "convinced that in fifty years [this entire] . . . ecosystem will be lost. . . ." The ecosystem at stake is as large as California, and includes the central flyway of most of the migratory birds in North America, the drainage of most northern-running river systems in the central part of the continent, a number of endangered species of animals, and Inuit, Cree, and Naskapi/Innu people, who have lived here for at least nine thousand years.

There are no longer "strangers" who devour the land. They are entrenched in the North, in the form of Hydro-Quebec, which put 4,400 square miles of land under water and wreaked ecological havoc in an additional 67,954 square miles. Hydro-Quebec and its counterparts in Ontario and Manitoba are taking a vast territory notable for running water, and essentially proposing to turn it into a vast territory of stagnant reservoirs—virtual toxic sinks.

Already there is spreading mercury contamination from James Bay I. Methane from decomposing plants and trees, which have been drowned in the flooding, converts the inorganic mercury already present in the soil into organic methyl mercury, a lethal poison. Because the process is enhanced in acidic conditions, the mercury levels in the reservoir system are up to six times the level considered safe for humans.

In the village of Chisasibi, downstream from one set of reservoirs (LG 1-4) scientists tested for mercury poisoning several years ago. Two of every three people were found to have excessive levels of methyl mercury already present in their bodies—30 milligrams per kilogram of body weight. Some elders registered twenty times the level deemed acceptable, and had developed symptoms of mercury poisoning such as shaking, numbness of the limbs, loss of peripheral vision, and neurological damage. Hydro-Quebec advised the Cree to stop eating river fish and instead to harvest fish from James and Hudson's bays. These fish, which are still relatively free from methyl mercury, are frequently contaminated with PCBs, a result of other "development" projects in the region and contamination now moving into the arctic food chain from industries to the south.

The Cree call it *nimass aksiwin,* "fish disease," and no other two words could have such a devastating effect on people. "*Nimass aksiwin* strikes at the very heart of our society. It's like being told that armageddon has started, and people are scared as hell," says George Lameboy, a Cree fisherman and trapper. "The scientists come in here and tell us we're getting better [by eating less fish], but hey, you can't measure the effects of *nimass aksiwin* by taking hair samples. How can you measure a man's fear? How can you measure your way of life coming to an end?"

As if the methyl mercury were not enough, the change in water levels in the rivers had devastating results in at least one case. Normally rivers run highest in the spring melt and lowest in winter. Since the flow of rivers is now determined not by nature but by the electrical demands of southern consumers, the order has been reversed; many times, it is increased or decreased dramatically to respond to the "power grid" of the south. In 1984 a sudden release proved deadly, as water was released out of the Caniapiscau Reservoir (now the largest lake in Quebec at 1,865 square miles) precisely during the seasonal migration of the George's River caribou herd. Ten thousand caribou drowned. Hydro-Quebec officials called the disaster "mainly an act of God."

The ongoing environmental problems have solidified Cree opposition to any more development in their territory, and strengthened their calls for a comprehensive environmental review of the first phase of the project prior to construction of any new dams. The Cree call to halt the project is now supported by a growing number of local, national, and international environmental and consumer groups who are deeply concerned about possible long-term consequences of the development. The Cree and other groups have joined in extensive and seemingly endless legal challenges to the project, which at this point have resulted in a court decision calling for an environmental inquiry. Unfortunately, neither the scope of the review nor its weight (that is, whether findings will be binding to the utility) have been determined, leaving many Cree and environmentalists frustrated and skeptical.

The Cree and other groups have consistently called for federal intervention. Cree Chief Mathew Coon Come points out the irony, saying, "When you have the largest project of the century in your backyard, and no environmental assessment . . . not one person monitoring the impact, there is an obvious failure of federal responsibility. . . ." Bill Namagoose, of the Cree Regional Authority, echoes his words, calling the federal sidestepping of the issues "environmental racism." Can you imagine a man who has lived his whole life in Paris—and one day awakens, looks out his window, and Paris is underwater? It just wouldn't happen. The Cree, Inuit, and Innu are far away, dark and different. That is one reason this project, like the exploitation of the Amazon and other rainforests, is planned to go ahead. If Hydro-Quebec proposed to flood the villages, farms, homes, and gravesites of thousands of French-speaking white people, well, it just wouldn't happen.

If the second phase goes ahead, the new dams would greatly accentuate the present environmental damage. At Great Whale, four smaller rivers will be diverted into a single large one. On the Nottaway, Broadback, and Rupert river systems, eleven dams would be built—with the Nottaway being diverted into the Broadback, then the Broadback into the Rupert. In total, the reservoirs will cover more than ten thousand square miles, an area the size of Lake Erie. The project, according to the National Audubon Society, "is the northern equivalent to the destruction of the tropical rainforest."

What is worse is that the Quebec dams are only one set of proposals for James Bay. Another huge hydroelectric project has been put in place on the Nelson River in northern Manitoba, draining into Hudson's Bay, and an undetermined number of dams are planned for the rivers in northern Ontario. Virtually every single river flowing into James and Hudson's bays is now proposed for some hydroelectric or diversion scheme.

This worries not only the native people, but also environmentalists and other people to the south. For although an environmental impact assessment is pending for the Quebec projects, there is no proposal as yet for a cumulative impact assessment for all projects in what is essentially one, unified ecosystem: James and Hudson's bays. As Alan Penn, an environmental advisor to the Grand Council of the Crees of Quebec points out, "There is no precedent for the manipulation of a subarctic watershed elsewhere in the world on the scale proposed here. The project represents a natural experiment, both ecological and sociological, on a massive scale."

Perhaps most horrendous is that this massive experiment is all about making money. Hydro-Quebec is the provincial government's chief economic tool for capitalizing its economy. Although the 125,000 jobs promised never materialized from James Bay I, Hydro-Quebec has all in all done well from its huge investments. In 1970 Hydro-Quebec had 12,000 employees, assets of $3.5 billion, and debts of $2.6 billion. Today the provincial utility has 23,000 employees, assets of $34 billion, and a debt of $23 billion. This corporation accounts for 20 percent of all new investments in Quebec.

A great portion of the scheme is designed to service electrical markets in the U.S. A number of U.S. utilities have accepted Hydro-Quebec's promotion of its power as a cheap, clean alternative to coal and nuclear generating. New York, for instance, has purchased Hydro-Quebec power, and the purchase has accounted for about 9 percent of the state's electricity supply since 1970. This figure is expected to rise to 30 percent by the year 2000. Seven U.S. utilities—the New England Power Pool, the New York Power Authority, Vermont Joint Owners, Massachusetts Power Authority, Citizens Utilities, Consumers Power, and Detroit Edison—have entered into long-term contracts with Hydro-Quebec and Ontario-Hydro to secure power for the next twenty years or more. These contracts, of course, enhance the utility's ability to raise the huge investments required for the new phase of development. In other words, U.S. consumers are clearly implicated in the destruction of this ecosystem.

Canadians, however, are far from innocent. According to Tom

Adams of the Toronto-based Energy Probe, "We are the single most inefficient consumers of electricity in the world. We are twice as inefficient as even the next in line—the U.S." And that inefficiency is buttressed by low rates: industries in Ontario, for instance, pay six times less for electricity than would their counterparts in Japan. Not only do provincial electric corporations subsidize the "hidden costs and dis-economies" of power production, but these very "cheap" rates discourage conservation and undermine any incentive to plan realistically. Energy analysts like Amory Lovins have frequently pointed out that conservation of electricity would make the dams not only unnecessary for projected demand, but cost a great deal less in hard cash. It is outrageous that "cheap electrical rates" are a justification to destroy an entire ecosystem and way of life.

As politicians, environmentalists, and economists speak of the future, "sustainable development" is the phrase most in vogue. While the meaning of that phrase varies with the person using it, the concept has validity for me. Some days I listen to my father-in-law talk when he has come in from his trapline—which is, incidentally, just west of the proposed Nottaway-Broadback-Rupert (NBR) project. He explains that he walked five miles one way to check his rabbit snares and his traps. And he tells me of reaching his hand into a beaver house, to count the number of beavers in the house. There is even a word for this counting in Cree. The point of the counting is so that no person will take more beavers than should be taken from a certain area. There is no word for this in English, only a long description. And it makes no sense whatsoever to explain to a Cree the concept of "sustainable development." My father-in-law and his ancestors have been harvesting and hunting this same area for thousands of years. It appears to me that "sustainable development" and a "sustainable economy" are scheduled for destruction only so that twenty years from now some southern expert can "reinvent" a sustainable economy for this region.

The problem is not Hydro-Quebec, Ontario-Hydro, and the U.S. energy contracts. The problem is "development," and the structure of Canada's (and for that matter, the U.S.) industrial economy. The Canadian economy has always been based on the exploitation of raw materials and resources from the "frontier." The North has always been the frontier, and continues in that role today. The Canadian economy requires this exploitation to prosper. The James Bay dams and diversions are only a small set of many such mega-projects presently underway or proposed for the North. All share a common denominator—a development policy based on capital-intensive, resource-extractive industries. The promise is jobs and prosperity but, as evidenced in James Bay I, the reality is stark and destructive.

At some point, there will be no more "frontiers" to conquer. There will be no more resources to mine, rivers to dam, trees to fell, or capital to invest. As we approach the year 2000, those who have an interest in surviving to the next century would say that point in time is now. And as I sit on my Arctic Ocean beachfront I think about that. I think about the testimony that is in this powerful book, and I hope that by a collective act of conscience, sanity, political and economic change, James Bay will remain saltwater and free of methyl mercury.

The Diaper Problem

Appeared in the TOWNSEND LETTER FOR DOCTORS, *January 1990.*

I'd like to talk about a sensitive and very personal subject: diapers. My son was in cloth diapers, but it was easy enough to put him in disposables. After two days of "Huggies" my garbage bags were full and I was forced to fight off my dogs to get to the garbage bin outside. That's when I noticed that disposables are a lot of garbage. And, the fact is, that they are not really "disposable." After all, you can throw away your coffee maker, or a broken television, but that doesn't mean it's "disposable."

These diapers are paper, plastic and chemical, and they basically don't go away for 500 or so years. So here we are, living in the pollution-free beautiful North, and within a generation we may be literally covered with diapers. The problem is not just on White Earth. Indian people have the highest birth rate in the country; and almost all those babies are in plastic diapers. So, most reservations are going to have to look at this concern sometime.

Is there a problem? Yes. According to studies by the American Journal of Pediatrics, disposables may create health problems for babies. Disposables also cost more than regular diapers, and the biggest problem is that they are literally toxic waste. According to the U.S. Environmental Protection Agency (EPA), the diapers may be filling dumps with disease.

ARE BABIES BETTER OFF IN PAMPERS?

Plastic diapers have been associated with health problems in babies—most notably rashes and a new form of "toxic shock" syndrome. A 1979 article in the *American Journal of Pediatrics* reported that 54% of babies in disposables had rashes, 16% of those rashes were severe. In comparison, only 18% of the babies in cloth diapers had rashes, and no baby had a severe rash. Part of the problem may be that since the diaper "feels dry" it is changed less often than a soggy cloth diaper might be.

The "dryness," however is cause for concern in other areas. A New York State consumer association petitioned the state government to stop the sale and distribution of the new super-absorbent diapers. This consumer association contends that the plastic diapers cause a "toxic shock" syndrome. The diaper itself initiates such a powerful absorption when it becomes wet that the skin may shrivel up and fluids from baby's body may be absorbed.

TOXIC WASTE PROBLEM

The biggest problem of paper and plastic diapers is the environmental one. How do you properly dispose of a Pampers or a Huggie? There are actually instructions on the box. Basically, you take the diaper apart, wash the icky stuff away, flush part of it away and throw away the plastic. If you follow directions, part of the problem would be in your toilet, your plumbing would be busy, and you would have done almost the same amount of work as if you had a cloth diaper.

Instead, most people (about 95%) just toss the diaper. This is the problem. Baby poop can contain over 100 viruses, including live polio and hepatitis from vaccines. That's what the U.S. EPA found in disposables at a landfill in 1972. And, that's not even mentioning that we're dumping untreated sewage (that should go into a sewage system) into a landfill. In turn, when rainwater goes through the dump, the viruses and bacteria can be carried into the streams and subsequently the water supply. Since many dumps are near water tables it is quite possible we are drinking our own waste.

How much of a problem is it? In a sample of one landfill, between 16 and 32% of the garbage was disposables. It is about the same here at White Earth. Think of it this way; assume there were 155 babies under 3 on the White Earth Reservation. If 90% of them use Pampers, then 140 will use about 7,400 diapers each in their "diapering years." That means 1,036,000 plastic diapers going to the dump in 3 years. That is a lot of garbage. That is also a lot of toxic waste.

HOW DID WE GET HERE?
My father-in-law was a moss baby. My parents were cloth diaper babies as were my brother and I. In 1970 Procter and Gamble released Pampers to the supermarket shelves. By 1976, about half the babies were in Pampers.

Not to be outdone, Kimberly Clark came out with Huggies in 1978. By the 1980s Pampers, Huggies and Luvs were bun to bun in the race for babies. At stake is a market that exceeds $3 billion per year—more than 21 billion diaper changes.

The trick is advertising: check it out. Some evenings during "prime time" six or more plastic diaper ads are on television. The most convincing ad brings us a pediatrician who is also a mother. She is sure to tell you her brand of disposables are best for babies. Who wouldn't believe her? As advertising agencies know, young parents are "easy marks" because they want what's best for baby. The industry spends over $100 million on advertising because it works.

By 1987, more than 16 billion diapers were being used annually, representing over 1 billion pounds of paper and resulting in about 3 million pounds of raw sewage dumped into landfills each year. This is one of the fastest growing toxic waste problems on the continent. Meanwhile, back on the reservation, we have a problem. Within a generation we will probably be swimming in plastic diapers. And by the time these toddlers have babies, the toxic waste problem may make our water unfit to drink.

IS THERE A WAY OUT?
We've been here for centuries. It seems a pity to bury ourselves under a pile of Pampers. Lucky for us, this problem has some solutions.

First, save money and do your own diapers. For around $200 (diapers and fancy pants that make changing fast) you can keep your baby in diapers. Add your time and detergent costs and you still have a deal. Compare that to the estimated $2,000 it costs to use disposables, and you can count your savings.

A second option is a diaper service. Many towns and cities have successful diaper services. Basically the service works like this: every week you pay $15 or less and get 70 clean diapers and a pail dropped off at your house. Every week the service picks up your poopy diapers and leaves you clean ones. This saves you money over plastic diapers, is easier than washing, saves on the environment and could create a new industry in your community. Something like this would need coordination with the local hospital or public health agency to make sure safe sanitation procedures were followed. Public health agencies could consider this an investment in "preventive medicine." The idea could be a big success in some of the communities in the north.

A third way is the old times. Moss (Spagnum moss) would not be such a bad idea, especially if the moss is put in the toilet. It's cheap and organic. In fact, northern reservations could even go into a new "organic disposable" business. How about "Mossies" as a new industry for economic development in the North? Think of it as a topic for those Indian conferences. This could be a truly Native business.

In any case, there is a light at the end of the tunnel. The plastic diaper industry has led many of us astray. But there is a return from Pampers. Native people are in an ideal position to "dig out" from under a pile of plastic diapers. And, once Indians have something good going, history has shown that the white people will be right there to join us.

The Council of Energy Resource Tribes:
An Outsider's View In

Appeared in NATIVE AMERICANS AND ENERGY DEVELOPMENT II,
by Joseph Jorgensen, 1984.

*"You know the cause of our making war. It is known to all
white men. They ought to be ashamed of it. . . ."*
—Black Hawk, 1832

Oklahoma Indian Territory was to become the homeland of 97 Indian nations forcibly relocated from the eastern seaboard and Northeastern United States in the wake of "Manifest Destiny." In the mid-1850s, oil was discovered in "Indian territory," with one oil well in production as of 1859.[1] In 1866, the federal government demanded new treaties with Oklahoma-based Indian nations—treaties which resulted in the loss of one half of the Indian Territory. By 1869, some 18,634 oil wells were in production in Oklahoma—what had been Indian Territory, was the source of the "black gold." The oil rush continued, and in 1899, over 69,673 oil wells dominated the landscape.[2]

During these same years, the Indian land base and Indian population dropped significantly. While in 1883, some 25 Indian reservations within the Territory encompassed over 39 million acres, by 1979, less than 546,879 acres of land remained "Indian." All but 22,000 acres of this, 5% of the original land base, has been leased out for oil exploitation. The Indian population decreased at the same time. According to figures of the Federal census, there were 170,000 Oklahoma Indians in 1883. By 1930, this number had dropped to less than 72,000.[3] Somewhere 100,000

Indian people were lost. Today the state of Oklahoma exists with just over 80,000 Indian people living within its borders.

One century later, we enter another era of energy crises in the United States. In a nation which encloses 8% of the world's population yet consumes 40% of all natural resources, consumption, once threatened, becomes a crisis. The U.S. is becoming increasingly dependent upon foreign sources of raw materials—a habit which is not easily broken.

"The U.S. Department of Interior has estimated that the annual gap between domestic production and consumption of all minerals, including energy materials, is likely to grow in constant dollars from $8.6 billion in 1970, to $31 billion in 1985 and $64 billion by the turn of the century. . . ."[4] Imported Arab oil has increased from 15% of annual consumption in 1974 to over 50% in 1977.[5]

Foreign "instability," "nationalism" and OPEC are thought of as having created an "energy crisis," yet the crisis is not as real as it appears.

While prices for Arab oil have gone up, the resources are *still* available, with enormous reserves remaining in the Middle East. The oil price increases have spurred the development of new oil areas, notably Mexico. Mexican president Jose Lopez Portillo announced on September 1, 1978 that Mexico has proven oil reserves of 20 billion barrels, and potential reserves totaling 200 billion barrels—on par with Saudi Arabia. Eighty percent of Mexico's current oil exports go to the United States.

A resource crisis assumes that there is an immediate scarcity of resources. The wells will eventually run out and the mines will some time soon run dry—the resources are undeniably finite. Resources will run out most quickly if consumption increases or is maintained at the same level.

Industry by far consumes the greatest amounts of electricity. In fact, petroleum, raw material and primary metals processing and a few others—termed "energy intensive industries"—consume one third of all U.S. energy produced, but supply only 10% of the jobs.[6] This paradox is exemplified in the Northwest, where over one third of all electricity consumed by industry is used by the aluminum industry; in the Southeast, uranium enrichment facilities operated by Union Carbide and the federal government consume the greatest portion of the electrical production.[7]

If the future of the United States is to be based on energy and capital intensive development and industrialization, the final "resource crunch" will arrive quite soon.

An "energy crisis" also assumes that the energy industry is part of a "fair market system." In other words supply and demand are factors in a competitive market. There is no industry controlled by fewer firms than the energy industry. Oil companies control not only the oil industry (which is becoming more selective each year), but also control the uranium and coal industries. Oil companies control over 74% of the uranium industry, and exercise almost one half of the market control in the coal industry.[8] Mergers and acquisitions in recent years have accelerated this trend.

While U.S. citizens were watching the meters go wild on the gasoline pumps, EXXON, CONOCO and Kerr McGee had "earnings" like never before. People were led to believe that the Arabs had created a shortage, while the majority of the price hikes were pocketed by the oil companies. To insure the market, oil tankers were docked at New Jersey ports until the price was right.

Nationalization of mining and oil industries in the third world took a serious psychological and political toll on the oil companies. The companies found themselves evicted from "stable" countries, and with fewer sources of production, their own stability was on the decrease. As the industrial stance of the giants faltered, the companies were forced to move back to North America—the "safest" place yet. Although these multinationals are among the most powerful forces in the world, when they are forced to return to North America, they come from a position of weakness. The energy giants, whether EXXON, ARCO-Anaconda, or Newmont Mining Corporation, *need* North American resources to survive in their current stature.[9]

North America contains vast deposits of coal and uranium,

among the greatest in the "free world." While these resources appear to be the key to Energy Independence for the United States, through the work of corporations like Westinghouse, Bechtel and General Electric, coal and uranium are destined to be exported—as the emerging energy backbone of countries like South Korea, Taiwan and the Phillipines.

These nations are the "export market" for the United States. Pacific Islands, Brazil, Argentina, and a host of other countries are looked to as "economic miracles." In reality, U.S. multinationals have created a demand for electricity in these nations by establishing industrial sites within a "host country's" borders—the Phillipines' "export zone," Ford plants in Brazil, and similar energy-intensive sites in the "developing nations." In turn, the U.S. energy industry supplies the newly created electrical demand with a U.S.-made nuclear reactor, or an American-engineered coal fired power plant.[10]

Of the 229 operating nuclear power plants in the world, 71 are in the United States. Nuclear power, however, largely as a result of citizens' opposition, is not expected to play a major role in the future of American Energy Independence. The uranium boom, nevertheless, continues with more exploration, mining and milling taking place today in the United States than ever before. The domestic market for uranium destined for nuclear power plants is contracting; this makes the uranium export market all that much more important to the nuclear industry.

The United States leads the world in uranium exports—in 1974, contributing almost one half of the world production supply.[11] This dominance has been downscaled in recent years with new mines opening in the uranium rich countries. The following table outlines estimated 1979 world uranium production.

While the table points out the importance of not only the U.S. in the world uranium market, but the increasing significance of other producers of uranium, a few other facts should be incorporated for careful analysis. Many mining areas and specific mining sites in the United States have been in production for decades and are

Country	Million Pounds U_3O_8		
	1979	1985	1990
Australia	1.3	13.4	22.4
Canada	17.1	27.4	27.4
Republic of South Africa	12.7	21.2	21.1
Other Africa*	18.5	29.7	30.3
Other countries**	6.9	13.4	15.2
Non-U.S. Total	57	105	116
U.S. Total	38	50	50
Total free world uranium production	95.00	155.00	166.00

*Includes Niger, Gabon, Namibia
**Includes Argentina, Brazil, France, Mexico, Spain
Source: NUEXCO, Memorandum to Nuclear Industry #34, September 30, 1979 Menlo Park, Los Angeles, Ca. 1.2. Table 5 A.

reaching the end of their productive years. The Anaconda mine at Laguna Pueblo (in New Mexico) is one example—after three decades of uranium production (beginning in 1952), the Anaconda mine is expected to be exhausted by 1982. Each day 5,500 tons of raw uranium ore was produced at this mine, which with the exhaustion of the reserve will create a gap in the U.S. figure for uranium production. Many other mining operations are to be found in similar situations, and it is therefore to be expected that although future U.S. production will not increase substantially, (in comparison to Australia and Africa), new mining projects will have to be opened if the current level of uranium production is to be maintained.[12]

Indian reservations and the areas bordering the reservations (allotted and Bureau of Land Management lands in many cases) will play an important role in the future of the uranium industry. Exact estimates as to the resources on "Indian land" vary greatly, according to who is asked. Between a low estimate of 11% of the U.S. uranium reserves and high estimates of 66% of U.S. uranium, the figures are cloudy—it's likely that only the companies know for sure.[13] Coal estimates are a similar problem, but one third of all western coal (one-sixth of total U.S. reserves) appears to be a constant estimate.[14]

More importantly, it is not a question of where the resources are located, but which deposits enter the production stage. In this light, Indian nations take a primary role. In 1974, 100% of all federally controlled uranium production came from Indian reservations.[15] Within the Canadian borders, uranium production has an ironically similar look—Indian nations in the north of Saskatchewan and elsewhere in "sparsely populated areas" are an important source of Canadian uranium. Rich Nafziger, in a 1976 report to Americans for Indian Opportunity discovered that if Indian nations were looked at as one nation we would be the 5th largest producers of uranium in the world.[16] These figures do not incorporate the production of Canadian Indian nations, which if combined with Indians within U.S. borders, the statistics could be revised upward again to the 3rd or 4th largest producers of uranium in the free world.[17] Coal figures denote a similar prevalence of Native American production. According to the Council on Economic Priorities, Indian coal reserves are the site of four out of the top ten largest coal mines in the United States.[18]

The future from the standpoint of production once again takes on an important color. Uranium production in both South Africa and Namibia is unstable, the result of Black liberation forces. Australian uranium deposits are anticipated to be in production by the end of 1980, but citizens' opposition to uranium mining has delayed the projects for many years already. Inside North America, Vermont recently banned uranium mining and initiatives are on state ballots this November in South Dakota and other states. British Columbia was anticipated by industry to be a future source of uranium for the Canadian reactors export market, but the industry will have to wait for at least 7 years. In February of 1980, a public inquiry into uranium exploration, mining and milling was cancelled by British Columbia Premier Bill Bennett. Bennett cited health and environmental reasons, combined with the political ramifications of uranium exports to the South Korean based Korean Electric Company as the primary motivations behind his decision.[19] Each of these events contributes to the uncertainty in the uranium market, as well as the pressure on Indian nations to proceed with development of uranium resources. These factors also make the actions of the Council of Energy Resource Tribes (CERT) more important than ever.

Coal production from the reservations finds the Indian nations in a similar situation. President Carter's two-pronged approach to coal and synthetic fuels—the energy mobilization board and the synthetic fuels bill—have not been entirely successful. If the energy mobilization board (EMB) had been passed, the federal government would have been able to supersede any state or local jurisdiction or regulation on "priority projects" designated by the EMB. In June of 1980, the bill failed, only after the House of Representatives had passed the legislation. The Synthetic Fuels bill, however, did pass. This bill authorized federal loan guarantees for synthetic fuels facilities, which are a big step toward the realization of 20 or so predicted synthetic fuels facilities in the west.

Several tribal councils applied for funding through the synthetic fuels bill. This fact, the presumed "willingness of tribes" to consider a "synfuels" plant will be a contributing factor to increased development of reservation coal reserves. The failure of the Energy Mobilization Board will also facilitate development of Indian coal reserves, since states and counties cannot be forced to house a facility, Indian tribes may be expected to.

While these pressures contribute to the general atmosphere of hysteria in the West, particularly on the reservations, they also put tribal decision makers in a position of increased power and responsibility. Not only are the decisions made for Indian people today, but for this generation and the generations to come. The future of the uranium market, domestically and internationally, are both at stake, as is the final test of synthetic fuels. The forces that exist today are similar to those in Oklahoma a century ago, but the times have changed drastically. Energy companies are powerful, but lessons have been learned. Indian nations have been faced with a history of long tests, but with 4% of the original land base remaining, the greatest test is yet to come. The intention of this author is to provide information to Indian decision and policy makers, with the understanding that knowledge is power.

CERT: CHANGING ROLES IN CHANGING TIMES

Most of the CERT reservations have been the site of active energy development for over 50 years—primarily oil exploitation. With the exceptions of the Navajo and Spokane reservations, and Laguna Pueblo—all of which are the source of significant uranium production—oil has been the primary resource produced from the reservations. CERT tribes, like other reservations, share a bond of bad leases negotiated by the Bureau of Indian Affairs, which lock the tribes into long-term agreements with minimal returns. As a response to the Bureau's leasing history, and the increasing development planned for the reservations, CERT came about.

In an interview with John Foster, Director of the Native American Natural Resource Development Federation (NANDRF), he stated that "The idea [for an organization] originated at a 1973 meeting held at the Fort Berthold reservation. Over 100 Indian leaders came together to discuss water rights and realized, in the wake of the Arab Oil Embargo, there was much more at stake. . . ."[20]

From this meeting of tribal officials, Indian organization leaders, and a few Bureau representatives, came the push for a coherent plan for reservation development. NANDRF was formed, working with 24 tribes on all aspects of development (including timber, agriculture, etc.), but within a year, CERT was destined to be the Indian development organization.

Specifically dealing in energy resources, exactly what the federal government was looking for, CERT surpassed even the National Congress of American Indians (NCAI) and the National

Tribal Chairmen's Association (NTCA) in recognition. The charismatic leaders of CERT brought increasing attention to the organization, as well as substantial funding. LaDonna Harris, President and Executive Officer of Americans for Indian Opportunity, has been dubbed the "Mother of CERT." According to the 1978 Annual Report of AIO, LaDonna's organization has served in an "advisory capacity" to CERT since the Indian energy organization came about. John Foster of NANDRF commented, "with the tremendous energy and great political contacts of LaDonna Harris and Peter MacDonald (Navajo Tribal Chairman), CERT took over the entire ball game of Indian development organizations. . . ."[21]

Peter MacDonald, Laguna Pueblo Governor Floyd Correa, and LaDonna Harris were the most noticeable spokespeople for CERT. One of the initial tactics of the CERT leaders was to create an image of the "Indian OPEC." Rumors of meetings with OPEC officials and Arab leaders (never substantiated) were circulated throughout the United States. The new force in Indian country raised eyebrows in Washington, and $2.9 million in federal funding dropped out of the sky into the CERT treasury.

Phase Two

Keeping up with U.S. energy policy and the weekly proposals from energy corporations for the reservations is a large job. The CERT staff of 60 is now headed by Ed Gabriel (Executive Director), formerly of the Federal Energy Administration's Office of Impact Assessment. Other staff members include Ahmed Kooros, former deputy Minister of Oil Affairs in Iran. The "OPEC" image began and ended with Kooros. The remainder of the staff are predominantly bright young Americans, with 12 Indian staff members. The responsibility of the CERT staff is to advise tribal chairmen on energy issues and options for the reservations.

After receiving enough money from the federal government to meet office and staff expenses, CERT leaders asked for a larger slice of the pie. Peter MacDonald, CERT Chairman, requested "One half of one percent of what the president was putting into his

"Energy Security Budget" from Carter. MacDonald's request amounts to $60 million annually for the next ten years for the CERT treasury.[22]

Washington did allocate some money for CERT, although not as much as MacDonald requested, but a substantial chunk. The announcement was formally made at the CERT annual meeting, held in December 1979 in Phoenix. John F. O'Leary, former Deputy Secretary of Energy, announced that CERT would receive $24 million in federal assistance coming from a variety of departments. MacDonald commented that "Santa Claus" had "come early," and the CERT board meeting continued.

The meeting itself was a colorful affair. Admission cost $250 for corporations and $100 for wealthy individuals. Somehow a few poor people got into the prestigious Adams Hotel in Phoenix, rounding off attendance at somewhere around 400 people.

Addressing the assembly was Robert O. Anderson, Chairman of ARCO, David S. Freeman, Director of Tennessee Valley Authority, John F. O'Leary, from the Department of Energy, and others with great interests in reservation resources.[23] O'Leary was given a special CERT Award of Appreciation for his work in channeling federal funding to the organization. CERT appeared to be interested in convincing the energy generals that "although the price will go up, we are still interested in talking. . . ."

During the course of the meeting, Peter MacDonald announced that six energy projects would be underway soon on CERT-represented reservations. Several months later, Ted Smith, Director of Economics and Finance for CERT, assured me that the organization was "not in the business of selling Indian resources."[24] The nature of the board meeting, however, and the circumstances which resulted make CERT appear to be a very good mechanism for developing Indian coal and uranium. For example, a "reception" sponsored by five corporations including Consolidation Coal (CONOCO), General Electric, and Gulf Oil was the setting for quite a few business talks. The "reception" consisted of a very well-stocked bar.

As Geoffry O'Gara reported in *High Country News*:

> *Leonard Burch, Chairman of the Southern Ute reservation in Colorado sat quietly at the conference table. A tall man in a gray suit, an oil company executive, leaned towards him . . . "If a few of us could get together with you," he was saying, ". . . we're down here, we're interested in what's happening here, and if you have the time. . . ." Burch quietly agreed to a later meeting.[25]*

Although no traditional Indian people were allowed to speak from the platform at the CERT meeting, a delegation of native people from the Diné (Navajo) reservation issued a press release in response to the CERT meeting:

> *We maintain that CERT is claiming to represent individuals of diverse intertribal groups that in fact, they do not represent. . . . We have come here in an observer capacity and can testify as individuals who live in, and whose livelihood is being affected in the land areas in contention. Through our observation here at the CERT meeting, we have witnessed that no testimony has been allowed to reflect the voice of the indigenous people who will be affected by the decisions made here. . . . We urge that the indigenous members of CERT realize their traditional and spiritual ways of survival and their responsibility to the earth and to their people to help assure their survival. . . .[26]*

The message from the reservation was clear. Whether the CERT representatives heard it is another question.

Phase Three
CERT: the "Department of Energy
with a tiny drop of redskin?"

The Department of Energy money, and that of other agencies funding CERT, is not designed for a priority on the development of "renewable" or "alternative" energy resources. An estimated $300,000 of the $24 million is destined for feasibility studies and educational expenses in alternate sources of energy.[27] Like the Department of Energy, CERT representatives have a substantial interest in synthetic fuels facilities, coal gasification, coal lique-faction, oil shale and the like. Several "feasibility" studies are underway on CERT reservations for these projects, and CERT Chairman MacDonald announced the possibility of the "first op-erating synfuels facility"—the "CERT contribution" to the Na-tional Energy Policy.[28]

The CERT leaders from southern reservations have thus far played a key role in CERT. Peter MacDonald and LaDonna Harris have successfully lobbied for federal funding, and Floyd Correa, former Governor of Laguna Pueblo and CERT Vice Chairman, now holds a high position inside the Department of Energy. These individuals, combined with some strong northern allies from CERT reservations and contacts in Washington, have set much of the stage for CERT.

The southern and northern reservations have some major dif-ferences, perspectives which may alter the future of the organi-zation in the years to come. It is crucial to learn from both the successes and failures of the southern reservations. Navajo and Laguna Pueblo are paving the way for "economic development based on energy development"—a lead which is enticing for northern reservations to follow. At the same time, noticeable op-position to development in the north is sprouting on several res-ervations. Alan Rowland, Northern Cheyenne Tribal Chairman, stated in an interview with a San Francisco–based journalist, "The uranium stays in the ground where it can't hurt anyone. No can-cer, no bombs, period. . . ."[29]

The Nez Perce Tribal Council rejected a proposal for a small-scale hydroelectric project—a renewable source of energy—after several feasibility studies completed by the CERT staff revealed that the tribe's fishing area would be jeopardized. In turn the Yakama Tribal Council is taking an aggressive stand on nuclear waste disposal. The Hanford Nuclear Reservation, where some two-thirds of U.S. nuclear wastes are currently stored, is located 20 miles from the Yakama reservation, well within their 1855 guaranteed treaty lands. In a statement to members of the Senate Subcommittee on the Environment, Councilman Russel Jim delivered a strong speech:

> *The Yakama Indian nation is deeply disturbed with the future plans for the Hanford Nuclear Reservation as presently put forward by the representatives of Rockwell International. . . . We feel strongly that steps of vital importance to the very existence of our people are being taken, and are about to be taken without proper regard . . . for the safety of all peoples within the area, and for the federal obligations contained in the treaty with the Yakama Indian people. . . . The Yakama Indian nation is an important part of the 50-mile circle around the Hanford reservation within which the law requires that workable plans for evacuation be developed. The Yakama Indian nation sees this concept of evacuation as a cynical and empty phrase when applied to our Indian reservation. . . . By placing hazardous radio-wastes near our reservation, they may well undermine our Treaty rights by threatening a destruction which the implications of the Treaty show to be illegal. Our lands may be contaminated irretrievably by action on nearby non-Indian Land or from faulty transportation of radioactive wastes. I believe any of you gentlemen will realize that for Native Americans, "Evacuation" from their lands is meaningless. . . .[30]*

Whether Tribal Chairmen involved in CERT will follow the lead established by Navajo and Laguna in the South and Spokane, Colville and Crow in the North, only time will tell. The outlook of the Acoma Pueblo, Nez Perce and Yakama provides a stark contrast, which should be carefully evaluated for future times.

Notes
[1] Angie Debo, "And Still the Waters Run"
[2] American Indian Journal, Institute for the Development of Indian Law, Washington, D.C.
[3] Debo, op. cit.

(Many of the following references were found in "The Hour is Late: Native Americans and Natural Resource Development," an unpublished senior thesis by David Weiss for the Board of Environmental Studies and Sociology at the University of California, Santa Cruz, March 9, 1979.)

[4] Al Gedicks, "Raw Materials; the Achilles Heel of American Imperialism," *The Insurgent Sociologist*, VII (Fall 1977). pp 4–6.

[5] Weiss, op. cit.

[6] Weiss, op. cit.

[7] See Bonneville Power Company Regional Power Study, 1979.

[8] Oil Chemical and Atomic Workers Union, "Economic Data for Nuclear Industry Bargaining Units," 1977, Denver.

[9] Analysis from interview between Weiss and Gedicks—Alternatives to Nuclear Conference, Laney College, Oakland California, January 18, 1980.

[10] See "500 Mile Island," publication of Pacific Research Center by Bello, Hayes, Zarsky. Volume X, #1 First Quarter, 1979, Mountain View, Ca.

[11] New Mexico Indian Environmental Education Project, *Report to Pueblo Governors*, April 1980.

[12] New Mexico Indian Environmental Education Project—analysis of uranium industry—Chavez, LaDuke.

[13] Low estimate comes from the Department of Interior, high estimate is from the National Indian Youth Council, Albuquerque, N.M., 1979.

[14] Council of Energy Resource Tribes, *1978 Annual Report*

[15] American Indian Policy Review Commission, 1976.

[16] Rich Nafziger, "Indian Uranium, Perils and Profits," *AIO Red Paper*, 1976.

[17] Analysis of data from Canada and the United States combined with Nafziger analysis—La Duke, 1979.

[18] Council on Economic Priorities, "Leased and Lost," 1976.

[19] See Robert R. Williamson, "7-Year Ban on Uranium Mines Hailed by Critics," Toronto Globe and Mail, February 28, 1980, p. 1.

[20] John Foster, telephone interview, April 16, 1980.

[21] Ibid.

[22] Sam Maddox, "Can 17th Street Make Peace with the Energy Tribes?" *Denver Magazine*, May, 1980.

[23] ARCO operates the uranium strip mine at Laguna Pueblo,has interests in Papago and Cheyenne reservations.

[24] Ted Smith, telephone interview, April 25, 1980.

[25] Geoffry O'Gara, *High Country News*, December 14, 1980.

[26] Delegation from Big Mountain, *Press Release*, December 9, 1979.

[27] Ron Zee, CERT Appropriate Technology director, interview, April 17, 1980.

[28] *Business Week*, March 24, 1980.

[29] Christopher McLeod, "Indian OPEC Laid to Rest," *Pacific News Service*, December, 1979.

[30] Russel Jim, Senate Subcommittee on the Environment, January 12, 1980.

Red Land and Uranium Mining: How the Search for Energy Is Endangering Indian Tribal Lands

Appeared in RADCLIFFE QUARTERLY, *December 1981.*

The women of Paguate awake early every morning. Almost daily they are busy making their bread, cooked in the same outside adobe ovens that they have used for generations. In many ways, from the summer dances to the winter storytelling, little has changed in the peaceful traditions of the Pueblo Indians. Even the language remains, despite more than 400 years of foreign visitors to the mesas of New Mexico. Like their cousins the Hopis, and their ancestors and neighbors at Acoma Pueblo's Sky City, the Laguna Pueblo people believe that their traditional life must continue if the precious rain is to fall, and the corn, beans, melons, and squash are to prosper annually.

Paguate, with its 300 residents, is quiet—almost too quiet at times. The dogs rarely bark and the horses barely move their heads. In the quietness of Paguate, everything surrounding the village has changed permanently. Where 30 years ago there were orchards and a peaceful Rio Paguate meandering through the Pueblo of Laguna, today there is a gaping crater grinning up at the village. The sounds of blasting still echo against the ravaged edges of dry earth. Even the Rio Paguate has changed from a seasonal clear stream to a pool of fluorescent green radioactive water oozing from the bottom of the crater.

In 1952, the Anaconda Company discovered a vast uranium deposit at the village of Paguate. Anxious to begin operation, Anaconda negotiated a mining contract with the tribal council of Laguna Pueblo—a favorable contract that guaranteed royalties from the uranium ore to the tribal treasury and jobs to the Laguna people at the mine. Both were needed at the Pueblo, where, as on many other Indian reservations, the tribal treasuries are barely maintained by a financial influx from the Bureau of Indian Affairs, a branch of the Department of the Interior. Unemployment, or more appropriately, lack of employment, hovers at an average of 50 percent. To both the Laguna tribal council and the Bureau of Indian Affairs, the uranium discovery looked like the light at the end of a long tunnel. The Atomic Energy Commission, which originally contracted the ore, looked to the mine as a critical contribution to the "Atoms for Peace" program.

The Laguna treasury began to blossom, and each year more Lagunas were drawn from the statistics of unemployed into the uranium mine. By the mid-'60s, Anaconda's Jackpile mine employed more than 300 Lagunas directly, and by the end of the '70s, the number had doubled. The tribe and company built a new housing project for the workers, a desperately needed community center, and a new government headquarters. Laguna investments in the stock market diversified the returns to the tribal treasury, and individual investments in pickup trucks, televisions, and appliances diversified the culture of the Laguna people. With almost two decades of prosperity as a developing Indian reservation, government and Indian economists would point to Laguna Pueblo as the model reservation.

"URANIUM IS A KILLER"

As the saying goes, however, all things must pass; and in the mining industry, this metamorphosis is particularly applicable. In 1981, the Anaconda Company began the phaseout of the Jackpile mine. Once the largest uranium strip mine in the world, the crater is only a monument to a boom that entered the inevitable bust of the cycle. With the closure of the mine, the Laguna miners are looking elsewhere in the uranium-rich region for jobs. And, with the closure, the Laguna people as a whole are facing some stark problems, which, unlike their benefactor Anaconda, will not disappear.

When the U.S. Environmental Protection Agency (EPA) came to Laguna Pueblo in 1973, both the Laguna officials and the company representatives were too busy to listen. The EPA found that the Rio Paguate was contaminated with radiation from the Jackpile mine, as was most of the groundwater near the village of Paguate, which now adjoined the mine. In 1975, the EPA returned again and found that not only Laguna Pueblo, but also the groundwater throughout the uranium-mining region of the Southwest was heavily contaminated with radiation. Everyone was still too busy. In 1978, when the EPA returned for the last time, the agency found that a number of building structures at the Pueblo were contaminated with radiation. The community center, the Jackpile Housing Project, and the tribal council headquarters all had been constructed with radioactive materials from the mine. The roads to the mine at Paguate, all carefully maintained by the company, had been repaired with low-grade uranium ore. Between the repairs and the escaping dust, much of the Pueblo was radioactive.

Radiation is a bit of an elusive subject. Not only is it invisible, but also the effects often take almost 20 years to appear in the general population. For the ill, the medical profession has found many ways to use the power of radiation beneficially, but for the healthy, high levels of exposure are detrimental.

Manuel Pino is a young Acoma Indian who lives downstream from the Jackpile mine. In a recent interview, he expressed some fear of the effects of the radiation on the Pueblo people. "One of our grandmothers just died from bladder cancer. Most of us Acomas live to be almost 100, but she died young. The only thing that could have caused it is that water—that radioactive water. It takes the old and the young, like the unborn babies, first. In the last two years, more of our grandmothers have died from that same thing. Their water is the same water—the water that comes from that mine and those other mines west of the reservation." Although some uranium is known to exist within the borders of the Acoma reservation, the Acoma government has been quite hesitant about opening up the reservation for any ventures. Acoma commissioned a reservation-wide study of water quality on the reservation, a study that confirmed suspicions of radiation contamination. "The difference with us," continued Manuel, "is that the Acomas don't mine, and if you get my point, we mind more. It's just because the uranium doesn't put food on our tables that we can call it what it really is—a killer. Uranium is a killer."

Although the national debate on the dangers of radiation exposure continues, for some isolated populations, like the nonmigrant populations on the reservations, there is not much debate. Elevated lung cancer levels among Navajo uranium miners, who worked for a Kerr McGee operation on the reservation (1952–68), have resulted in a legal suit. Stewart Udall, former secretary of the interior, has taken the suit, which seeks compensation for almost 100 miners and the families of the deceased. All of them died of various diseases that they associate with radiation. Udall's case is supported by studies done by Dr. Joseph Wagonner, formerly with the National Institute of Occupational Safety and Health (NIOSH). The studies by Wagonner and by Arell S. Schurgin and Thomas C. Hollacher (Brandeis) and others all link high levels of pulmonary cancer among uranium miners with radon gas emissions from the uranium ore.[1]

In a 1978 report by Los Alamos Scientific Laboratory, it appeared that the United States government was also aware of the dangers. The report suggests that "perhaps the solution to the radon emission problem is to zone the land into uranium mining and milling districts so as to forbid human habitation."

This problem of radiation contamination is by no means restricted to the mesas and canyons of New Mexico, where, with 52 operating uranium mines, the problem is not a small one. In 1979, a joint report by the OECD Nuclear Energy Agency and the International Atomic Energy Agency noted that uranium production from the 368 operating mines in the United States had reached the level of 14,800 tons of processed ore per year—an amount that is predicted to double by 1985. With many closures in process, or pending at the older uranium mines, domestic exploration had reached a record $340 million by 1979. The majority of this exploration has been in the West, a great proportion of it on federally-managed lands.

EXPLOITATION OF TRIBAL LANDS

Continuing a trend that began in the mid-'70s, for both economic and geological reasons, Indian reservations have been a site for extensive exploration. In 1975, the Federal Trade Commission reported that 360 uranium leases had been issued on Indian lands, as compared to four on public and acquired lands. The economic reasons have primarily centered on the mining agreements acquired by companies from the tribes—low royalties and extended lease periods. According to a 1977 report issued by Albuquerque-based Americans for Indian Opportunity, Indian tribes received 60 cents per pound of uranium ore, valued at the market at $30 a pound—two percent of market value. Currently, on all federal lands, natural resource royalties are mandated by law to be a minimum of 12 percent of market value; but the older leases negotiated with the tribes, many of them just coming into production now, make Indian resources sound financial investments for the companies. In addition, most of the leases hold the clause ". . . for as long as the ore is producing in payable quantities . . . ," meaning that the tribes receive the same royalties, no matter how high the market value of the ore.

Geologically, Indian reservations are located in what is known as the "western energy corridor," a stretch of resource-rich re-

gions from the Colorado Plateau to the northern Rockies. Estimates by the Council of Energy Resource Tribes (CERT), an
Indian energy development organization with 28 separate reservation governments participating, indicate that one half of all
United States uranium resources and one third of all western low-
sulfur coal lie under Indian lands. To the Bureau of Indian Affairs, and organizations such as CERT, these resources are seen as
the ladder to economic development of the impoverished reservations. Per capita income remains at one fourth the national
average, infant mortality rates and malnutrition are high, and the
tribal treasuries under the Reagan Administration have just hit
rock bottom. These resources, if managed carefully, are thought
to be the answer.

OUTCRY

An increasingly vocal contingent of Indians, however, believe
that the resources should be left in the ground. When 26 mining
corporations began uranium exploration on the border of the
Black Hills of South Dakota in 1978, the companies were met with
an outcry from the local Indian and non-Indian residents. In this
case the companies had picked a particularly sensitive spot. The
Black Hills are an extremely sacred place to the Sioux people,
land which the Sioux nation has been fighting a court battle to
regain control of for almost a century. In any case, the Sioux say
the land is not for sale, and the local ranchers who need water for
irrigation and livestock say that the water is not going to be contaminated. Elsewhere in North America, similar opposition to the
uranium industry is active. The state of Vermont has banned uranium mining, and the province of British Columbia has placed a
seven-year moratorium on uranium exploration.

On the reservations, the case is not so clear-cut. Many of the
western Indian tribes are faced with growing populations and
increasing pressure to develop, from both inside and out. The
greatest pressure is from the companies; the Reagan Administra-

tion, particularly Secretary of the Interior James Watt; and American consumers. To the Indians, it appears that all three are demanding the natural resources as a sort of God-given right.

Precariously balanced on the brink of development, the tribes hold their breath as they watch Paguate and other places where the companies have already been. This generation of visitors to the mesas and mountains has permanently changed the land. And, if even the government is discussing zoning laws that may make the reservations unoccupiable by their original inhabitants, the uranium industry does not appear to be a welcome guest. After all, the older Indians have always said that when the people and animals cannot drink from the water, there will be no more Indians.

Notes

[1] A 1975 study by Schurgin and Hollacher found that "From 1950 to 1967, lung cancer killed 62 miners out of a sample of 3,000." According to the study, this number represents six times the number of miners predicted to die from radiation-induced lung cancer.

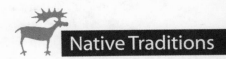
Native Traditions

Who Owns America?
Minority Land and Community Security

Delivered at the UNIVERSITY OF WISCONSIN, MADISON,
June 6, 2001.

Akiing is the word for land in our language, and in the indigenous concept of land ownership or the Anishinaabeg concept of land ownership, it is much more a concept that we belong to that land than the land belongs to us. And that is perhaps the outset of my remarks, which is that land tenure itself and concepts of land ownership are of course a concept of culture—they are a concept of your teachings, a construct of how you are raised and how you live in your community. And so when we discuss these things, I always remember where we come from and our experience with that in our own words. . . .

As we look around our territories, the Anishinaabeg people—as other indigenous peoples—have different concepts of the places that are there. Perhaps there is a story of the place where the great giant sleeps. That is a story in the part of creation; it is a part of our history. Or the story of the places that we stopped in our migration from the east to the west. Those are the places that we know in terms of our land or our *akiing*—the land that is out there. Other nations have similar stories. The place where the great race was run as it surrounded, perhaps, the Black Hills. Or the place where the young people ascended into the sky from the great horned butte. Those stories are a part of our oral history—the places on the land. We repeat that knowledge and that relationship through our oral histories, and also often through our ceremonies. Our religious practices in our community—and many indigenous communities, I think, on a worldwide scale—are practices where we are always reengaging in this relationship with our *akiing,* because that is from which we get our life. And so it is those concepts of land ownership that are embedded in many indigenous communities.

European concepts of land ownership are of course quite a bit different. Our concepts of land ownership, traditionally, are collective ownership or a collective relationship to the land and individual or family use rights—that's what "usufruct" land is. But a lot of you work in these issues of land and so you are familiar with that term. But that is quite a bit different from the concepts of land ownership that we must deal with in this day and age. And those concepts come quite often out of the church. That is the origin of much of the land tenure pattern and the land ownership patterns that we have today. The church itself in its "heyday"—I'm talking about the Catholic Church—had a very significant impact on land ownership on a worldwide scale and of course on land tenure patterns. And this is something that needs to be discussed in terms of honesty. The honesty of it and what we are dealing with in terms of the laws today.

For instance, Papal Bulls in the 1400s issued edicts from the Pope that encouraged people like Columbus and Cook (of course Cook was many years later). But these early guys, who were called "discoverers," went to claim land on behalf of the church, on behalf of God. And there was a view at that time which is, to a great extent, maintained today: that only those Christian nations had rights to the land. That only those who were in the folds of the church and were in the folds of Christ had rights to the land, and the rest of the vast majority of the world, who were not Christians, did not have rights to land on par with those who were Christians. That is why the church became a "handmaiden to colonialism." The Catholic Church was one of the architects of colo-

nialism as we have come to know it today, because it provided
the philosophical and religious underpinnings through which
colonialism could continue and be justified in the eyes of God.
That process itself has had significant impact, and those impacts
continue to this point in time. It continues even to considerations
in terms of international policy or to the Holy See, the Vatican,
which is the only religion that has a seat at the United Nations. It
has a seat of power that is similar and equal to the seat that is
held by the country of Switzerland. I've always wondered why
the Dalai Lama doesn't have a seat if the Pope has a seat. But it is
a holdover from the historic power of the Catholic Church. It is
also perhaps why indigenous peoples struggle . . . and not just
Indian people in North America. On a worldwide scale, there are
5,000 nations of indigenous peoples. Whether they are the Masai,
whether they are the Wara Wara or the Anishinaabeg or the Diné,
indigenous peoples on a worldwide scale and in terms of the
United Nations struggle continuously—struggle for basic rights
to self determination, basic rights to territorial integrity, basic
rights to determine our destiny at the United Nations, while the
Holy See itself has a seat at the United Nations.

It is also translated in terms of the land tenure patterns that
we have today. Land tenure patterns emerged initially from the
Catholics and from the Pope; then it became English common
law; and today we have a situation where American legal institutions, British legal institutions, Canadian legal institutions, and
Australian legal institutions all hail to their common foundation
of British common law and these initial cultural biases on land
tenure as to who could own land and who could not own land.
That is why today we find circumstances where, by and large,
aboriginal title is not viewed, quite often, as having the same par
as private property under the law. It is these initial foundations
of land tenure that we must consider when we talk about justice
in the terms of land tenure issues today—because the reality is
that this is the land tenure system that we have inherited in the

United States, the land tenure system that exists in Canada, the land tenure system that exists.

And we know this land in term stories of "that is where the giant sleeps," or "that is where the spirits rose out of the lake," or "that is where the spirits lived in the lake." You know my reservation has a lake, and we talk about how the spirits lived there. Those names were changed by people, largely because of their cultural bias against indigenous religions and indigenous cultural practices. So, for instance, you have a place like Spirit Lake in North Dakota, which until recently was known as Devil's Lake, North Dakota—renamed by the Christians with the perception that if those people saw spirits there, and if they had a history of having a spiritual practice, that must be the devil. Or the place where young children ascended into the heavens after they were chased by a monster was for many years know as Devil's Tower in Wyoming, a place that has its own name in the language of the people who live there, whether they are Lakota or Cheyenne.

I tell you that because it is one of the things that indigenous people find incredibly offensive: the naming process of America. It is kind of a question of who has the right to name. How did that right come about? Who gave them those rights? Where did those names come from? And it is, in my humble estimation, one of the things that we must begin—not only in the spirit of justice, but also in the spirit of what is right—the process of recovering those traditional names and supporting them . . . whether it is the Ho-Chunk Nation, with their renaming of themselves in their own language, or whether it is Spirit Lake or whether it is Mount Denali in Alaska.

Which brings me to another subject that I always found horribly offensive: How come there are so many mountains named after small men? Who were these guys? Why did they get these mountains named after them? You go out there and these little puny men have mountains named after them, and some of these men were really, really bad guys. You know, Harney Peak—that

guy was a butcher, the guy committed massacres against the
Lakota people, and he's got a little peak named after him—Harney
Peak. Or one of my personal favorites, because I was educated in
New England, is Amherst. Lord Jeffrey Amherst was one of the
initial purveyors of small-pox-ridden blankets. In this day and
age, are we going to name towns after Hitler? Probably not . . .
but, you know, you have a number of towns, cities, and colleges,
named after guys who were basically mass murderers. And it is
really offensive as indigenous people, but it is also offensive as
humanitarians to consider that we continue to aggrandize individuals whose crimes are crimes against humanity. And that is
one of the challenges we face, not only in terms of the structures
of land tenure, but also in terms of the framework and how we
consider the land upon which we live. It's points of reference. So
that is a little bit of my philosophical thinking about some of the
history of these issues, in terms of not only indigenous people
here but elsewhere, and the moral and ethical issues surrounding land tenure in North America.

Having said that, there are many practical aspects of the transformation of land tenure in the North American continent, with
which we live today. The reality is, as the saying would go, that
theoretically Indian people or indigenous people should be the
richest people in the country and we are the poorest people in
the country. For every social and economic statistic you don't
want to have, we have it. Theoretically, we should actually be the
richest people in the country, because a while ago we pretty much
were the only people that were here, right? But there is this saying in Indian country that I think is true, which is that, a long
time ago, when the white people came, the Indians had the land
and the white people had the Bibles. And now the Indians have
the Bibles and the white people have the land. And that is pretty
much true. That is pretty much true in Indian country.

But there is a practical application of that which has to do
with the nature of who holds land and who needs land. Indigenous people traditionally have been the people who have lived

on the land, but the predator/prey relationship that exists between America and the land is one that has caused the constant erosion and taking of the indigenous land base in the Americas. And it has caused the constant erosion and the taking of other people's land outside of that context as well. The reality is that there is a direct relationship between the "development" of the United States and the "underdevelopment" of Native America. Just as much as there is a direct relationship between the development of Europe and the underdevelopment of Africa; and the development of the United States and the underdevelopment of Africa. Some get rich and some get poor. Some take other's land, natural resources, and people, and some are left to deal with the consequences of it. Which is the history. So whenever someone talks about developed countries, I always remember the kind of the things that my grandmother used to say to me, "They didn't pay Union wages when they built that"—and they didn't. They didn't pay those people for that land when they took it. They appropriated it. Some got rich and some got poor, and that is a worldwide circumstance, which is why the developed countries are termed as such. The developed countries have appropriated those lands and resources of others. This is not news to most of you, but what I will say is that it is important to always recognize that when we talk about issues in the North American context.

You know, one of the problems with running for the office of Vice President of the United States is that, by and large, most of the predecessors in those offices of President and Vice President were land speculators, people who took land from Indians. And so it is kind of problematic sometimes, when you are talking about these issues and you are coming into, basically, the arena of the thief. The reality is that the founding fathers were land speculators. The fact is that you couldn't vote in this country if you did not own land, and that basically you had to be a white man who owned land. Now how did they get that land? They basically had to steal it from someone, and that would probably be the Indians. And so most of the initial founding fathers, while they may have had some really nice ideas about democracy, had a lot of issues with people of color. They had a lot of issues with people who held things that they coveted.

In my own community, I always say that the White Earth reservation in northwestern Minnesota suffers from having bad neighbors. In 1889, Minnesota ranked second in the country in logging, with the northwestern portion of the state leading the state's production in 1889 through 1890. Eleven million board feet of timber were taken from the White Earth Reservation; in the next year 15 million feet were cut, followed by another 18 million in the 1891 and 1892 seasons. Just as a footnote, a couple years ago the timber production for the entire state of Minnesota was 4 million board feet. So we are talking 15 million board feet taken from one area of 837,000 acres of land. That would essentially be deforestation—a very rapid deforestation of an area. Some were made rich and some were made poor.

In the early 1890s, we had a guy who moved to Little Falls, Minnesota, just south of us—his name was Frederick Weyerhaeuser. Frederick was the son of a brewer, and he saw the great pine trees of northern Minnesota and got what my friend Ralph would call, "corporate welfare"—which is also what I would call it when you get a railroad that goes from your mill to the timber- and tree-filled land in Northern Minnesota, and it is paid for by the United States government. He took those trees, and by 1895 he owned more acres of timber than anyone else in the world. He was considered the richest and brainiest of the lumber millionaire chiefs. His logging company sawed enough lumber in one season to six times encircle the globe if it were cut up into one-inch strips. Not bad. Some get rich, some get poor, and the consequence of Weyerhaeuser's interest in our land was that by the 1910 period, 99% of the White Earth Reservation was held by non-Indian interests. A good portion of it was actually held by logging companies affiliated with Frederick Weyerhaeuser.

Sometimes in my work—well, quite often in my work—I talk

to all kinds of people. And whether it is the Rotary Club of a town that is a border town to a reservation or whether it is testifying in a hearing on a mill expansion, I find that these things do not change. Quite often it is said to Indian people that we should get over it. That it happened a long time ago. I have heard that a number of times in my life. "You guys should get over it, it happened a long time ago." You cannot get over it if you are still in the same circumstance as a consequence of what happened a hundred years ago. You cannot get over it if you are still in exactly the same relationship as you were a hundred years ago. Because while my great-grandparents were faced with Frederick Weyerhaeuser, today the single largest timber interest on my reservation is the Potlatch Corporation, which is a direct descendant of the Weyerhaeuser empire. And so it is this intergenerational dysfunctional relationship that exists between the Weyerhaeuser empire and the people of White Earth that does not go away. Some try to keep their trees and some try to take them.

The white man, or the American government, has a way of saying they are sorry, which is to pay you. That's pretty much their approach. Now what our elders have said in our reservation and in Indian country in general is that actually the only compensation for land is land. That you cannot pay us with money that you took, that you made off of our land. That's kind of the analysis that goes behind that. Because the only thing that is actually of value to our community is the land itself. It is not the compensation.

The federal government set up a form of reparations in the 1920s called the Indian Claims Commission which was more like, as our elders—whether it is Frank Fools Crow or George Aubid from my own community—have said, it is more like the court of the thief. That is, a court in which the federal government realized that they had taken land and not paid for it, not kept their part of the treaty—what they said instead was, "Go ahead. You know what we are going to let you do? We are going to let you sue us in our court. And when you sue us, we are going to pay you for that, and you are going to feel a lot better about it, and then we are going to say we cleared title." And through that process they secured basically the continental United States for 800 million bucks. That is the Indian Claims Commission allocations that were given—about 800 million dollars. Which is pretty darn cheap real estate, is what it is. What does it average out to? I don't know—11 cents an acre? 17 cents an acre? 5 cents an acre? Minnesota was between 5, 11, and 14 cents and acre. I don't know about Wisconsin. But I know this has been a huge sore point in Indian Country because it is, in fact, the court of the thief. Where the thief actually gets to set the price that they will pay in compensation for something that they stole.

What the Indian community has maintained, the two most outstanding cases that many of you probably know are the Lakota Nation and the Western Shoshone Nation who have said, "Actually, we never said it was for sale. You took it, you return it." Which is pretty much correct, in terms of my house—I have three kids of my own, seven kids in my house in total, and one thing I teach my kids is that you don't steal. If you steal you return. That's kind of like basic decency. But the United States doesn't behave that way. The United States says, "Yup, we did steal, but what we'll do is, we'll pay you. One-millionth the value of it. And we'll pretend like you think that's OK. And then we'll say we cleared title." Which is the story of the Indian Claims Commission.

These are issues that are at the center of our hearts. These are issues at the center of this country here. And not just this country, but every other settled country in the world. These are issues that must have some redress in terms of justice. It is incumbent upon us to consider how to begin this process, this multifaceted process of addressing the injustice of the historic patterns of land tenure, and the appropriation of land from others, and the naming. So we must address the issues and deconstruct the culturally biased land tenure system. Oh, that would be like the next couple years, huh? I suppose it might take a little longer than that. But I suggest and I ask you, I implore you, to have the courage to struggle with these issues. Not just to struggle with the issue of land tenure in terms of the Euro-centric colonizer, but also to struggle with land tenure issues in terms of the actual deconstructing and the honoring of traditional land tenure systems and their relationships.

So whether it is the naming—as we look across Turtle Island we see that there is one name after another of indigenous people who are taking back their names and naming their places again; and remembering those names and reminding us of what those places are. Or whether it is the indigenous nations in Canada and elsewhere who are recovering their territories, and explaining the difference between the land tenure systems and recovering their own land tenure systems. These are stories that warm our hearts and remind us of the lengths that we must go in addressing these issues.

These are fundamentally issues, of course, of justice, and they are issues of survival; because the reality is, if you do not have the ability to sustain yourself on your land, you do not have the ability to sustain yourself. That is it in the end. This *akiing* is the land to which we belong. It is indeed that. It is not our land. It is the land to which we belong.

Native Auctions and Buyer Ethics

Appeared in the PARK RAPIDS ENTERPRISE, *March 28, 2001.*

A Bureau of Indian Affairs corpse tag was to be auctioned off this weekend at a Park Rapids, Minnesota, auction. The tag was reputed to be a replica, rather than an original tag. I presume that the original tag would have been attached to the body of a Native person in the Wyoming territory. To me, the auction of a BIA corpse tag is essentially the equivalent of selling a tag from the corpse of a Jewish person who died at Auschwitz. At the very least, such a sale is something we should consider to be in very poor taste; it also raises many concerns regarding what we should and should not sell to (and buy from) each other. The proposed auction of this item—along with many others—brings into question the morality of Indian collectors and the ethics of auctioning Indian-related objects. Fortunately for my own sanity, and for the rest of us, auctioneer Randy Jokela pulled the tag off the auction block, after we talked.

According to the auction bill, the corpse tag was joined by several sets of fully beaded ceremonial moccasins, a medicine man's beaded leech fetish, several religious pipes, a sacred *"midewin* medicine or pipe bag," and a number of other "sacred and religious objects." A couple of those items were also pulled off the auction, after a discussion with the auctioneers, as well. The initial representation of the items and the sale of "ceremonial" items and those related to deceased Native people caused me a great deal of consternation. The other items on the bill, however, did not. Those included both new Native beadwork and a usual collection of western memorabilia, pictures, and pawn jewelry.

The problem in this sort of "Indian Art Market," for both the buyer and the original owner of the items, is that many of these objects have dubious origins. Such methods of obtainment include looting from graves, collection as "war booty," and trading by unscrupulous individuals. The present owner may or may not have had any part in these dealings. Nonetheless, legal and ethical issues persist.

In the North Country, "Native American and Alaskan primitive artifacts" are hitting the auction block in increasing numbers. There are laws that govern the sale of these items; in particular, there is a national law called the Native American Graves Protection and Repatriation Act (or NAGPRA), which was passed in 1990. The law was intended to address the hundreds of thousands of skeletal remains, sacred items, and "items of cultural patrimony" looted from graves, stripped from bodies at massacres, or simply shipped off to museums and collectors around the world.

Prior to the 1970s, there wasn't much of a market for these items, as they were usually viewed as anthropological specimens. Since that time, the interest in Indian-related objects has translated into more and more auctions and sales, many of which raise serious ethical questions and concerns.

The NAGPRA law is primarily intended to address public collections. Consequently, it has aided in the return of numerous sacred and family items to the tribes and families from which they were taken. Such acts of reclamation return not only the bodies of our relatives to our communities, but allow us to bring our sacred items back into ceremonial use, which is essential to the health and well-being of our people.

One of the best examples of this process was the 1999 return of parts of Ishi, a Northern California Native man known as the Last of the Yahis to his people. It turns out he wasn't the last of his kind; but as it was, the Smithsonian Institute had his brain in a jar for around seventy years, and just now found it after a lot of requests and looking. Think that's kind of macabre? That's pretty much the tip of the iceberg.

Consider that numerous items today finding their way onto auction blocks came there in pretty awful ways. For instance, an auction might include "a Lakota or Sioux beaded bag and Cheyenne leggings, children's moccasins, etc. 'collected by Captain Alfred Mason Fuller (1852–1902) while serving with the Second Cavalry in Montana and Wyoming between 1876 and 1882.'" Now, you and I know that Captain Fuller wasn't an art collector. More likely, those items were probably taken off children, women, and men after battles, possibly massacres, and are now purchased and sold as "art."

Then consider the story of the Survivors and Descendants of the Wounded Knee Massacre Association, ancestors of the 1890 massacre of three hundred unarmed Lakota in southwestern South Dakota in the depths of winter. The children who lived through that incredible era found that their parents' clothes, moccasins, and even sometimes hair, fingers, and breasts had been severed and collected. For instance, Cheyenne women's breasts were known to have been severed and collected by U.S. Colonel John Chivington and his soldiers at the Sand Creek Massacre in 1864 and turned into tobacco pouches. (Jeffrey Dahmer had only a few bites on these people.) The Wounded Knee massacre victims' items are now sitting in a museum in Barre, Massachusetts, and the collector is unwilling to negotiate their return to the community.

These stories are the stories of America's brutal history. They are stories that need to come to an end. We should not pride ourselves in buying these sacred items or profiting from their sale; they are items that often have been stripped from graves or stolen from those murdered in the heat of massacres.

The NAGPRA law as it applies to individual collections (like the one being auctioned off next Sunday in Park Rapids) specifically states that items taken from federal trust land or Indian land are not to be bought or sold.

Do you know the origins of all items in your possession? Their histories? The people who had them? The descendants of those people? Native Americans are people. Not items. Not mascots. Today, these auctions raise important ethical issues, issues that remind us of—and return us to—our history and of the need to shape our future. My thanks to the Jokela family for pulling some of the items off the auction block. My concerns for future auctions, however, remain.

There are plenty of Native American rugs, jewelry, arrowheads, and products historically produced for common use (as opposed to ceremonial use) and trade. More important, there are many incredibly gifted Native artists today who need to be supported through the purchase of their work. There is a growing Indian art market nationally and internationally that should be patronized by those interested in collecting Native art.

In the end, I'm pleading: *It's not only "Buyer Beware," it's also "Buyer and Seller Be Ethical."* Increasingly, private collectors, auction houses, and even eBay are reaching agreements with Native communities. These agreements allow for alternative ways to gracefully return items to where they should go, whether through sale or donation. That's what needs to happen in Park Rapids and in the entire North Country.

The auction season for the summer is heating up. We can do the right thing.

The Spirit Powers of Ojibwe
and Odawa Art

Appeared in AMERICAN INDIAN, *Fall 2000.*

Manitoulin Island rises like a thundercloud from the depths of Lake Huron. It is here in the heart of Anishinaabeg (Ojibwe and Odawa) territory that imagery and art are reborn. Alternately called Woodland or Legend painting, the art of Blake Debassige, Zoey Wood-Solomon, and Mishibinijima (James Simon) pleases the Anishinaabeg eye much as the sounds of paddles slicing the calm waters of a lake or rice sticks gently knocking on stalks of *manoomin* (wild rice) soothe the ear. It is both quintessentially Anishinaabeg and absolutely modern.

Woodland or Legend painting is an art tradition and style practiced primarily by Ojibwe, Odawa (Anishinaabeg), and Cree (Eeyou) artists, from the northern woods of the continent. It is a form that has become more prevalent and revitalized over the past two decades and whose origins are imbedded in the legends and oral tradition of these peoples. "The teachings and legends depicted on my canvases," explains Mishibinijima, "have been handed down by the elders." The canvases bring new light to the relations of the Anishinaabeg to Mother Earth. "Man must understand Mother Earth," Mishibinijima continues. "He must look at animals, plants, and fish to find answers. He forgets he is only a part of this chain of living things." Those relations are graphically illustrated in the culturally based style of Woodland painting.

For generations, the Anishinaabeg have surrounded themselves with these images. Thousands of petroglyphs, or paintings on stone, are the handprint of the people on the land and the rock. Scattered on cliffs surrounding the Great Lakes and usually renewed periodically, they tell stories of the relations between humans, the spirits, the supernatural, and animals. Although the subject matter is diverse, certain stylistic elements pervade, like the outlined figures, the spirit lines emanating from both the interior and exterior of various figures, the depictions of spiritual power, and the relationship of the being to the greater world and to other beings.

The same figures and other forms also appear on birchbark scrolls—an ingenious and primarily Anishinaabeg record-keeping and mnemonic system depicting oral histories, creation stories, songs, ceremonies, and migration records. Kept safely within the caches of traditional Anishinaabeg spiritual practices, primarily the *Midewin*, or Grand Medicine dance, the sacred teachings have been passed down for centuries. Birchbark as a medium is amazingly hardy. "Left in water or buried in the ground, this bark will remain intact for decades, even centuries," writes birchbark scholar Selwyn Dewdney, who cites a 1,000-year-old birchbark scroll remnant. Today, these design elements and recountings of history appear in the art of Manitoulin Island. It is a new millennium, yet art of perhaps two millennia and many generations past is today transformed and represented by these artists, each in a unique way.

The reawakening or remembering of the art form is attributed to the eyes and hands of Norval Morrisseau, widely credited as the founder of the Woodland School. He was born in 1932, on the Sand Point Reserve in northern Ontario, with the traditional name Miskwaabik Animiiki, or Copper Thunderbird. Morrisseau's grandfather passed on oral tradition and imagery to his grandson from their land on the shore of Gull Bay at Lake Nipigon, Ontario. There, raised by his maternal grandparents, Moses Potan

Nanakonagos and Veronique Nanakonagos, Morrisseau found the core of Anishinaabeg art forms. A short stint in boarding school in Ft. William, Ontario, and a fourth-grade education were the extent of his "formal teachings."

At 19, Morrisseau was afflicted with tuberculosis, a common disease in Native communities, and he was sent to a long-term care hospital at Ft. William, where he began to paint. It was also there that he met his wife, Harriet Kakegamic, who inspired him in his work and taught him Cree syllabics, a form of writing used commonly in the North and reflected in Morrisseau's own signature of his works. Teachings of his grandfather Potan, joined with a series of dreams and visions, became the muses that Morrisseau said called him to be an artist. "My paintings are icons, that is to say, they are images which help focus on spiritual powers, generated by traditional belief and vision." Upon recovery, Morrisseau traveled to visit many traditional Ojibwe villages and petroglyph sites, to nourish his artistic development and put it on canvas. His early imagery, like *Two Bulls Fighting*, is at the Glenbow Museum in Alberta, and paintings depicting shamans were donated as graphics to the once-leading Native publication *Akwesasne Notes* (in Mohawk territory at Rooseveltown, New York). Much like the original art forms, his art has been scattered through the communities he visited, often left as gifts in acknowledgment of the hospitality he had received. True to the birchbark and petroglyphs, Morrisseau uses traditional art styles of outlined figures and employs imagery like "X-ray anatomy" and "spirit power lines" that radiate from the spines of animals. His images show balls or seeds of "spirit power" reminiscent of the most sacred art. New representations of these elements are seen in the work of some modern Ojibwe artists, including Blake Debassige, Mishibinijima, and Zoey Wood-Solomon, who all have roots on Manitoulin Island.

Manitoulin Island is the largest freshwater island in the world and home to five Anishinaabeg reservations, including the

Unceded Wikwemikong Reserve. Morrisseau's work was shared with young Ojibwes and Odawas from Manitoulin Island reserves in 1971 at an art camp known as the Scribben Island Summer Art Project. Native artists like Carl Ray, Daphne Odijig, and Frances Kagige exposed the teenagers to the art not only of European masters but also of Ojibwe masters. Blake Debassige (from the West Bay Reserve) remembers a light going on when he first saw Morrisseau's work. It was like "a thick curtain being lifted. I saw that we do have our own culture and art forms, and yes, it is possible. I totally embraced this style because it spoke to me."

Those paintings and images also spoke to Zoey Wood-Solomon and Mishibinijima, both from the Wikwemikong Reserve at Manitoulin. By then other Native artists like Cecil Youngfox (now deceased) and Peter Miigwan had begun to paint. The artists continued an emphasis on collective, group, and community as their techniques developed and influenced each other. Wood-Solomon remembers "seeing some of the paintings and thinking, 'I'd never be able to afford them.'" As if to say that the art belonged to the whole community, not to the individual, she recalls, "Peter Miigwan handed me a blank canvas and said, 'You're an Indian, so go ahead and paint!'"

"All of us worked together as a group, as opposed to as individuals," Debassige remembers. The artists often shared techniques and teachings. "I'd ask Cecil Youngfox," Wood-Solomon says, "'How are you doing your backgrounds now?' He'd just smile and start painting. I would just watch him." Debassige recalls, "Listening to elders, and researching legends was my schooling." The art grew "exactly the same way grandmothers taught their children: by experience, by oral history." Debassige is quite proud of the cultural collective that brought about and nourishes the art—a community base, which is quite different from the individualism so often encouraged in today's modern art world. Debassige's *Birth of Nanabush,* and paintings of various flowers from the region, often graphically represent the oral tradition on canvas, providing a fountain of cultural preservation, while accentuating individual interpretation and expression. All of the artists also often teach art in the community, passing on the cultural wealth they have accumulated to future generations of Native artists.

Living within one's own community offers both a wellspring of artistic and cultural material and a set of responsibilities. Mishibinijima looked to traditional Ojibwe symbols as a foundation of his work. "I'd ask the elders, 'Can I use that in my paintings?' They'd say, 'What's your intention?'" The artist took the hint and left some of the most revered and sacred symbols out of the public realm of his large acrylic paintings. Instead, Mishibinijima developed his own symbols, which reflected some traditional forms.

The land and waters, too, tell the stories, which may come to life in the paintings. Dreamer's Rock is a traditional place for prayer and vision-seeking for the Anishinaabeg people of the region and is reflected as an animate spirit in Mishibinijima's work. Other sacred sites are depicted as perhaps a spirit woman looking upward from inside the mountain. Wood-Solomon's *Mishibiiju* (Great Panther) portrays the great mystery of the Underwater Panther, which, it is said, provides food for the thunderbirds and alternately watches and lurks in the waters of the Great Lakes. It is this rich oral history of great waters and land mysteries that provides a wealth of material for traditional artists.

Each art work by Debassige, Wood-Solomon, and Mishibinijima carries on these traditions and yet represents the avant-garde of Ojibwe art. Wood-Solomon's paintings often reflect simpler, black-outlined forms, filled in with brilliant colors, and depict the Ojibwe cultural experience, from jingle-dress dancers to cultivation of corn or the agony of colonialism. Debassige's work ranges from outlined plants and animals to surrealistic paintings like *Tree of Life* and closely etched spirit beings like *Twins of the Self*. Mishibinijima's intricate detail and use of symbols, adapted from birchbark scrolls and petroglyphs to represent various elements of his art and teachings, are brought to life with vibrant colors. Each artist's work spans personal dreams and visions, traditional teachings and stories, and avant-garde imagery. Common threads such as "spirit lines," "spirit balls," and X-ray anatomy run through their work and identify the imagery as founded by the Legend or Woodland School.

Wood-Solomon (born in 1954), lives in Sault Ste. Marie, Ontario. Wood-Solomon's experience as an artist spans two decades and has included a number of public and private collections, including *Three Sisters* at the Oneida Casino in Green Bay, Wisconsin, and the Algoma Collection in Sault Ste. Marie. She also has some pieces at the Institute of American Indian Arts Museum shop in Santa Fe, New Mexico. Debassige (born in 1956) was a participant in the original 1971 Scribben Island Summer Art Program. His career of almost three decades spans the mediums of painting, lithographs, serigraphs, acrylics on birchbark, and wood carvings, which he signs as "Debosegai." He joins his wife, acclaimed playwright and director Shirley Cheechoo (Cree), in creating set designs, props, and costumes. Blake's work has been exhibited in Geronimo's Studio in Munich, the Royal Ontario Museum in Toronto, and Canada House in London, and is contained within the exhibits of the Heard Museum, the Royal Ontario Museum, the McMichael Canadian Art Collection, and many private collections. Mishibinijima (born in 1954) is widely represented in Canadian and European collections, including the Royal Ontario Museum, the Mashantucket Pequot Museum, the Vatican Museum, and the Mishibinijima Art Gallery in Germany.

As the new millennium begins, Ojibwe people respond with imagery and beauty, reflecting the wealth of the community in their art. The art of the Legend and Woodland School is a reminder of that immense tradition, proving that much of the Anishinaabeg world remains as constant as the rocks of the Canadian Shield and the waters of Lake Huron.

Buffalo Nation

Appeared in SIERRA, *May/June 2000.*

In February, 1999, Rosalie Little Thunder and Joseph Chasing Horse led some 40 Native people on *Tatanka Oyate Mani*, the Walk for the Buffalo Nation, from South Dakota's Black Hills to the stone archway of Yellowstone's northern entrance. It was there that Yanktonai Lakota Gary Silk danced for the buffalo as Horace Axtell, a descendant of Nez Percé Chief Joseph, prayed and sang with his sons, their clear voices resonating to the mountains. Through sleet, wind, and blizzards, Little Thunder and the other Tatanka Oyate Mani participants walked a 507-mile spiritual journey along seemingly endless yellow lines through the Northern Plains, jostled by barreling semi-trailers, and prayed for the restoration of the Buffalo Nation.

To Native America, the buffalo is the elder brother, the teacher. In Lakota culture, it is said that before you kill a buffalo, you must perform the Buffalo Kill ceremony. You must offer prayers and talk to the animal's spirit. Then, and only then, will the buffalo surrender itself. Only then can you kill the buffalo. "The First People were the Buffalo People, our ancestors which came from the sacred Black Hills, the heart of everything that is," explains Chief Arvol Looking Horse, one of the Lakotas' most revered holy men. "I humbly ask all nations to respect our way of life, because in our prophecies, if there is no buffalo, then life as we know it will cease to exist."

There is a similar teaching in my own culture, the Anishinaabeg. During midwinter ceremonies, an elder's voice will rise as the drum quiets. "The buffalo gave their lives so that we might live," she will say. "Now it is our turn to speak for the buf-falo, to stand for our relatives."

The fate of the buffalo has vast implications for native ecosystems as well as Native peoples. Buffalo determine landscapes. For thousands of years, the Great Plains, the largest single ecosystem in North America, was maintained by the buffalo. By their sheer numbers, weight, and behavior, they cultivated the prairie. It is said that their thundering hooves danced on the earth as they moved by the millions; their steps resounded in the vast underground water system, the Ogallala Aquifer, stimulating its health and seeding the prairies. And their destruction set in motion the ecological and economic crisis that now afflicts the region.

In the mid-19th century, 50 million bison ranged the prairie. There were then more than 250 types of grass, along with profusions of prairie dogs, purple cornflower, prairie turnips, mushrooms, and a host of other species listed today as endangered or protected.

This natural balance has shifted considerably. Biological diversity has plummeted. Those 50 million buffalo have been replaced by farms and 45 million cattle. Due to massive cultivation and irrigation, the Great Plains' topsoil is eroding and its groundwater dwindling. The prairies are teeming with pumps, irrigation systems, combines, and toxic chemicals. Much of the original ecosystem has been destroyed, and what remains is in a precarious state. No other biome on the continent has suffered so much loss.

The Great Plains region spans 40 percent of the United States but holds just a small fraction of its population. Roughly one in four counties are in economic and demographic decline as well as social distress, and have reverted to what is technically called "frontier status," with fewer than two residents per square mile. The historian Frederick Jackson Turner declared the frontier closed in 1893, but he may have been a bit premature: The frontier, as determined by population, is in a permanent state of flux. In

North Dakota, the frontier zone shrank to 21 percent in 1920, but over the past 50 years has stretched again to cover three-fifths of the state.

In 1990, delinquency rates for holders of Farm Home Administration loans hit 26 percent in North Dakota, 42 percent in South Dakota, and 28 percent in Nebraska; rates for production loans exceeded 40 percent in all three states. Average net cash returns per farm in North Dakota, for instance, were just over $13,000 in 1997, down 37 percent from 1992 and roughly on a par with average farm incomes after World War II. Beyond these chronic troubles, bad years can bring drought, floods, and wheat scab. Little wonder farmers are calling it quits.

Yet an ironic reversal of history is taking place here. While non-Indians, farmers and otherwise, are fleeing the rural areas, Native populations are increasing. Montana, North Dakota, South Dakota, Nebraska, and Oklahoma all suffered net population losses between 1985 and 1990. Yet many Indian reservations populations' have doubled during the past two decades. These new demographics offer hope. What we are witnessing may be nothing less than the return of the Indian and the buffalo, the ebb of the frontier, and, in its own way, a regional reversal of Manifest Destiny. In the minds and hearts of the buffalo peoples, the prairies are where the buffalo are meant to be, the place where the wind calls their names. Buffalo are the animals of the past, yes, but they are also the animals of the future.

As your eyes scan the Pine Ridge buffalo pasture in southwest South Dakota, one thing stands out clearly: prairie. Native prairie grasses and plants blanket the uncultivated tribal land. This is also the case on Yankton, Cheyenne River, and a number of other Northern Plains reservations. Simply stated, some of the last vestiges of the region's historic biodiversity are found on its Indian reservations.

Nationally, 41 separate tribes now belong to the Intertribal Bison Cooperative, whose sole mission is buffalo restoration. On reservations from Taos Pueblo to Standing Rock in North Dakota, Native communities are actively welcoming home their relations.

The Ironcloud family brought their first buffalo home to Pine Ridge in 1997, and now have a small herd in a 1,200-acre pasture. Ethelyne Ironcloud's brother, Edward "Buzz" Ironcloud, is in charge of the Knife Chief Buffalo Project near Porcupine. The Knife Chief Project, like the Seventh Generation Buffalo Cooperative on the Standing Rock Reservation, is founded on the restoration of small herds, using methods employed successfully by the Arkansas-based Heifer Project—like donating calves to families who, in turn, pass along one of their gift animal's female calves so others can breed herds of their own.

Richard Sherman is a lanky wildlife biologist with the Oglala Lakota Parks and Recreation Department on Pine Ridge. I try to keep up with him as he strides purposefully through the largest of several pastures for the Oglala bison herd, a 17,000-acre expanse of real-live prairie. He stops to point out various buffalo delicacies: prairie turnips, sage, mushrooms. The pasture is a model of Sherman's vision for Lakota land stewardship, "a culturally appropriate system based on the values and philosophy of the Lakota people."

"It doesn't seem to take too long to heal the land," Sherman tells me. "It's happening right here in our buffalo pasture."

And not only here; buffalo restoration is taking root across the prairie. Pine Ridge's Akcita Buffalo Society, for example, now provides buffalo for four projects, each of which has received a "seed" herd of cows and bulls to start full-fledged herds of their own. The projects keep 60 percent of all new calves, and give the rest to Oglala Parks and Recreation. The society is hoping to seed additional herds over time.

Farther west, Ben Sherman, Richard's brother, has a vision of his own. He found a buffalo jump site near Beulah, Wyoming, in the northwest corner of the Black Hills region, where more than 20,000 buffalo are believed to have been killed over hundreds of years by ancient buffalo hunters. Ben wants to establish an interpretive center here, modeled on Head Smashed In Buffalo Jump

Interpretive Center in Alberta. But history is only the beginning. Over the past few years he has cultivated a relationship with the Nature Conservancy, which has purchased 2,000 acres in the area and is interested in restoration. "We want to run buffalo up there," he says. "I'd just like to see buffalo back in the hills again."

To the south, Taos Pueblo in northern New Mexico has maintained a buffalo herd since the 1930s for traditional subsistence and ceremonial purposes. With Taos buffalo program director Richard Archuleta, I wandered out for a closer look at these beautiful animals. They are relations. Today, the tribe's herd numbers 170, double its size a few years ago, and resides on 500 acres.

Such developments flow directly from the wisdom of Native teachings. The Braveheart Women's Society, or *Inhanktunwan Winyan*, has spent the past six years working closely with more than 70 young women on the Yankton Reservation to keep alive and restore the traditional ways. "The primary role that women had was dividing up the buffalo once the buffalo were killed," explains Faith Spotted Eagle, a Braveheart mentor. "When women had the relationship with buffalo we were able to learn from that, and pass that on to younger women. The underlying teaching is the primacy of the relationship with buffalo."

Rosalie Little Thunder, an artist and longtime activist, tells a story about the 1855 Little Thunder massacre in Nebraska, when General William Selby Harney came to the Lakota community and was greeted with the truce flag and a meal of salt pork and hardtack. "While this was going on, there was a grandmother standing there with her ten-year-old grandson. She told him to hide where the tall grass was. They started shooting down the people then. And when she was shot, she threw herself and her shawl on top of that little boy. That way she hid him. She hid him and died.

"That little boy," she adds, "he was my grandfather."

Nearly 70 people were killed that day. A century and a half later, a buffalo slaughter in Yellowstone National Park brought it all back for Little Thunder. "I had my ten-year-old grandson standing next to me," she says. "And they started killing the buffalo. Just like that, shooting them down. I covered his face with my shawl and told him to go move."

On March 5, 1997, Little Thunder and a small group of spiritual leaders, including Arvol Looking Horse, were among 75 people who congregated around 147 bison in a holding corral to pray for the buffalo spirits. During a lunch break they heard the shots. The Montana Department of Livestock had killed eight buffalo a mile to the north. Little Thunder and several others wanted to go to the site to pray, but sheriff's deputies warned them about trespassing on private land. Little Thunder walked forward to talk to one of the deputies and, as the would-be prayer group looked on helplessly, was arrested, handcuffed, and taken away in a patrol vehicle.

The arrest was the spark for a burgeoning movement to halt one of the most brutal wildlife slaughters in recent history: the killing of 1,100 bison that winter, followed by sporadic killings each year since. The cause of all this killing is Montana ranchers' fear that diseased bison will give their cattle brucellosis, which can induce spontaneous abortion. (According to the National Academy of Sciences, interspecies transmission has been demonstrated in only a few controlled situations.) That the movement to stop the slaughter has caught fire is clear from the actions of grassroots groups, a barrage of litigation, and the outrage of some 65,000 people who have spoken out at public hearings on the future of the Yellowstone herd.

It's a high-stakes mission. The killings, says Ethelyne Ironcloud, are "really devastating to not only Buffalo Nation but to the Indian nations as well. We believe that the way they treat the buffalo is the way that they treat the Indians." That is why the Yellowstone slaughter cuts to the heart of the Lakota and other buffalo cultures of the Great Plains.

No one argues that Yellowstone, an island of wildness in a sea of civilization, is ecologically ideal for buffalo. "Because biology has been absent from design decisions," writes conservation biologist Reed Noss, "park boundaries do not conform to ecological boundaries and most parks and other reserves are too small to maintain populations of wide-ranging animals over the long term or perpetuate natural processes."

Buffalo are a serve-yourself sort of critter, which means they must leave the park as conditions demand. Noss considers that a reserve of under 250,000 acres might sustain a viable population of small herbivorous and omnivorous animals, but says large carnivores and ungulates, such as buffalo, need reserves of anywhere from 2,470,000 acres—already larger than Yellowstone—to ten times that size.

Noss' notions on saving wild species are best described graphically. He and the Wildlands Project, with which he works, are focused primarily on core areas where major populations would reside or, in the case of the buffalo, roam. Connective corridors, protected by buffer zones, would link primary genetic pools, or herds, with other herds, allowing for some genetic diversity. Based on a review of empirical studies, Noss has concluded that an average population of 1,000 animals "must be maintained to assure population viability of species."

Where would the land for such preserves come from? Buy up some private farms and ranches, add in some Native reservation holdings, and you've got a pretty good start. In central South Dakota, for example, Lakota landholdings total over 7.5 million acres, more than twice those of the U.S. government. In his book *Ecology and Economics of the Great Plains,* Daniel Licht proposes creating "ecoreserves" by buying out struggling farmers, noting that reserves make better economic and environmental sense than costly farm subsidies. All told, Licht's proposed refuges would cover more than 27,000 square miles, an area he says could support 25,000 buffalo, 300 wolves, 10,000 elk, 15,000 mule deer, and over a million prairie dogs.

Richard Sherman and others on Pine Ridge believe that a buyout of land from ranchers in the Badlands might be the key to restoring the prairie. They suggest that everyone could tear down their fences and allow buffalo to roam on the collective holdings, which would have a fence around the perimeter. Ranchers, Indians, and federal agencies could then hold shares in the herd.

"There should be some alternative besides killing them in this day and age," says Little Thunder.

In fact, there may be no other alternative than to save them. Such a dream is only fitting. Buffalo are born for the plains. Their massive heads make them uniquely equipped to plow through snow; unlike domesticated cattle, buffalo face the wind, and the wind-chill. The hardiness that enabled bison to survive the severe climate of the plains is especially impressive when compared with the vulnerability of cattle and other livestock. The deep snow and searing cold of the winter of 1996, for example, left more than 450,000 head of livestock dead on the Great Plains, but took the lives of fewer than 20 bison.

According to Lakota prophecies, should Earth, the Mother of All Life, ever be shaken to crisis by the people living upon her, then White Buffalo Calf Woman will return. In the summer of 1995, a female white buffalo calf, "Miracle," was born in southern Wisconsin. Thousands of prayer offerings fluttered on the fence surrounding the calf, now a cow with offspring of her own. Miracle's birth signaled new hope to the buffalo peoples of the Great Plains. The return of White Buffalo Calf Woman symbolizes the dawn of a new era, and with it the promise of the restoration of the prairie, the buffalo cultures, and *Tatanka Oyate*, the Buffalo Nation itself.

Native American Faces in South Africa: The Parliament of the World's Religions

Appeared in NEWS FROM INDIAN COUNTRY, *January 15, 2000.*

It is a long road to freedom, as South African leader Nelson Mandela will tell you. From small village to hard labor, twenty-eight years of prison for "supporting the aims of a banned organization," to the almost unimaginable social, economic and political brutality of apartheid. To see that all change, within the eighty years of a man's life, is an amazing gift.

It was also a long road for Native American delegates to the Third Parliament of the World's Religions, held in early December in Cape Town, South Africa. Twenty hours of flying time for most of us. Native delegates from traditional Native religious practices, as well as various introduced faiths, joined with some 6,000 international delegates and 2,500 South African delegates to grapple with issues of faith, values, and the future of the Earth. Delegates also challenged dominant religions to address fundamental inequalities between religious practices, the lack of religious freedom in Native America, and the Vatican's complicity in violation of religious freedom of Native people and their sacred sites.

Joanne Shenandoah—Oneida songbird, Nammy award winner, and Grammy award nominee—led off the first day with an adaptation of a prayer turned to song. Lakota and Dakota delegates (including Pat Locke, her son Kevin Locke, and Darlene

St. Clair) presented informative panels on issues related to Native language restoration, and the status of Native women. Other presenters included Herman Agoyo (San Juan Pueblo), Professor Jennifer Joe, and Omie Baldwin (both Diné) on issues like the relationship between environmental degradation, threats to spiritual practice, the status of Native women, and repatriation.

A large Native American delegation came with Kifaru Productions/DreamCatchers Inc. (Director Gary Rhine), which organized a ten-part dialogue between Native people, and renowned world religions scholar Huston Smith. Panel members included Doug George (Mohawk), Frank Dayish (Diné), Walter Echohawk (Pawnee), Charlotte Black Elk (Lakota), Lenny Foster (Diné), Anthony Guy Lopez (Lakota), Tonya Gonnella Frichner (Onondaga), and others who presented on an array of issues for the Parliament, and for a documentary, under production by Kifaru. Kifaru's past productions include *Your Humble Serpent* (on Native American Church Leader Reuben Snake), *Wiping the Tears of Seven Generations (Big Foot Memorial Ride)*, and *The Red Road to Sobriety*, among many others. The documentary is expected out in late 2000.

In the panel's sessions of "America's Shadow Religions," presenters discussed the historic and present absence of religious freedom for many native American people, challenging world religious institutions to recognize the integrity of Native spiritual practices, and exhibit not only a tolerance for these practices, but also preserve these practices.

Walter Echohawk, a Pawnee attorney with the Native American Rights Fund, charged, "Will these Indian religious practices survive? It's how the U.S. addresses these issues that will show what the country's character is, more so than what the U.S. says." Echohawk, a veteran of many legislative and legal attempts/successes at protecting religious freedom, urged protection of sacred sites, and domestic legal and social policy to "return some of these places like the Black Hills to the people."

Frank Dayish (Diné), past president of the Native American Church of North America, talked about the tenuous thread of protection of the Church, and continuing persecution of Native American Church members. Dayish urged the Indian Health Service to stop the practice of designating babies born into the Church as "peyote babies," earning the infants possibly a preconceived stigma of "drug babies" and urged a formal recognition for the Church by government agencies.

Lakota attorney Charlotte Black Elk described the significance of the Black Hills to Lakota spiritual practices, noting that many parts of the Creation have "pieces of the song" but, "all of the song is contained in the Black Hills." Black Elk urged respect for other religions arguing against the "globalization" of religious thought.

Lenny Foster, Diné and long-time advocate for Native American prisoners' religious freedom, recalled to all present that the "liberation of the mind, body and spirit can only occur with spiritual practice and spiritual freedom." Foster works with over 1,500 Native American prisoners in struggles over use of the pipe, sweatlodge, "final rites," and right of Native inmates to have long hair, and urged protection for those who have the least ability to pray, have ceremony, or retain any semblance of human dignity.

In between the panels, Kifaru Productions had arranged for the Native delegation to meet with traditional and political leaders of the South African community. I watched Lenny Foster's eyes flicker with both recognition and amazement, as we walked between cellblocks at Robben Island prison, one of the most notorious prisons in the world and home to many of South Africa's political prisoners—including Nelson Mandela for two decades, and most leaders of the African National Congress (ANC), the party now in control of South African government. Today, that same prison is a National Heritage Site, a primary school, a classroom of history, and an example of South Africa's courageous steps towards reconciling the nation. Its transformation, from one of the most brutal regimes in modern world history (the apartheid regime of South Africa) to the beginning of a democracy, is, in itself, a miracle in modern political development. Echoing the need for this type of transformation on a worldwide scale, religious leaders from around the world called upon the world's guiding institutions to reassess and redefine their roles in order to assure a just, peaceful and sustainable future. His Holiness, the Dalai Lama, exiled head of the Tibetan Buddhists, reiterated these words in our ears, talking about the need for compassion, forgiveness, community and love.

Perhaps two of the larger challenges to the morality of present major religions came from Tonya Gonnella Frichner (Onondaga) and Anthony Guy Lopez (Lakota). Frichner, an attorney, presented concerns about the Human Genome Diversity Project (HGDP), and the macabre study of the genetic make up of humanity which includes 440 Indigenous communities. Frichner urged a more active role in opposition to the international project by the world's religions, questioning the ethics of genetic manipulations, and the often-uninformed consent involved in taking genetic materials (blood, tissue and hair samples). Frichner also, referring to a number of pleas by Native organizations and nations, urged people to reject the term "endangered populations" used by the Human Genome Project, and called for increased financial support for medical programs in these communities, on par with the expenditures of the HGDP. Frichner pointed to the historic Christian doctrine which considered Native people as less than human (Papal Bulls in the 1490s to mid 1500s), and urged all Catholics present to call on the Pope to rescind the Bulls.

Similarly, Guy Lopez challenged the Catholic Church, in relationship to the Mt. Graham Telescope Project. The project impacts an Apache sacred site in Arizona. Representing the Apache Survival Coalition, Lopez reiterated a decade of opposition to the telescope. The project is sponsored by the Vatican, the University of Arizona, and recent partners including the Notre Dame

University and the Max Plenke Institute, which is located in Germany. Three telescopes presently scar the sacred site, with proposals for an additional set.

The Cape Town Parliament of the World's Religions is the third such gathering, the first held in Chicago in 1893, the second a century later, also in Chicago. The first parliament did not have any Indigenous representation, while the second included a large Native delegation of presenters. The gathering was meant to be a place for world religions to grapple with issues of society at the cusp of the millenium. The Cape Town, South Africa Parliament, in its keynote document "A Call to our Guiding Institutions," continued a tradition born in Chicago in 1893, in calling together religious leaders, scholars, theologians, and other representatives of the world's religions to ponder the "place of faith and spirituality in the modern world. As the deliberate formal encounter of many religions, East and West, this unprecedented gathering marked the beginning of modem interreligious dialogue," they wrote. The 1993 gathering continued this tradition, developing a document, entitled "Towards a Global Ethic, an Initial Declaration," setting forth four fundamental commitments which remain powerfully relevant today: nonviolence and respect for life, solidarity and a just economic order, tolerance and a life of truthfulness, and equal rights and partnership between men and women. The Parliament calls on the religious community to actively move towards these roles in order to assure a just, peaceful and sustainable future. Participants discussed a range of issues, from the ecological crises of ozone depletion, over-consumption of resources in northern countries, to the rise of AIDS, and issues of globalization, child labor and sex trades.

Set against the backdrop of a new South Africa, one which five years ago was democratically transformed when Blacks were finally allowed to vote, these issues seemed all the more real. Immense poverty stands within a mile of incredible wealth. A pursuit of justice underlies public policy, yet social peace is not yet apparent, in a country with a high crime rate (of individual against individual, as opposed to the previous, governmentally imposed crimes against humanity). Decades of courage, and an equal challenge permeate the culture. While the Parliament covered these issues in discussions, the South African society as a whole is engaged in a deep and delicate process of reconciliation. This process of reconciliation is illustrated, in part, by the Truth Commission, and its multiracial task of unraveling the horror of political and economic violence.

Native American delegates reminded the world's dominant religious institutions that these same issues must be taken up in home countries. As we stood and cheered for 80-year-old Nelson Mandela, we see that the long walk is possible. And, by our own delegation's words, we are reminded, as Mohawk Doug George explained, "that we are survivors, only so far as we maintain our practices, our responsibility to those yet unborn, up to the seventh generation from now."

Honor the Earth:
Our Native American Legacy

Delivered at the NINTH ANNUAL WESTHEIMER PEACE SYMPOSIUM, WILMINGTON COLLEGE, WILMINGTON, OHIO, *October 20, 1999.*

Something about our Ojibwe that's kind of unique, is that we are a language of verbs—eight thousand verbs. That's a lot of verbs, eight thousand verbs. That's what I always say, though—I say that we're a people of action. . . .

I am motivated, as many people in my community are, by our teachings. I think about those people who had such a hard time before me. All of us look back, and it was not an easy life for most of our ancestors. They had to struggle. People today are now in such luxury—it is called the luxury of consumerism or the luxury of the petroleum age—that we've forgotten, perhaps, what it was like for our old people; that they had to struggle to have some dignity in their lives. I look at that, and in that process I am always reminded of our teachings. That is what drives a lot of our work in my community and in our own indigenous community.

I'm going to share with you tonight one of our prophecies, which is the prophecy of the people of the seventh fire, or the prophecy of the seventh fire. The reason I'm going to tell you this story is because it is something that very much is in the Anishinaabeg world—it's one of the important things that we think about. But I also tell you this story because I am quite cognizant that in the larger society, not only do most people not know very much about indigenous people, what they know is quite often untrue—whether it is romanticized or whether it is

kind of compartmentalized, or however you want to look at it—
that's what it is, and it is not seen in the holistic view within
which we view ourselves. For instance, I'm an educated person, I
went to college, and I find that indigenous people's work is not
in fine arts, it's in anthropology. Much of our literature, until
recently, was over in anthropology. Our stories that we hold most
sacred to us are viewed as folkloric, as things that are of interest,
perhaps, but not as having that wellspring of teachings that would
guide a culture.

In my life and in the life of my family, many of us in our community find that those teachings are not about the process of
going back, but that's kind of the mythology that surrounds the
view of native people—it's that "those Indians want to go back
to how it was a long time ago." That's not very realistic. It's not
about that at all. It's about recovering that which the Creator gave
us as instructions, and then walking that path which the Creator
gave us—because that's the path that we were intended to walk
in, and it's a lot easier if you walk that one than if you try to go
on those other ones. If you don't, you're kind of assuming that
you know a way better. I've learned that that's kind of a faulty
assumption.

So let me tell you our teaching of the people of the seventh
fire. A long, long time ago they say that these prophets—each
society has prophets—came to our community. These prophets
said to our Anishinaabeg people that these times will come and
will be signified by fire. They said, a time will come when you
will move from the East. They said, you will follow a great shell
in the sky and you will move to the place where the food grows
upon the water. That's what they said. And that food is wild rice.
That's what that is and that's where we moved. They prophesied
that such a time would come. And they prophesied that we'd be
doing pretty well, but every once in while we wouldn't do too
well. We're just like every other society, you know, we just really
botch it up sometimes. I don't want anyone to think that I would
argue that we are perfect.

You know, they say that a long time ago, maple syrup used to flow from the trees all year round. And then the Creator came down and saw our people, and our people were laying on the ground underneath the trees. And the Creator said, "That's really lazy of you. That's kind of shameful. You want to tell me what you're supposed to be doing, laying under the trees and licking up the syrup?" The Creator said, "We'll fix that, and what we're going to do is that sap is going to not run as syrup, it'll run as sap." Forty gallons of sap make a gallon of syrup, for your information. And in only one part of the year, and you've got to work if you want to taste that sweetness. This is one of our teachings: Don't be lazy. Learn how to live the right way and respect what was given to you. . . .

We were also told that people would come to our land and some of those people would have fair skin. And some of those people would be good and extend a good hand toward us, and some of those people would not be so good. That's true, you know. Some people are just goodhearted and some people are just greedy. That's the way it is. You know, we learn that lesson. We learn that.

And then they foretold that a hard time would come to our people. That's the time of the fourth and fifth fires—epidemics and plagues and people almost disappearing. A ninety percent reduction in our populations. We are survivors. The unmentioned Holocaust of America is the Holocaust that occurred to our people. Almost entirely disappeared, our peoples. But they said we would survive that, and then we would have a continuing hard time where things that were ours would be put away or taken away. And we'd look all around and where are all our ancestors? Our ancestors are in museums, many of them still, taken away from our communities. Our drums, our sacred items, all our things taken, stashed away, hidden away. They said that that would happen to us and that it would cause us great grief because we could not heal. We could not conduct our ceremonies—we're in disarray when we lose those things. They said that those things would happen to us.

And then they said this time would come, this time of the sixth fire when we would start reawakening, and we would look and start to find and bring back those things which had been put aside, had been lost, had been taken, and we would start recovering them and becoming full people again. That's what they say, becoming *Oshki Anishinaabeg*, that's the word—the new people. We would start becoming those people and in the process we would stand up again and say, "We are Oshki Anishinaabeg, we are those people and we are going to carry on our way." And they said the time would come then, the time of the seventh fire.

They say that that is the time now, the time of the people of the seventh fire, the time of the seventh fire. And during that time these Oshki Anishinaabeg, they would have emerged and would be standing up straight and then they would say, "You have two choices. There are two paths ahead of you." One path, they say, is a well-worn path but they say that it is scorched. That's what those old people say, that it is a scorched path. And the other path is green, that's what they say. They say that now is the time of choice.

We have a choice between these two paths. And this is the time of the seventh fire.

So I share that prophecy with you because that is something that was told to our people, a very, very long time ago. And that is something which informs our work, it informs how we think, how we view things. It is not something that is far away, distant, romanticized, or trivialized. It is a core of what we believe—that we have these choices. I also share them with you because it is our teaching that those choices are not unique to us, that we all have these individual choices, like these new people, these Oshki Anishinaabeg.

So I tell you that as kind of what drives our work in our communities, this question of being a responsible parent, this question of recovering that which you have and trying to walk, this question ultimately of being a person at the end of the cusp of the millennium here at the twilight of this century, and saying that as a person, as a woman, I'm the one who has the right to determine what my destiny is. I'm the one. I take that responsibility. I do not relinquish that responsibility to someone else. I keep that, because that is what the Creator said. The Creator said, "You are full human beings with that integrity, and you have that right to determine your destiny."

That is the challenge, however, that we face, because that is not a simple thing. If you take that responsibility, you have to take all the consequences and all the pieces that go with it. But that is what forms our work, the body of our work in our community.

I'm not a specialist in all indigenous peoples. I want to be really clear about this. There are over five hundred federally recognized tribes in the United States. I come from one community. I know our teachings. I'm pretty good in our teachings. My elders, they say, "You go out there, you speak well in English. We want you to talk a little better in Ojibwe." That's how they talk to me. So what they say, though, in our teachings, is that natural law is the highest law, higher than the laws made by nations, states, or municipalities, and one would do well to live in accordance with natural law.

That is our biggest teaching, that natural law is the highest law, and it would be folly to figure that you can outwit natural law. That is the challenge that many of the earlier speakers were talking about, the idea that we over time have a society which has figured out how to trade pollution credits. Have you ever noticed this thing on radiation standards? You can't even figure out what they mean anymore. They keep changing what they mean, or changing the terminology. We cannot do that. You can change the terms, you can change the allowable limits, you can do the risk assessment—all these things—but in the end, the fact is that you and I drink that water. You and I breathe that air. You and I live here.

So we can say whatever we want to in our little human minds, but in the big picture of things, it is natural law in the end. We all walk down the same path. We all have to live here. So we say that natural law is the highest law, higher than the laws made by nations, states, and municipalities.

How do we know what is natural law? Two sources of our knowledge. . . . First, intergenerational residency. Observe nature over a long period of time. I laugh because in northern Minnesota we have this argument about wolf reintroduction. These guys come up there, and they have all their scientific models. They figure out what's going to happen with the wolf. They know how many wolf packs there are, how many wolves can be here, and they've got it all projected over a ten-year period. Do you know what happened? About five years in they had to toss their model out. That was just totally great guys, great model. A wolf is a wolf. They're going to go where there's something to eat. They're going to go where they like it. That's what they're going to do. We could have told them that, but they didn't ask us. They came up there with their models. Intergenerational residency; you observe how your relatives live. That's a good way to know what natural law is.

Another source of our knowledge is spiritual knowledge, spiritual practice. . . . We all have our own wellspring of our spiritual practice and that's a good thing. But what I would say is that in our community, I think it is really important to always emphasize that, because a lot of times it is associated with a place. We practice our religion at a certain place, a sacred site; a lot of the sacred sites are endangered in this country today. All over this country our sacred sites are in danger.

We practice our religion. Until 1978, did you know it was not legal to practice your religion as a native person? The American Indian Religious Freedom Act passed in the United States in 1978, kind of late for a country that was founded, allegedly, on religious freedom. I say that because it's a big issue to our community that we are allowed to practice our religion, because that's how we know what we're supposed to do. That's how we know, how we practice our religious beliefs. How do we know? By natural law. One thing we know is that most things that are natural are cyclical, they're cyclical. That is the tide, the moons, the seasons. . . . We understand that they're cyclical.

I say that quite often, that's one of the conflicts we have in this society, because this society is not based on a cyclical worldview. Instead of being based on a cyclical worldview it's based on a linear worldview. Time is the best way to describe that. How you can talk time in this country—did you ever notice? Timeline. Did you ever see a timeline? Even in school to this day you go over there and they start that timeline, 1492. They continue it from there on out with some dates that are of importance to someone. I never figured out who that someone was. You ask them—you know me, I always have to ask the questions—about pre-1492. They call that prehistory. What does that mean, if you're me? That didn't really happen, that was before history. But that's the linear view. It's associated with a set of values; the driving value in this society is progress. Got to have progress. Don't want to throw it out. Progress is what you want to have. Progress is defined in this society, largely, by technological advancement and economic growth. Those are the two primary indicators, I would say, of progress in this society.

In other societies we might not have those same indicators. For instance, if we wanted to look at a number of people in prison, we wouldn't call the United States very far along in progress. Status of women, number of people in poverty, not very far along. But instead, technological growth, Dow Jones, doing pretty well. Those things are good. It's a different system.

But even in its essence, the production system is linear in this country. And that is one of the challenges we face. You take raw materials, natural resources, capital, put it together, produce product and produce what? Waste. Waste. Linear production system in this country. It's not really, we make the argument, it's not quite in keeping with natural law. It's one of our challenges. That's why we've got some problems there. We keep producing waste. Linear system. You can say whatever you want to, but the more you build it up—nuclear waste, perfect example—the more you build it up, the more there is.

Cyclical thinking. That's a part of our concept of natural law.

Another concept of natural law is the recognition that most things are animate. In my language of eight thousand verbs, most of our nouns are animate. Many of them are animate. The word for stone, *asin*, is animate in my language. A lot of things around us, all those things are animate. What that means in our conceptual framework is that they are alive, they have standing, they have spirit. That's what that means when it's an animate noun. Even, ironically, the word for car in my language, *odaabaan*, is animate.

But you compare what has happened to our language, the English language, and what you see is over time it's mutated—when we used to talk about corn or water. I spend a lot of time arguing about on my reservation with loggers in Becker County, and they look up at my reservation full of trees and they refer to it as "timber resources." Inanimate. It's inanimate. I say no, excuse me, that's a forest with trees. No: timber resources, board feet. Of value in terms of its beneficial use to man. I'm saying this because it's a really important conceptual difference between worldviews, and I believe at the cusp of the millennium we must grapple with these issues. Water. Look at the West—"beneficial use of water," that's what you want to have. Water in the river is not necessarily a beneficial use of water. Allocation of water rights, all in terms of beneficial use. "Agricultural products." We used to call it corn. Now we call it an agricultural product. It moved from being an animate to an inanimate noun. It's important, what's happened even to the language, to recover the language. In my view, most of these things are animate.

Finally, I would say one of our last teachings—to be really simplistic about our teachings, of which there are many—is the teaching of reciprocity. When you take something, you give something back. So when I go harvest wild rice on my reservation—I'm a big harvester, I pick a lot of stuff up there—I always offer tobacco. I offer that and ask that rice to give itself to me because it feeds my family. It not only feeds my belly, but it feeds my soul. That's what we say. You offer something to give thanks that it gave its life to you to nourish you. That's one of our teachings in our community. It's an important part, because that way you're respectful and you're asking it to give itself to you all the time. Because we do not create. Try to live without food. Try to live without water. You cannot make it. . . . You have to have that, but you have to give thanks for it.

So I say that to you, because that is also a little different than the practices we have. One of the challenges that we have in America is that America is a society based on conquest, not on survival. It is a society, by and large, based on the concept that there is always a West, always a frontier. There will always be someplace to go. We don't necessarily have to give thanks for where we are because we're moving. That's what has happened in this America, is this conceptual framework—there is always going to be someplace we can go or something else we can buy.

I would suggest to you that that practice is not sustainable. That, in fact, the only societies that really have experience with living sustainably here are our societies. You cannot make an argument to me that the United States is sustainable. You cannot. You cannot make an argument to me that the United States is sustainable, because there is no way that a society that causes so much extinction—an industrial society that caused the extinction of over two thousand nations of indigenous people—is sustainable. . . . A society that causes so much extinction is not a society that is nourishing.

That is the challenge we find ourselves in at the cusp of the millennium. This conceptual framework between one worldview and another worldview, indigenous and industrial, or land-based and predator. That's what we call it sometimes—the predator. The predator worldview. It is, in fact, manifest in how we live here. And every ecological crisis we have today is a direct consequence of that—and the human crises that we have as well. Our communities have seen that and we are still here. We survive.

Life of a Powwow Emcee:
Vince Beyl, the Man behind
the Microphone

Appeared in NEWS FROM INDIAN COUNTRY, *March 31, 1998.*

It's mid winter, and Vince Beyl is tapping his foot to the sound of traditional drum music. That is one of his favorite things to do—all year round.

He's a big guy with a winning smile that seems to be given out freely. He's not stingy with laughs either. From him, you'll hear those laughs and that voice of authority—not like the authority of those nuns at boarding school, but like a guy who knows what he's doing and is going to help you out.

Vince Beyl is a powwow emcee. White Earth reservation's very own emcee. That is his other job when he's not Director of Indian Education for Bemidji Public Schools, where almost nine hundred Native students are his concern. It is the emcee job, however, which takes him from Toronto to Saskatchewan, throughout Minnesota, the Dakotas, Wisconsin and Michigan.

Somewhere between a religious instructor and a square dance caller is an emcee. There is actually no simple way to describe the job—it is as fluid as the motion of a grass dancer, and as subtle as the movements of a woman's traditional dance. The emcee is the voice behind the powwow, the one who rouses dancers and drums in the morning, encourages the shy and interested to join the circle, and then occasionally chides the brash. His job commands a great deal of responsibility and demands an equal amount of respect.

Zongun Cumig, Stands Strong Ground, is an apt name for Vince Beyl. As an emcee he is perhaps the most versatile individual at a powwow. The emcee is often asked to explain the significance of eagle feathers, the origins of diverse dance styles, or the meaning of various songs. On an occasion or two, an emcee might facilitate a wedding, naming ceremony, or more commonly, a giveaway recognizing the passing of a family member or an honor in life.

Vince does all that and more. "All of my life I went to powwows. My grandmother took me to the powwow at Red Lake on the Fourth of July, Mille Lacs, White Earth, and all the different ones, from the early 1960s on," he remembers. "I was a traditional dancer for many years and an original member of the Red Earth Drum. But for the past fifteen years, I've been mostly an emcee."

As one of eight regular emcees in the state, and White Earth's most prominent, Vince keeps his datebook busy, as traditional and competitive powwows last every week from May to September and are scattered through the remainder of the year. His last powwow in 1997 was the Toronto Skydome, Thanksgiving weekend. His first this year is right in his own home office turf—the Bemidji High School powwow in February. Then come spring, he's on the road, ready to call for those drums and introduce dancers.

Why does he do it? "It's my way of giving back to the Circle, doing something for the people—I do it for the people that come. They come together for a few days and in that time I try and be a special host. It's about the circle, the ceremony and healing."

To those of us who attend and dance at the White Earth powwow, we have noticed how it has grown and flourished over the recent years. The numbers have grown—until last year almost four hundred dancers in all catagories were registered—and new hand drum and moccasin game competitions round out the activities. "It's hometown kind of stuff," he says and smiles. "The reservation powwow has more enthusiasm. . . . It's one of the largest traditional gatherings in the state, and a lot of families focus their vacations on that. It's a great thing."

The gift is making a huge event run smoothly. Think of it this way. The complexity of other rural cultural events does not compare to the activities underway at one time during the powwow. With square dancing, all the dancers are dancing the same style, and hopefully in unison. With a rodeo, each event is in sequence, and, with a little luck, all of the competitors are divided correctly by each event. In an auction, we are talking about things, not about 350 dancers and 12 drum groups. The average powwow runs two nights and two afternoons. So, in its own right, a powwow is a marathon of dancing. Add competition to it, and you have another element—and all the scoring, judging, and drama that corresponds to it.

Vince Beyl's challenge is to make this marathon run smoothly and, hopefully, ensure that people enjoy themselves. An emcee like Vince can do that because he has some experience, confidence, a little help from the spirits, and a computerized list he runs off. Vince is proud of his list. It includes the names of the drums, the drum order, intertribals, processionals, grand entries, invocations, introductions, welcome addresses, special events, and any contests that are a part of the schedule. That system is kept in a sort of grid chart that makes sure all the drums get to perform a variety of songs and that all the protocol is taken care of. The names of dignitaries, elders, and "visiting royalties," or representatives from other communities, are all on his list, so he doesn't have any false steps in introductions, an important consideration on the microphone. That's where if you make a mistake, five hundred people notice it.

The powwow circuit gives back to Vince as well. "It keeps me fresh, and I'm always learning," he says. "The first nations of Ontario often hold their traditional drum ceremony before they start their celebration. This includes blessing and feasting of the dance grounds and drum. Then, as they need to, they hold their doctoring and healing throughout the four-day celebration. These drums and songs have always been amongst the Anishinaabeg people, and are very much still maintained today."

The fact is that all the powwows are different. Each reflects the local culture and practices of each community, and their history. "There's a lot of knowledge in powwows. Each person has their own style, there's a lot of hard work involved in it, and it's sometimes unstructured. The challenge is that people expect you to be professional."

"There's immense responsibility for everything in it. There are a lot of traditions in these powwows and sometimes they are different. As an outsider you can't impose your way in a community. There's etiquette in this all. There's also the protocol of the powwow itself—flags, Eagle staffs, Veterans' songs, eagle feathers that have fallen, all of that. You need to know that. There's also the specials, honor songs, memorials, giveaways, namings, all of them."

What's the secret of being a good emcee? That, I have a feeling, Vince only divulged in part. "The rhythm . . . sequence and rhythm, keep it going and flowing, that's what we want to do. Rhythm, that's what you want. The rhythm of the powwow gets the people and dancers all geared up to really want to dance. The challenge is to get to that level."

There are also, it seems, some helpful traits for emcees: patience, foresight, and sense of the crowd, peripheral vision and peripheral hearing. "It's important that announcers have a lot of confidence. You have to be able to go through these things, explain what's taking place, and sometimes to clarify what someone—like an elder—is saying. You can set the tone of how it's going. Sometimes you gotta say no." An emcee also, it would seem, should know how to let the dance continue when the people are really enjoying themselves. I asked Vince when he knew if he was doing a good job. "When people enjoy themselves, way up 'til Sunday night. Then the people are still there, and the dancers want to keep dancing. Then I've accomplished something. Those times, I'll say, let's retreat those Eagle staffs early, so that the elders can get back to their camps. Then we'll keep dancing and keep going."

Closing lines from the big guy behind the microphone? "The significance of powwows is to express beauty and elegance through song and dance."

The phone rings and there's a request to emcee a powwow. "I'd like to help you, but I'm heading out that weekend. Here, try Murphy Thomas."

Then the big man is gone. Out of the office, and off to the next powwow.

What Others Say: Sacred Sites, Fishponds and the National Park Service

Appeared in INDIAN COUNTRY TODAY, *May 7, 1996.*

Mahealani Pai wades out into the waves and makes his offerings, then turns towards the *heiau*, a traditional Hawaiian temple. He is the caretaker of the heiau at Honokohau near Kona. The Pai family has cared for the heiau and the adjoining traditional fish traps for four generations. Now the National Park Service (NPS) is seeking the Pai family's eviction since the family does not hold fee simple title to the five-acre parcel. Negotiations in mid-April will decide NPS's position.

My family and I wander through lava-strewn back roads near the Kona harbor, trying to find Mahealani Pai. After three or so tries, we succeed, directed to the Pai family land by one of many homeless families in this state, where rents in the largest city, Honolulu, are on par with Manhattan, and 80 percent of the population is people of color.

As I walk past porta-potties and the heiau, I see some tents, tarp cooking-dining areas, a couple of pole houses on a jetty between fish traps and a group of twenty or so people. A man stands with flip chart behind him. As we approach I hear the man with the flip chart discussing litigation and organizing strategies used by the Environmental Justice Movement and the Pai family. An environmental justice workshop from the University of Hawaii is underway. A tall husky man with a long ponytail stands and walks toward us, extending a hand, Mahealani Pai.

Hawaii has so many land problems with Native people that you can just about name the district and a number and come up with a land struggle and arrests. There is only so much land on an island, and in Hawaii, like elsewhere, power and money dictate who gets the land.

That's Mahealani Pai's problem. His family has battled eviction threats from the NPS ever since the federal government bought parts of an area for the Kaloko-Honokahau National Historic Park in 1988. The Pai *Ohana* (family), unlike the NPS, have cared for the land, fish traps and heiau since before 1848. The family, however, does not hold fee title to the property although the park is intended as "a center for the preservation, interpretation and perpetuation of traditional Native Hawaiian activities and culture." Now it seems the NPS no longer requires Native Hawaiians to preserve, interpret and perpetuate their own culture.

Add to that a proposal by Nansay Hawaii to construct a "destination resort development" with 1,000 rooms, 330 multiple-family residential units, 380 single-family homes, golf course, health club, commercial businesses and infrastructure and you get the real picture. This, I assume, is NPS's idea of complementary multiple use of public lands.

"We know this is where all of them came from, where they lived and where they are buried. Ownership of land? We know we don't own it but we know that we belong to it," Mahealani Pai said.

The Pai Ohana has maintained the fish traps, ceremonial sites on land and water while paper title is transferred between owners. The last owner before the NPS maintained a cooperative understanding of the Pais.

"All they asked us was to keep up the place. They understood how special this was to our family, and they knew who the old folks were."

But when the NPS took over the site area in 1988, Mahealani's family was coerced into signing "a paper that would not allow the family to continue living a life-style we've been living up to now."

That document was a "tenant disclaimer" acknowledging that the person (family) is a "permissive occupier" of the land being sold to the U.S. government and the signer agrees to relocate upon demand by the government, waiving all claims to just compensation.

The Pai family never dealt with land title issues until shortly after the NPS requested they sign a "special use permit." On January 24, 1994, the NPS began a process to remove the Pai family from their land because Mahealani and his father refused to renew a special use permit with the Park Service. The permit, according to the NPS would allow the Pais continued residency for five years.

So the Pai family ended up in court, first against the Nansay Hawaii Corporation, which poses an immediate threat to their fish traps and ceremonial worship. Although the case seemed innocuous in the form of the question, "Should a public interest group called Public Access Shoreline Hawaii be given a contested case hearing by the Planning Commission over a permit request by Nansay Hawaii?" it is not.

And the court decision was not so easygoing. Not only did the August 31 decision allow Public Access Shoreline Hawaii and its primary plaintiff Mahealani Pai, a hearing, the court also held that the right of Native Hawaiians to practice traditional activities on privately owned land has always been accommodated in the law and that the state, and by extension the private property holders, are required to do whatever is necessary to preserve and protect these rights. Or in this case, if Hawaiians are gathering shrimp and fish from anchialine ponds sitting on a resort's property, Nansay may have to provide them with access and preserve the ponds.

As it stands, Mahealani Pai isn't too interested in collecting fish and shrimp or in praying at the heiau in the shadow of a luxury resort development.

Now the Pai family is looking at the NPS. The federal government has a stronger role in controlling land in Hawaii. First of all, consider that the Department of Defense controls a good portion of the land that the tourist industry does not control. There are over 100 military installations in Hawaii with fully 10 percent of the state and 25 percent of Oahu under direct military control. Then there's the strange story of Kaho'olawe the eighth Hawaiian Island, one of two you'll never visit (unless like me, you consent to being tossed off a boat to swim to shore, or can talk yourself onto a military helicopter). Kaho'olawe was the only National Historic Monument used as a bombing range, until about three years ago, when after 20 years of protest, ceremony and political struggles, the entire island is being restored to some yet undefined Native Hawaiian sovereign entity.

Put that all aside and think about it. The NPS is trying to evict the Pai family from a park created to preserve Hawaiian culture and which has a temple.

"What we are trying to say to the NPS is that you cannot curate a temple," Mililani Trask, Kia Aina of Ka'lahui, a Native sovereignty group said. "You can curate a national historic site, not a sacred site."

This has national implications. The Timbisha Shoshone in Death Valley National Park are in a similar situation. They always lived there and had a national park created around them. According to James Kawahara, a staff attorney at the Native American Rights Fund (NARF), the National Park Service at Death Valley, Calif., was told by Congress in the recently passed California Desert Protection Act (one of the only so-called "environmental laws" to pass Congress in the Clinton era) "to prepare a report to congress on the homeland issue."

"Now the NPS is saying," Kawahara explains, "'to start this discussion first, your homeland is outside the park, then we'll talk to you.'"

"Indigenous people have always been there, including their sacred sites, burial sites. The park was created around them." Now Kawahara and NARF are concerned that the NPS policy is to "subordinate their [Indigenous peoples'] needs to natural and archaeological resources. The people have in fact lived there and cared for the land for generations. If Native people are subordinated in this manner, we'll have to ask the Clinton Administration to overhaul the policy."

This brings other sacred site issues to mind. HR 563, for instance, will amend the National Historic Preservation Act to "prohibit the inclusion of certain sites on the National Register of Historic Places," especially those with no visible sites, a point which seems to be interpreted at the whim of the government. The bill is targeted at public lands, most notably Mount Shasta.

Mahealani Pai's situation brings other sacred sites into the discussion. "If the NPS cannot curate a temple, should it," as Miliani Trask wonders, "be able to curate Mount Shasta, the Medicine Wheel, the Sweetgrass Hill or the Black Hills?

"Native curators, not federal agencies are likely better suited to care for religious sites," she said.

As my eyes scan Mahealani Pai's fish traps, heiau, shrimp ponds and beach, the work of generations to build and maintain an area for 150 years is clear. The only ones who can care for an area so well are those who have prayed there for a century. But, as the courts and federal agencies discuss the matters over the next months, I am not sure that opinion is held in Washington.

Don't Cheapen Sovereignty

Appeared in THE CIRCLE, *March 1996.*

*"The man who is to be chief must have certain qualifications.
He must be a man who is honest. He must have 'Hoeyianah' or
the 'good mind,' as we say. He must have great concern and do
the right thing by his people. He must not be a womanizer. . . .
The clan mother can remove a chief. If he is guilty of 'forcing a woman'—we don't say 'rape'—or stealing or of taking
a life, the chief is deposed instantly, without even being
forewarned. . . ."*

—Dewasenta, Onondaga Clan Mother

In this era, there seems to be a lot of talking about sovereignty,
but not many sovereign actions. As an Anishinaabe, I'd like to
see more of the latter than the former. "Talk," frankly, has become cheap and all this talk, whether from Skip Finn, Darrell
Wadena or various White Earth enrolled members who elect to
avoid child support payments, cheapens the values our parents
and grandparents stood for all the more.

Three circumstances recently turned my stomach. Minnesota
Senator Skip Finn pleading that the state had no jurisdiction to
prosecute him on embezzlement charges, based on his sovereign
status as an enrolled Leech Lake tribal member. Then the White
Earth tribal council members pleading sovereign immunity to the
forty-four Federal indictment charges—not saying they were innocent, just arguing the Feds could not prosecute. There are also
a series of White Earth men, many of whom have voiced opposi-

tion to the Wadena administration, parading in front of the Becker County Courthouse with their sovereignty, arguing that the state has no jurisdiction to secure their child support payments.

There is an immense amount of talk about rights. But what of our responsibilities? Our sovereign rights, our hunting rights, our rights to our children. . . . Let me ask some questions:

If our sovereign rights are so important, why did/does the White Earth Tribal Council enter into "acts" with the state relinquishing a sales tax exemption on the reservation, or the right/ responsibility to regulate hunting and fishing licenses within the reservation? If sovereignty is important why would the alleged election fraud occur? If our sovereign rights are so important, why did the White Earth Chairman agree to WELSA (the White Earth Land Settlement Act), in spite of the implications for Indian land title on this reservation?

How about hunting and harvesting rights? There is a fish consumption advisory in effect for a number of lakes on White Earth, Leech Lake and Red Lake reservations. That means that women of childbearing age, for instance, should only eat so many fish because there is mercury or other heavy metals in those fish. This gets worse every year, as it is cumulative. That mercury and heavy metals contamination comes from coal (usually burning Indian coal from northern Cheyenne) and incinerators like those in Perham and Fosston, north and south of the reservation. There is little point in fighting over rights to fish that you cannot eat. (I say that to Trout Unlimited and Bud Grant and all those sport fishermen as well as the White Earth Tribal Council and the *ogitchidaag* of our nation.) Where are all these people fighting about spearfishing, when there are state hearings to increase the allowable mercury levels and emissions?

And the children's rights. What is the point of an Indian Child Welfare Act when there is so much disregard for the rights and well being of the children? Take these *ogitchidaag* for instance. An Indian guy has a few children with a few women. No problem. Except that traditionally, native men took care of their children and those women—all of them. Now some of these guys from White Earth are saying the state has no jurisdiction to extract child support payments from them. Do they pay on their own—to these women? I don't think so. I know better. How does that equation better the lives of our children? How is that sovereignty?

The U.S. Federal government is so hypocritical about recognizing sovereignty that we (the native community) seem to fall into it all as well. I would argue the Feds only recognize Indian sovereignty when a First Nation has a casino or a waste dump, not when a tribal government seeks to preserve ground water from pesticide contamination, exercise jurisdiction over air quality, or stop clear-cutting or say no to a nuclear dump. "Sovereignty" has become a politicized term used for some of the most demeaning purposes.

How does the present White Earth Tribal Council's exercise of sovereign immunity help our people? The fact is that our ancestors and our leaders fought and died for the principles of our nations, our cultures and our sovereignty. George Aubid (Mille Lacs) stood up to the State of Minnesota on land taxes on White Earth—and opened up this era of the land struggle. David So Happy (Columbia River) went to jail and died over a right to fish. Buddy LaMonte got a bullet in his head over the Oglala people's right to determine their destiny.

How do the actions of today's alleged leaders and *ogitchidaag* warriors stack up against tradition, against our values? Not well.

Let us change the tide. The Northern Cheyenne reservation enacted a very strong tribal code on child abuse—let's follow in our communities with a code to protect and nourish our future generations and ensure their father's support. Let tribal governments or First Nations secure child support for our own tribal members. Let us also secure labor laws so that tribal workers may be free from recrimination. That's sovereignty.

The traditional Seminole Nation of Florida continues to speak its language, practice ceremonies and shun America, while they struggle for a land base. As a matter of fact, they refuse Federal recognition and won't enroll their tribal members, even if they are full bloods, saying that is their business, not America's. They have no casino, no programs; but they certainly practice their sovereignty and have their dignity.

Some Anishinaabeg from Red Cliff and elsewhere in northern Wisconsin are looking at a Seventh Generation amendment to the U.S. Constitution. The amendment to any tribal constitution or traditional law would say that "all decisions now must be considered in light of the impact on the Seventh Generation from now." That would rule out nuclear waste, toxic waste and clearcutting. That, it seems to me, is an honest practice of sovereignty.

I'll challenge the White Earth Tribal Council and all who oppose it to act and live by a standard that denotes sovereignty, not cheapens it. Let's be people our grandchildren can be proud of— good minds, good hearts, good actions.

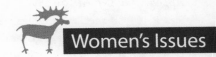

Women's Issues

Ingrid: Ogitchidaakwe Mikwendaagozid
A Warrior Woman Remembered

Appeared in INDIGENOUS WOMAN, *Volume III, Number I, 1999;
a special tribute issue honoring the memory of Ingrid
Washinawatok-El Issa, co-chair of the Indigenous Women's
Network, who was killed in Colombia on March 4, 1999.*

It is always hard to express in words decades of a relationship—
hopes, dreams, laughter, and tears—all the quilt pieces of memories that remind me of my friend Ingrid. She was, and remains,
beloved. While some strive to develop a place, a presence, a balance in the world of chaos, Ingrid possessed it all. Her heart, her
laughter, her voice beckoned you closer, and called to you across
the room, in a shriek, in a voice, which announced . . . always, I
am here, I am alive, I am full of joy. It is that memory that reso-
nates with me to this day, which I remember in my head, in my
heart. It is the memory of those decades—admiring her stamina,
her ability to move between diverse circles of people without
batting an eye, her ability to make us all feel like we were her
best friend—that I remember. Yet, amidst the most nurturing of
personalities was the sharpest of analysis, a perception of political direction that could find a path, no matter how small, through
the smallest of openings in the forest. Or the one who would
make the path. It was the wellspring of her heart and personality
which opened the doors, and it was that same charisma which
would give others the comfort to follow her through them. She
was a true leader, an *Ogimaakwe*, and an *Ogitchidaakwe*, one who
defends the people. Those many gifts she brought lovingly to all

her work, but since its inception, she brought them to the Indigenous Women's Network.

When we were young, there was a group of young women who were of similar ages: Lakota Harden, Sherry Means, Marcie Gilbert, Aggie Williams, Bena and the other McCloud girls, Ingrid, Lisa Bellanger, myself and others who were to come of age in the movement that was in the late 1970s and early 1980s. It was a time of great change in the Native movement, from the resistance marked by watershed occupations like Alcatraz, the Abbey at Menominee, and Wounded Knee, the BIA Takeover, the political repression illustrated by the ongoing trials, the Peltier, Butler and other trials, convictions, etc. Our movement was forced to move into political arenas with which we were all unfamiliar— national policy and international arenas. This growth in the demands of political work and skills would continue to resonate with broader political organizing strategies like the Longest Walk, which took the occupations and political resistance to the American public forum, and the alliance-building strategies of the Black Hills Alliance and the two gatherings in South Dakota. All of these events nourished our spirits, provided us with the teachings that can only come by experience, and set the stage and tone for much of the work we were to do in the early internationalizing years that followed. In these years, Ingrid and I, and some of these other young women, would be called to action; called to work for our people in ways that we could not have imagined as children.

I always remember looking across the room at Ingrid, admiring her height, her presence, and her easy laugh. After our early years working in the movement, the sophistication of our work seemed to grow, as did what we had to do. As I moved to the east coast for college, and began my initial work with the International Indian Treaty Council, I recall the political transformation required of all of us. At the UN NGO Conference on Discrimination Against Indigenous Peoples of the Western Hemisphere, our community had one of the first opportunities to speak in large numbers to the UN forum and begin to break the isolation of the oppression, of the dialogue on colonialism. As we as young women and young men looked to those who had struggled through hardship to bring us out of the silence—Phillip Deere, Bill Wapepah, Oren Lyons, Thomas Banyaca, Nilo Cayuqueo, Jimmie Durham, Janet McCloud, Mathew King, Audrey Shenandoah, and so many others—we felt an immense responsibility to sharpen our skills and our vision to serve a community better. We looked to those with big hearts and keen memories who had undergone so much hardship, yet could still always give a smile to us young people, and were immensely thankful for their guidance and cognizant of our responsibility to do what we could to take those words forward.

We slept on the floors of the generous and eccentric in New York, borrowed cars and subway money to get to work, and somehow worked diligently to provide the administrative support, the writing, the information sharing, the fundraising, to make the international movement move forward. We ate tortillas and beans, fry bread and mac soup, and were always hopeful that someone could take us to lunch. We worked odd jobs—Ingrid was a coat checker, I was a waitress and a librarian; all of it was how we supported our early political work.

My friend Ingrid was saintly in her work, laughing at our circumstances, our pitiful practices, and our tiredness. My friend Ingrid was the most patient. While some of us couldn't stick with New York City, Ingrid could—a big city girl off and on during her childhood, she could muster the city; in fact, she would thrive. Margo Thunderbird was her savior, showing her the City and introducing her to the ever-growing Indian community of the Big Apple. In a way, while all of us would be forced to develop skills, strategies and ways of working that would respond to the conditions in which we found ourselves, some would excel and shine in their new places: Ingrid was one of them. With her studies in Cuba, she gained immense international knowledge, and that invaluable skill of the Spanish language. With it all, she found her life companion, Ali El Issa. When she would come back from her big travels, from her visits to Lebanon, she would share with us stories about the people, their hearts, and their conditions, and we would sit and listen; wide eyed and mesmerized by the adventure of it all, by her courage and bravery, which humbled us in its immensity. In New York, and in international work, she found a place for her big laugh, her full-hearted hugs, and her joy for life, which surpassed all of our potential.

As we did work to bring the issues of Indigenous peoples to the international forum, we craved a way to strengthen the work and the thoughts of women. We remembered and were instructed of the traditional women's societies in many of our communities, and welcomed a process of restoring them. At the same time, there was growing, by necessity, a "pan Indian" movement, which would break the isolation of certain communities and provide a way for us all to become aware, politicized, and recognize the commonness of our struggles. As we looked across the continents, we saw similar circumstances; the African peoples struggled against these same oppressions of colonialism, and we saw that the women of these movements also had organizations. In 1979, WARN, Women of All Red Nations, was formed as a way to meet the needs of some of these women—to insure that we would be able to increase our dialogue as women, hone our political skills, our voices, and in the international arena, meet with our peers, the women's organizations which were a part of: SWAPO (Southwest African Peoples Organization), the ANC (African National Congress), the Palestinian Liberation Organization, the POLISERIO (representing the nomadic peoples of the Saharan desert), and so many other movements of indigenous peoples, who demanded, like us, the right to self-determination.

As we walked down this path, looked out there and saw relatives across the water, across the continents, our needs grew. We held three gatherings to bring together the Indigenous Women's Network, founded on the premise that we would be guided in our work by the "visions of our elders." We knew that our work would be diverse, but that it was ultimately about recovering those traditional relationships, the respect, the responsibilities and the rebuilding of our nations, as the partners, mothers, sisters and daughters of our peoples. At our San Francisco planning meeting in 1985, facilitated by Aggie Williams, (who worked, at that time, for the International Indian Treaty Council's Information Office) Ingrid came, her belly full with Maehki, her son. We worked hard and laughed harder, strolling through San Francisco's Castro Street on Halloween night—all of us enjoyed the celebration. All of these experiences brought us to our founding conference, at Janet McCloud's community in Yelm, Washington, where hundreds of Native women came to share, to tell stories, to learn from each others' experiences, and to grow: not only for ourselves, but for our communities, for our children—like Maehki—who were coming along.

Ingrid's role since the founding of the Indigenous Women's Network was to bring all of that experience and knowledge, to grow a way to encourage women, to build our capacity, our skills, and increase the volume of our voices, our presence in all arenas that impact our lives. Her work in the international arena flourished; she was a constant participant in the Working Group on the Rights of Indigenous Peoples, intervenor at the Commission on Human Rights, and maintained a growing presence in New York, where she, Ali, and Maehki would live. Her international experience, and compassion for people far from her Menominee homeland, was renowned and exemplary.

You build and restore community where you are, whether it is in the rural and reservation communities or in the urban areas, where many of our people have come to live. Ingrid, with her good friends Margo Thunderbird, Rosemary Richmond, Rudy, and others, nurtured a cohesiveness in the urban Indian community, which is challenging, because of the very diversity of those communities. Ingrid's ultimate presence, nurturing abilities, and love would bridge gaps between the most ancient of arch rivals, and provide the security for those who still would come out of their shells of isolation. The grace she carried with her, some would strive for their entire lives—she would possess it innately.

As we walked down this road together at the Indigenous Women's Network, Ingrid was always the strategic and patient voice. Rising above my impatience and directness was her voice of care, always referring to what the "guys are doing," the "ladies need," or the "folks are asking for." She drew from her international experience, her constant ministrations to the immense, intricate and oft convoluted processes of the international arena, to move carefully the work of the Network forward—always her feet on the ground, her eyes watching the horizon in Guatemala City, in Beirut, in Havana, or at Menominee. We raised our children together, as all the Aunties do, small bands of children marauding through the woods at the conferences, laughing, listening intently, and playing hard until they all dropped, exhausted under tables where their mothers still sat, talking late into the night. We could not bear to part with our children, so we brought them, almost always, and Ingrid's maternal love was so readily apparent—Maehki's special pancake breakfasts, her cuddling of him that flowed with such ease. She was the example of love, in all ways.

Often the struggle for dignity, for self-determination, will exhaust us. Although the wars may seem different than those of a century ago, they are also exacting. Ingrid, like Lisa Bellanger, Lori Pourier, myself and others from the Network, found our solace in dancing, in ceremonies, and in the Elders' conferences. Ingrid's new traditional outfit shimmered in my line of sight at the Blackfeet National Powwow, and later at Schimitzen, where her eyes gleamed with the pleasure of dancing and the honor of the celebration of life. It was the same need—to nourish the spirit, the soul—which brought her to the Big Drum Societies, the Midewiwin Lodge, where she would find the instruction and comfort for her lifeway, a pledge she made in June of 1998.

It was her big heart that drew her to the U'wa people in the end, her breadth of international travel that made a treacherous trip seem possible to her, and her courage that allowed her to go into someone else's war. In her work with the U'wa people, and the tragedy of her death, she brought them and the immensity of their struggle into our line of sight—something which Ingrid always did, and with an ability unsurpassed.

Ingrid walked into the war, in a country with the highest kidnapping rate in the world, where between 1988 and 1995, there were a total of 67,378 people who died as a result of the violence, or an average of 701.9 per month, 23 a day. She walked into a country where the military, the paramilitary, and ultimately, it seems, the FARC—the Revolutionary Armed Forces of Colombia—are all so beset with violence that there is no voice of reason in either the political or the military arena.

The U'wa people of northeastern Colombia number around 5,000, of which some 4,000 threatened to commit mass suicide if oil development would precede in their land. The proposed oil development (Occidental) at this point is slated to continue, and with it the Embera-Katio Hydroelectric dam, initiated in 1993. Some 3% of the population controls some 70% of the land in that country, and U.S. military and political interests continue to increase: The U.S. is interested in a U.S. model of stabilization in Colombia, based in part on an interest in oil and natural resources, in part on an interest in securing an alternative to the Panama Canal, should the U.S. lose control over that strategic shipping route.

It is in the tyrrany of the violence, of the drug lords, the oil lords, the "revolutionaries," and the struggle of simple people for dignity that Ingrid found herself once again fulfilling a part of her journey on this earth. It was from here that the FARC took her—just another faceless, nameless victim of the endless violence—silencing her physical voice, but leaving us with the immense legacy of her presence and her teachings, and a knowledge of people far away who need our continued support in their struggle for dignity, for self-determination.

At her March funeral at Menominee, I was grateful for the dignity of the Big Drum ceremony, the Menominee Warrior's Society recognition of their sister, and the men who danced in her honor for four days. I was also immensely grateful to the women who cared for our sister in a ceremonial way, before they returned her to the ground. Those bravehearted women took care of our fallen *Ogitchidaakwe*, fulfilling that traditional role of our women in being the hands that touch you at your birth and at your death.

I remembered a poster from the Guatemalan Civil War that hung for years on the wall of Ingrid and my friend Faye's house. The poster depicted a Mayan woman walking past tanks and bullet-ridden walls. Altogether we have more death than they, but altogether we have more life than they. As Lisa, Dorene, Sharon, Orlan and I danced one last dance for Ingrid in her beloved Three Fires Lodge this summer, we honored her life, her love, her commitment, and feasted for her in the next world. That place is without violence, without pain, and without sorrow.

A young woman named Kim told me a dream Ingrid left her in her death. As she and Ingrid walked in the forest, some huge trees had been torn from the ground, and tipped over by a big storm. Kim asked Ingrid what happened, and she responded, "a big storm came and blew us over." That is what happened: a storm of hate, of military, of violence, blew them over—all of them. But, there in the roots of the toppled tree were flowers, lovely purple flowers growing everywhere. Ingrid was the tree, and Ingrid was the flowers.

It is this legacy that we remember in the Indigenous Women's Network, in all of our memories. The laughter, the joy, the zest for life, and the prevalence and continuity. In her death, we pledge to honor her and continue her work against the violence and for justice and life. We pledge to do so with bigger hearts, with more patience, with stronger will, more courage, and always laughter.

I Fight Like a Woman:
The UN Conference on Women in China

Appeared in INDIGENOUS WOMAN, *Volume II, Number III, 1995.*

They came from far away. Reservations, small villages, big cities, and small islands in the Pacific. All colors, sizes, religions, cultural beliefs, and income brackets. From the super rich like Jane Fonda, to the women of Rwanda, victims of war, genocide, and international policies. The UN Fourth World Conference on Women in Beijing, China brought together more than 30,000 women and 3,000 organizations in the largest UN conference ever. This conference was an attempt to find common ground for women and to advocate for and protect the fundamental human rights of women. Far from the sparse and often trivialized coverage in mainstream American media—one magazine had a one-page layout on the conference and a three-page layout featuring the Miss America Pageant—Native women found the conference eye opening and empowering.

"For me it was really personally empowering," says Lori Pourier, an Oglala Lakota who attended as a part of the Indigenous Women's Network delegation. "It also really opened my eyes as an Indian woman living in the U.S. as to the human rights abuses against Indigenous peoples in so many countries like Tibet, and all of Central America."

The stories told, strategies shared, and tears cried resonated with the Indigenous women. Around forty Native women came from North America and one hundred fifty or so from around the world. As one woman, Corrine Kumar from the Asian Women's Human Rights Association explained simply, "From the periphery of power, human rights look different."

"It was the 1982 massacre in Lebanon, September 17. I was seventeen, my brother was twelve. We were on our way to a shelter, we were hiding," a Palestinian woman explained in testimony. She stood with two canes, her head covered with a long scarf. "We saw bodies along the way with blood flooding everywhere. The soldiers were everywhere. I heard them screaming, 'You dogs, are you still alive? Aren't you dead yet?' I heard someone say, 'Only God can end our lives.' I asked the soldier how he could take more after they (the Israelis) took our land, our most precious thing, our land. The soldier hit me, I hit him back. They started shooting. My sisters and brothers, eight, seven, three, one-and-a-half years, were all killed. The twelve-and-nine-year-olds were safe. I was wounded, paralyzed. The soldier thought I was dead, so he left me. Then he came back, three of them, raped me in front of my father. Then he shot me in the head and my father passed away as he watched. Before he died, he said, 'God be with you.' Then they shot me in the head twice." She cries now from the podium, she is full of rage and tears. "I laid there til the 19th of September, I pretended to be dead. Finally a soldier came, covered me with his coat and took me to the hospital. They wouldn't admit me, because I was Palestinian." She goes on with her story, explains how for almost a year, she lost the ability to speak, and now speaks out.

Her story melts into others—Rwandan women, Bosnian women, victims of war, victims of policies. "They are living the life of the decisions that other people made. Decisions they had no control over," Lori Pourier tells me. Somehow in the sound of these women's voices, and their faces, tears and rage, all that is American seems to become so trivial.

In the face of 7,000 delegates from the U.S., and a vast disparity between levels of income in U.S. delegations and most other delegations, I wondered at the process that brought women to this conference.

I asked myself, "How do these women do it?" How do these women from small islands in the Pacific or poor villages in India and Lebanon get to the United Nations? What are their hopes and dreams?

"Nineteen of my cousins died because they refused to be French." Susanna Ouneai is a Kanaki from New Caledonia, one of the many islands in the Pacific that France claims as its "domain." "We have stopped to be ashamed. That's what we have done, stop to be ashamed." She is defiant. Susanna is a black-skinned Melanesian woman, whose culture remains after a hundred years of French colonialism. "It started in 1853," she explains. "The French thought they discovered savages, the lost race of Melanesia. They find our beautiful land, our islands, and see nickel, gold, copper, and magnesium. And they kill our people, over 200,000 of them, for our land."

For the past decade the Kanakis have been in an armed struggle against the French, each year taking lives. The French in the meantime represent that they have diplomatic solutions, a referendum is scheduled at the end of the century. What the French neglect to tell outsiders, however, is that the French are transplanting French citizens to New Caledonia in an attempt to shift the demographics favorably towards the French. "A few years back there were 72,000 Kanakis," Susanna explains, "and 55,000 French. Now we're 43% of the population."

The Kanaki situation is that of much of the Pacific, "give us back our dignity, values, and land, that is what we want." She tells me, "Today we claim back all of what they have done to us, to our parents." And they plan on continuing their struggle. "Denuclearization is the same as decolonization," Susanna explains as she, with the other 30,000 women at the conference watched in horror as the French detonated an atomic bomb on September 4 near French Melanesia in the Pacific. "If they are so rich to make nuclear bombs in French Melanesia, it is because they got it from us—New Caledonia." To Susanna the issues are related—denuclearization and decolonization. "Since Algeria's independence, France can't test in the Sahara Desert so they want to keep French Polynesia and Melanesia. That is the only way, by uniting with people of the Pacific to decolonize."

What about the roles of women in the struggle for liberation? "We will not fight the violence of the colonizer and endure it at home. Kanaki women and men are a part of the same struggle, working side by side, going to prison, getting killed. I am often given the compliment by my male counterparts in the movement that I fight like a man. I don't, I fight like a woman! Together we have paid and are paying an important price. We did not fight and die in the struggle for nothing. There is no point in achieving liberation if we are going to turn around and colonialize our own women."

Susanna's determination springs from her history. "As a Kanaki woman, I know the specific struggles of women against colonialism, rape, violence of all kinds, sickness in watching our children butchered by guns and drugs. A few puppets of the colonizers get rich, while our people continue to live in slum housing." She believes in the future. "They give me back my house and land then we will bring back peace."

Vicki Corpuz is an Igarok woman from the Philippines, head of the Cordillera Women's Association. This tiny woman is dressed in what she calls her "battle gear." A traditional Igarok skirt and sensible, yet stylish walking shoes. Since I met Vicki almost five years ago, she has always been a great inspiration. We sit talking in the Indigenous Woman's Tent #49 at the conference.

"I became an activist in the late '60s in Manila. I received a scholarship from our village to the University and it was right at the height of the student movement in the Philippines. I was really thinking about how our people are going to be extinct. I kept seeing all the educated people go off and never come back. I asked, what is going to happen if all the intellectuals never come back? That made me question the world. Then we organized. We kept on working to throw out the Marcos regime." She laughs, "Well, after you have done the organizing to fight a dictatorship what can you do?"

I watch this tiny woman as we sit and visit. Gracious, that is what I would call her, gracious. Two or three people came over while we are talking; she organizes a later meeting, reimburses for some copies and turns back to me. She laughs, "I went home and got married. I am a nurse, so I decided to set up a community based health program. At that time martial law was declared, so the only way you could organize was with very innocent activities. We had three children, including a new baby, when our house got raided by the military. My husband was working with the mine workers, as an engineer and labor organizer."

Vicki is from a small village in the Philippines—central to a region that is faced with huge mining projects and has successfully fended off a huge World Bank dam project, the Chico Dam, in the late 1980s.

I asked her how and why she does international work. "I got involved in the women's groups in the early 1980s and went to an international women's conference in Australia in 1988. I did not want to do international work," she says, and giggles. "But I had no choice."

"We found that a lot of our problems were related to transnational corporations and institutions. And we thought it was time to get more accountability from them. We can do basic empowerment work here but all the decisions are actually made elsewhere. They should have to look at us in the face when they make those decisions."

And so, Vicki Corpuz and a group of women from the remote areas of the Philippines scrape together enough money to attend international meetings and look face to face at people. Vicki's primary focus now is the World Bank and so-called "structural adjustment," wherein small countries often find their entire economies re-ordered to meet debts to the World Bank. This problem is disproportionately born by women and children, frequently from Indigenous communities. Yet, as Vicki points out, "Even if we have acknowledged men are spokespeople, women should be equal participants from the beginning."

It was several years ago, Mililani Trask, Kia'aina (Head of State) of the Native Hawaiian Nation changed her mind about international work. "The real reason why all Indigenous people have to be apprised of, or involved in the international arena is because their individual land based struggles will be impacted by these nation states and international interests." We are flying through the bicycle-filled roads of Beijing in a taxi, one of the many rides we take together back and forth to the UN forums. My pen scribbles furiously on pages as she gestures and cajoles me. "I changed my mind you know," she tells me. "I used to say, let's stay home here and do our work, but how can we live. The world has become such a small place."

She tells the story of migratory birds from Hawaii, the state in the U.S. with the most endangered and threatened species. "Twenty-seven species of our endangered birds nest in the Arctic Refuge and whales spawn in Hawaii. We cannot protect our endangered species if we cannot preserve the Arctic National Wildlife Refuge from oil companies." It is all the same, and from her vantage point it is necessary.

Do things change? An Indigenous woman, Rigoberta Menchu, won the Nobel Peace Prize, and we have a Decade of Indigenous Peoples. Yet, decades after UN work started aggressively by Indigenous "peoples" (the Iroquois were at the UN when it opened), a U.S. State Department representative announced that the U.S. supports adding the "s" to Indigenous "peoples" and then retracts it.

A common thread is in all the voices. Palestinian, Kanaki, Igarok and Hawaiian. The needs of their land, their people and their children are great enough to demand extreme measures and commitments. They are women who came to Beijing to tell their stories, to look in the face of those from far away lands. They speak directly to those who make decisions effecting their villages and they are women who go home to continue their fight, empowered by the courage of others. They are women that will tell you that Indigenous people are nations and deserve that same right to self-determination accorded other nations and that neither the rights of Indigenous people nor women are the exclusive jurisdiction of states.

These women will keep telling their stories and working. And maybe someone will see or hear them. As a parting shot, Lori Pourier tells of an older Chinese woman, curiously walking by the conference site. "She walks towards the gate. Just that quick there were three or four security guards, they walked and carefully pushed her across the street away from the conference site. I was watching her, and all that time, her neck was craning. I saw her looking over her shoulder just curious about all these women."

These are stories we all should be curious about, and yearn to hear. These are women who can teach us all.

Mothers of Our Nations: Indigenous Women Address the World

Delivered at the NON-GOVERNMENTAL ORGANIZATION (NGO) FORUM, *Huairou, China, September 1995.*

It is a great honor as a young mother of two to be invited to speak to you sisters today, women who have great courage and commitment, women who are peers and leaders, and whom like myself are the Mothers of Our Nations.

The Earth is our Mother. From her we get our life, and our ability to live. It is our responsibility to care for our Mother, and in caring for our Mother, we care for ourselves. Women, all females, are the manifestation of Mother Earth in human form. We are her daughters, and in my cultural instructions we are to care for her. I am taught to live in respect for Mother Earth. In indigenous societies, we are told that natural law is the highest law, higher than the laws made by nations, states, municipalities and the World Bank; that one would do well to live in accordance with natural law, with those of our Mother, and in respect for all our relations.

One hundred years ago, one of our great leaders, Chief Seattle, stated, "What befalls the Earth, befalls the people of the Earth." And that is the reality today, and the situation of the status of women, and the status of indigenous women and indigenous peoples.

While I am from one nation of indigenous peoples, there are an estimated 500 million indigenous peoples or some 5,000 nations of indigenous peoples worldwide. We are in the Cordilleras, East Timor, New Zealand, Australia, Tibet, New Caledonia, Hawaii, North America, South America, and beyond. We are not populations nor minority groups. We are peoples and nations of peoples. Under international law we meet the criteria of nation states with each having a common economic system, language, territory, history, culture, and governing institution—conditions under which indicate nations of peoples. Despite this fact, indigenous nations are not allowed to participate in the United Nations.

Nations of indigenous peoples are not represented at the United Nations. Most decisions today are made by the 180 or so member states. Those states, by and large, have been in existence for only 200 years or less, while most indigenous nations, with few exceptions, have been in existence for thousands of years. Ironically, there would likely be little argument in this room, that most decisions made in the world today are actually made by some of the 47 transnational corporations and their international financiers whose annual income is larger than the gross national product for many countries of the world.

This is the centerpiece of the problem. Decision making is not made by those who are affected—people who live on the land—but the corporations with interests entirely different from that of the land and the people or the women of the land. This brings forth a fundamental question: What gives corporations like Conoco, Shell, Exxon, Daishowa, ITT, Rio Tinto Zinc, and the World Bank the right which supersedes or is superior to my human right to live on my land, or that of my family, my community, my nation, our nations, and to us as women? What law gives that right to them? Not any law of the Creator or of Mother Earth. Is that right contained within their wealth? Is that right contained within their wealth, which was historically acquired immorally, unethically through colonialism and imperialism and paid for with the lives of millions of people, species of plants, and entire ecosystems? They should have no such right. And we clearly, as women and as indigenous peoples, demand and will recover that right—the right of self-determination, to determine our own destiny and that of our future generations.

The origins of this problem lie with the predator/prey relationship that industrial society has developed with the Earth and, subsequently, the people of the Earth. This same relationship exists vis-à-vis women. We collectively find that we are often in the role of the prey to a predator society whether through sexual discrimination, exploitation, sterilization, absence of control over our bodies, or being the subjects of repressive laws and legislation in which we have no voice. This occurs on an individual level, but equally and more significantly on a societal level. It is also critical to point out at this time most matrilineal societies, societies in which governance and decision making are largely controlled by women, have been obliterated from the face of the Earth by colonialism and industrialism. The only matrilineal societies that still exist in the world today are those of indigenous nations. Yet we also face obliteration.

On a worldwide scale and in North America, indigenous societies remain in a predator/prey relationship with industrial society. We are the peoples with the land—land and natural resources required for someone else's development program and amassing of wealth. The wealth of the United States, the nation that today determines much of world policy, was illegally expropriated from our lands. Similarly the wealth of indigenous peoples of South Africa, Central and South American countries, and Asia was taken for the industrial development of Europe and later for settler states which came to occupy those lands. The relationship between development and underdevelopment adversely affected the status of our indigenous societies and the status of indigenous women.

Eduardo Galeono, the Latin American writer and scholar, writes: "In the colonial to neocolonial alchemy, gold changes to scrap metal and food to poison. We have become painfully aware of the mortality of wealth which nature bestows and imperialism appropriates."

Today, on a worldwide scale, we remain in the same situation as one hundred years ago, only with less land and fewer people. Fifty million indigenous peoples live in the world's rainforests. In the next decade, one million indigenous peoples are slated to be relocated because of dam projects (thanks to the Narmada Project in India, the Three Gorges Dam Project in China, and the James Bay Hydroelectric Project in northern Canada). Almost all atomic weapons which have been detonated in the world have been on lands or waters of indigenous peoples, most clearly evidenced here in China and in the Pacific with France's obscene proposal to detonate atomic weapons this upcoming month. This situation is mirrored in North America. Today, over 50 percent of our remaining lands are forested. Both Canada and the United States continue aggressive clear-cutting policies on our land. Over two thirds of the uranium resources and one third of all low-sulfur coal resources in the United States are on indigenous lands. We have huge oil reserves on our reservations. Over 650 atomic weapons have been detonated on the Western Shoshone Nation. We have two separate accelerated proposals to dump nuclear waste in our reservation lands, and similarly over 100 separate proposals for toxic waste dumps on our lands. We understand clearly the relationship between development for someone else and our own underdevelopment. We also understand clearly the relationship between the environmental impacts of types of development on our lands, and the environmental and subsequent health impacts on our bodies as women.

We also understand clearly that the analysis of North versus South is an erroneous analysis. There is, from our perspective, not a problem of the North dictating the economic policies of the South, and subsequently consuming the South. Instead, there is a problem of the Middle consuming both the North and the South. That is our situation. Let me explain.

The rate of deforestation in the Brazilian Amazon is one acre every nine seconds. Incidentally, the rate of extinction of indigenous peoples in the Amazon is one nation of indigenous peoples per year. The rate of deforestation of the boreal forest of Canada is one acre every twelve seconds. Siberia, thanks to American corporations like Weyerhauser, is not far behind. In all cases, indigenous peoples are endangered. And there is, frankly, no difference between the impact in the North and the South.

Uranium mining in northern Canada has left over 120 million tons of radioactive waste. Since 1975, hospitalizations for cancer, birth defects, and circulatory illnesses in that area have increased dramatically—between 123 percent and 600 percent. In other areas impacted by uranium mining, cancer and birth defects have in some cases increased to 8 times the national average. There is no distinction in this problem caused by radiation whether it is in the Dene of northern Canada, the Laguna Pueblo of New Mexico, or the people of Namibia.

The rapid increase in dioxins, organochlorides, and PCBs (polychlorinated biphenyls) in the world as a result of industrialization also has a devastating impact on indigenous peoples, indigenous women, and other women. Each year, according to Environmental Protection Agency statistics, the world's paper industry discharges from 600 to 3,200 grams of dioxin equivalents in water, sludge, and paper products. This quantity is equal to the amount that would cause 58,000 to 292,000 cases of cancer every year. According to a number of recent studies, this has significantly increased the risk of breast cancer in women. Similarly, heavy metals and PCB contamination of Inuit women of the Hudson Bay region of the Arctic indicates that they have the highest levels of breast milk contamination in the world—28 times higher than the average woman in Quebec and 10 times higher than that considered "safe" by the government. Consequently, it is clear to us that problems are also found in the South due to the export of chemicals and bio-accumulation of toxins. These are problems that emanate from industrial society's mistreatment and disrespect for our Mother Earth, and are reflected in the devastation of the collective health and well-being of women.

In summary, I have presented these arguments to illustrate that these are very common issues for women, not only for indigenous women, but for all women. What befalls our Mother Earth, befalls her daughters—the women who are the mothers of our nations. Simply stated, if we can no longer nurse our children, if we can no longer bear children, and if our bodies are wracked with poisons, we will have accomplished little in the way of determining our destiny or improving our conditions. These problems, reflected in our health and well-being, are the result of historical processes and are inherently resulting in a decline of the status of women. We need to challenge these processes if we want to be ultimately in charge of our own destinies, our own self-determination, and the future of our Earth, our Mother.

I call on you to support the struggle of indigenous peoples of the world for recognition as peoples who have self-determination. I ask you to look into the Charter of the United Nations, which states that "all peoples have the right to self-determination. By virtue of that right, they may freely determine their political status and freely pursue their economic, social and political development." "All peoples" should be construed to mean that indigenous peoples have that right, too. Accord us the same rights as all other nations of peoples, and through that process, allow us to protect our ecosystems, their inherent biodiversity, human cultural diversity, and the last remaining matriarchal governments in the world.

Finally, while we are here in the commonness of this forum, speak of the common rights of all women and the fundamental human rights to self-determination. So long as the predator continues, so long as the Middle countries of the world continue to drive an increasing level of consumption, there will be no safety for the human rights of women, of indigenous peoples, and the basic protection of the Earth from which we get our life. Consumption causes the commodification of the sacred, the natural world, cultures, children, and women. And unless we speak and take meaningful action to address the high levels of consumption, we will never have any security for our individual human rights as women.

This is not a struggle for women of the dominant society in so-called "first world" countries to have equal pay and equal status if that pay and status continues to be based on a consumption model that is unsustainable. It is a struggle to recover our status as Daughters of the Earth. In that is our strength and security, not in the predator, but in the security of our Mother, for our future generations. In that, we can insure our security as the Mothers of Our Nations.

Debbie Tewa: Building a Future
with Her Community

Appeared in INDIAN COUNTRY TODAY, *August 1, 1994.*

It's a sun-baked mesa in northwestern Arizona. Debbie Tewa straps on her toolbelt and hardhat. She clambers up a ladder onto the flat roof of a two-hundred-year-old stone house. She looks out over a hundred miles of desert, and takes a deep breath. She glances across the village, sees the sun glinting off of roof-based panels, and smiles. She is the Hopi Foundation's solar electrician, and she is home.

In the past three years, this community-based Native foundation, "Lomasumi-nangwtukwsiwmani," in their language, has placed photovoltaic solar panels atop fifty houses on the reservation. All of them were installed by this woman—a thirty-two year old Coyote Clan resident of Hotevilla. This project, like others of the Hopi Foundation, is embracing both the past and the future.

It makes sense. One third of Hopi villages have refused to accept electrical power lines into their village areas. The Hopi object to the electricity on several grounds. Village leaders are concerned about preserving their sovereignty as village entities. They see their people becoming "hooked" on public utility power, only to be compromised when the people are unable to afford the ever-increasing monthly payments. "They don't allow powerlines into the villages, because the utilities will also have the right of way," Debbie explains. Village leaders "think that if we don't pay up the bills, they'll take even more land. So when you get your own system, it's yours, there's no powerline, no right of way into the villages, so we have our own land."

Other arguments against the power are spiritual and cultural. Staff at the Hopi Foundation explain that "the force field of electricity emanating from the powerlines is considered to be disruptive to the atmosphere, ambiance, and balance of the plaza and ceremonial areas, at the same time blocking the aesthetics of the sky and the panoramic vistas of the mesas."

THE LONG ROAD

And so, each day before climbing onto the rooftops, Debbie begins with a cup of coffee at the office, lining up her schedule, and her equipment. Debbie came into this job down a long road.

Raised by her grandmother on the Hotevilla plaza, Debbie moved later to nearby Tuba City with her mother until the eighth grade. She graduated valedictorian from the BIA boarding school (Sherman Indian High School) in Riverside, California, and returned to Arizona to go to school at Northern Arizona University, in Flagstaff. "I wasn't doing too well in school so I quit," she laughs. "Then I went selling Avon for awhile, til I got this job, as the coordinator for the summer youth at Hopi (Moencopi) in 1983."

Debbie started thinking about trade schools when a recruiter for the Hopi Tribe began interviewing her summer youth students. "I asked her if girls could apply, and she said yes, so in 1983, I got accepted to go to a trade school," where she ended up in electricity. "I went to school for a nine-month course, and then I got a job with the Gila River Housing Authority, changing devices in the HUD homes."

So began a string of jobs with various electrical companies in the Tempe area. She got contracts, showed some real talent, and then more and more jobs. "Eventually I ended up with this company called Delta Diversified (in Tempe), and I worked with them for about three years. I started out as an electrical helper, and then eventually was promoted to a foreman. I stayed there about a year, and then I quit, because they were building a PHS hospital at Gila River, and they paid more money. It was a federal job. So, I stayed there for a couple of months, and then eventually got laid off, and was more or less on my own for awhile and got odd jobs. I wired houses for people here and there, had a contract with the Home Improvement Program, and then the Hopi Foundation got ahold of me. That was in late 1989."

Debbie ended up in a solar energy training program in Carbondale, Colorado. When she returned, the Hopi Foundation had started their program, part-time in 1989, and then slowly speeding up. In 1991, she began full-time work at the foundation, which now employs three people: a manager, a secretary, and an electrician—Debbie.

The Hopi Foundation, at its core, represents a way of dealing with the physical, social, economic and spiritual consequences of change in communities. The Hopi believe that there is a strength in the preservation and revitalization of culture and self-determination. The Hopi Foundation recognizes that members of their community have increasingly demonstrated their desires for modern conveniences, which are powered by electricity—a reasonable expectation for those living in the twentieth century—but the foundation believes there are ways to do that without destroying a way of life, or an ecosystem. That solution, in Hopi land, is solar energy. But, that is energy, which is, frankly, put in with a conscience, not just with a powerline.

Debbie talks about the change in perspective brought around by solar energy. "We're so accustomed to the conveniences of having the electricity, having some guy come over and hook you up to have power. With this system, you purchase it, and it's yours. It teaches you to be conservative, because you're getting your power from the battery, you can't just leave your hallway light on for three or four hours. It teaches you to be independent."

Solar energy and the Hopi Foundation also changed Debbie's life. She gets to work in her own community. "I really enjoy working at home. Just the interaction with the customers, the people— I get to talk my language, that's nice. I get to learn a lot up here, especially with the older folks. When you're out in Phoenix and you talk to people, you get fired, or get these looks. Here you get to talk to people. I don't mind hauling water, or getting through the mud to get to work. Sure beats driving in the big city traffic to get to work. I don't miss that one bit. We don't just do photovoltaics—I do trouble shooting. I can add on, or if they're hooked up to the grid, I can help them with that."

RESTORING CEREMONIAL HOMES

The foundation is interested in addressing some deep needs in the community, not just in solar energy. The foundation has worked to rebuild some traditional clan (ceremonial) houses. The clan houses are the most ancient, continuously occupied structures in North America still used to this day, yet, like anything which is four hundred years old, face deterioration from the elements. The gradual deterioration of these centers of Hopi life and the continued incompleteness of these houses that need rebuilding are, in the foundation's words, "a constant source of sadness. They stand as visible reminders to all about the toll that change has brought to the Hopi community." So it was under the authority of a matriarch of their Snow Clan at Shungopavi village that restoration of the three-story Snow Clan ceremonial house began in 1990. The Hopi Foundation, in a careful relationship between Clan leadership, architects, donors, and young Hopis, restored the house this past year, and now plans on other careful work. It is this type of project that has implications long past a "grant year" for a foundation.

"Like any community, we want to be self-sufficient. We know the government is there to help us, but it usually doesn't work out that way. So that's why the foundation was formed—we're separate from the federal government and tribal government." Debbie reminds me, "This foundation and all of their work is about the future. They aren't getting a handout—it's your own power system when you pay it off, it's your free power. It's our community."

"We look up to the sun a lot, and that's how, in a way, in this century it's helping us—not just with our fields, it's helping us with our electricity, too. So, when you get your own system, it's yours. There's no powerline, no right of way into the villages, so we have our own land."

WOMEN'S WORK

Debbie's work influences high school students in the village. She said, "You could do whatever you want to do. Whatever job you want, go for it."

"I have some respect from the kids, too. They say hi to me, and ask me questions about being an electrician, and stuff."

She feels support from the community, for the most part. "I get a lot of encouragement, especially from the old people, and that's a really good boost. They say something like this in Hopi— 'You're taking care of yourself. It doesn't matter how you do it. It's your own thing. Nobody's giving you the money to do this and that.'"

There are some young women who may be following in her footsteps. "There was one girl who was thinking of going into carpentry, and there was another girl who wanted to get into the electrical field in Hotevilla. So that's a start."

To other Indian communities, Debbie offered these words. "A long time ago, the Native Americans were all ecologists, and, if you really think about it, solar energy conserves, and it fits into that environmental scheme. Because you don't use the electricity from generating plants, you aren't damaging the environment. I think it's something that each community should look at.

With solar hot water heating, you can heat up the water through the sun, with these panels on your roof. The water goes up to the roof and comes down hot."

Women, according to Debbie, also can have a big impact in this area. "Women usually take care of the household and they have a job," she said. "They can look into solar energy, and they can educate themselves about the environment. I educated myself about the environment and this can help a lot. The women in the house are paying the bills. They can invest in some of these products and that can save them a lot of money. That can improve the efficiency of their house. They could get into this field to help their community."

As for herself, Debbie lives in a one-room house with an outhouse. "My kitchen, bedroom, living room are one room, and they're hooked up solar." Last year, she invented a solar shower (since there's no plumbing in her house) and she's thinking about a composting toilet. She's definitely on the cutting edge of Hotevilla, but that edge is something that appears to be carefully crafted. We may all be able to learn something from her, and this community.

The Salmon People: Susanna Santos

Appeared in INDIGENOUS WOMAN, *Volume II, Number I, 1992.*

I have known her a good portion of my life. Now as I watch her, it is past midnight. She seems dark, tiny, and weary. Yes, weary. I never thought I would describe Susanna as such—she has always been taut as a big cat in between springs, and in possession of unending creativity. It is not the time of night at all. It is the time of the land and of her river, the Deschutes. She is wearied, it appears, from the seemingly infinite battles, yet somehow she smiles at me, laughs again and reassures me that she is alive, she is still resisting.

"The people are the salmon." It is that clear. Spanning the Pacific Ocean from Prince William Sound to the Klamath River, salmon and people are intertwined through centuries of ceremony, creation stories, sacred sites, sustenance, economics, and ecosystems. Nineteen ninety-three's Salmon Summit (Portland) of West Coast Indigenous peoples brought it home through words and strategies, and as I sit and watch her talk, pace, laugh and cry, I am reminded, over and over again . . . the people are the salmon. . . .

"Celilo or Tixni, means the Falls of Women's Hair," Susanna translates for me the heart of Salmon culture on the Columbia River, a location now spanned by the Dalles Dam complex. "That's why I came back to fish. I wanted to dance the salmon, know the salmon, and say goodbye to the salmon. I grew up on that river (the Deschutes) in a tent, so it's not like I went away very long. Now, I am looking at the completion of destruction. The destruction of salmon by all of them—Exxon Valdez, Trojan Nuclear Power Plant, Hanford, logging and those dams. Commodities, that's the future of Indian foods here. To me that's the future."

Susanna Santos, artist, historian and fisherwoman is from the Tygh band of the Lower Deschutes, a resident of the Warm Springs reservation in central Oregon. Her band today includes a scant thirty families, endangered peoples themselves struggling to continue their instructions and relationship to the salmon. This past year, some seventeen fish were caught off the scaffolds on the Deschutes. The stories of the people and the fish are not so different.

"We are on the brink, and we're looking down into the abyss," exclaims Geoff Pampush, director of Oregon Trout, a sportsman and environmental organization that has joined in concern over the salmon. One hundred and seven stocks of salmon have already become extinct in the Pacific region, and 89 others are "at high risk of extinction."

Indigenous peoples speak of salmon as plentiful for as long as people can remember. American scientists estimate that 100 million salmon a year once emerged from the rivers along the coasts of California, Oregon and Washington. Today, these fish are extinct in southern California, and the remainder of the region produces perhaps 15 million annually, most of them from hatcheries.

Stocks, or runs, of salmon are those of a single species that emerge from the same freshwater spawning grounds, travel to the ocean together and return to spawn again at the same time. That means there can be hundreds of separate stocks, which the government typically regards as genetically distinctive creatures under the Endangered Species Act (ESA), although there are only five actual species of salmon in the northeast—chinook, sockeye, coho, pink and chum. Closely related and also suffering in the region are the anadromous steelhead and the sea-run cutthroat trout. It is no coincidence that virtually every river has a people, each as distinct as the salmon species.

Traveling down the "Oregon" coast 150 years ago, starting from the Columbia, one would have found a distinct language at almost every river mouth on the way. Clatsop at the Columbia, then Tillamook and Siletz, Yaquina and Alsea, Sivslaw and

Ukmpqua, Hanis and Miluk, Coquille, Tututni, Shasta Costa and Chetco. In all there are six families of languages which belong to the land and peoples of Oregon, none intelligible to the others, and all now, not unlike the salmon, on the verge of extinction.

"At one time we had 1,400 people. Then relocation happened. The government tried to force us to move. Our people kept relocating back to Shugar's Bridge (named after a so-called "discoverer"). My grandmother and her brother hid out in the hills. At night they killed almost everyone. A couple dozen people were hiding out in the hills there at Sheers Falls. They killed a lot of women. . . ."

Today, it seems little has changed. Susanna is understandably angry. "There are only two families fishing here on the Deschutes, and they've closed us down. We are still fighting them." She pauses, then continues, "What they are trying to do is genocide. They don't want us to fish and we're a strong matriarchal family. To take away our fishing rights and customs is the process of genocide. Part of that is the self-hatred and racism. Since the destruction of Celilo Falls, men's humanity becomes predatory— every species grasping for the little food left."

The listing of the salmon as threatened and endangered finally forced Northwest residents to acknowledge the problem. Years of talk, and political and social struggle over forests and owls, has left this region keenly aware of what happens when the economic practices of manifest destiny come into conflict with biological sustainability and, more recently, laws like the Endangered Species Act.

In response to the congressionally mandated studies, a series of dams were proposed to be built along the Columbia River. The Bonneville Dam was the first dam to be built in accordance with the Corps of Engineers proposals. Construction of the Bonneville Dam inundated the river tribes' fishing grounds from the dam site to above The Dalles, Oregon. In 1939, a settlement agreement was reached between the tribes and the United States relative to the flooding. This agreement, approved by the Secretary of War in 1940, provided that the War Department would acquire approximately four hundred acres of lands along the Columbia River and install ancillary fishing facilities to be used by the treaty tribes. After 20 years, the Army Corps of Engineers had provided 40 acres of "in lieu" sites, not 400. One of those sites—Lyle Point—is now the subject of a major confrontation between developers and Indians.

UNKEPT PROMISES AND THE FUTURE

Environmentalists argue that more water needs to be released according to the schedule of the salmon, not according to the electricity demands of the aluminum companies. Some go further and insist that the only way to save the Columbia River salmon is to pull down some of the great dams.

In a late spring ruling by 9th Circuit Federal Court Judge Malcolm Marsh, the federal government will have to do more to care for the salmon of the Northwest. Ruling in favor of lawsuits brought by Idaho, Oregon, Indian tribes and environmentalists, declaring that the National Marine Fisheries service and the Bonneville Power Administration had violated the Endangered Species Act, March required the federal agencies to make some dramatic changes. Susanna waits to see, one eye on the river, and one on her canvas.

It is a macabre scene. Against the stark background of hills, power lines, and nuclear power plants, Yakama Indians are tending fish in cooling ponds at the Hanford Nuclear reservation in Washington State—a facility battled for years by Yakamas (on whose treaty land the facility is constructed) and environmentalists. Hanford is the single largest source of radioactive contamination of the region. More than a half-million chinook salmon smolts are being released into the river in this project—fish that have tested free of radionuclides.

Throughout the Northwest, many runs are now so depleted that some Washington treaty tribes are having to purchase "farm fish" for their annual First Salmon ceremonies, which are events

of central cultural importance to Salmon peoples. "These fish are
our hope," says Jerry Menick, Yakama Tribal Chair. "They (the
ones reared at Hanford) are our future. If the salmon survive and
return to spawning the Columbia, we may again someday have a
real harvest."

Works in Progress

It is a time of ultimate ironies. I wander through Susanna's house,
into her bedroom and studio. At my home, her paintings fill my
walls with their vibrant colors. Today I look at her newest works
in progress. All of them dark, filled with shadows, pain. There is
a painting of a white man caught in a fishing net; one of the
"impacts" of so-called "ecotourism."

Susanna's family was on their fishing scaffold when the white
man came down the river, "drinking and partying." She saw him
drown.

The man was in a party of river rafters who, like so many
others, whitewater down the river whenever they feel like it, Indians fishing in ceremony or not. "In the drowning he violated
us by rafting down the river in front of us. That's like a person
opening the doors of a longhouse. I might have pulled him up,
but it would have torn my arm off." She sighs, then gives a dis-
gusted look. "I pulled his shorts up in my net."

To the north of her on Lyle Point, a familiar battle between
Indians and affluent developers rages. Seventy miles east of Portland, fishing scaffolds at a so-called "in lieu" traditional fishing
village on the Columbia River have become inaccessible, as gates,
walls and utilities push through for a housing development. Some
33 half-a-million-dollar homes are planned at Lyle Point by developers from the Columbia Gorge investor Limited Partnership.

Columbia River fishing people call the area Nanaimi Waki
Uulktt and vow to resist the development and expansion of a
wind surfing area in their traditional territory—so-called "in lieu"
(the meager 40-acre) sites guaranteed after the big dams devastated the traditional sites. "I have fished here forever, through

my ancestors," says Margaret Palmer, a member of the Yakama Nation. She stands by an ancestral fishing scaffold, where she has staged an encampment to protect her fishing rights along the Columbia. Margaret and other tribal members find the 100-foot allotment provided by Lyle Point developers, as access of fishing sites, unacceptable. "This is where fish come to give up their spirits. It is a sacred place," she explains. "I will not come to fish for my family next to tennis courts and the swimming pool of a luxury home development."

I look at Susanna's artwork again. The dark shadows punch me in my gut. Susanna breaks into my thoughts. "I am just boiling inside. I want to explode. I have to tell these stories in my paintings. As an artist, I have to take responsibility to rid myself of this pain and the impact on the people that are seeing it. I don't always live in this world. I live in the other world.

"Nothing can prepare you for the death of the salmon," she says. "It couldn't. What are we going to do? The fish is the spiritual food, the brain food, and without that fish, that food, the elders are going to die. They are now. I feel like we are going to go through another cycle of genocide, suicide and all that. Now is the calm before the storm.

"That is why I paint. I am trying to document history. To document us. To document we are alive. We're going to protect sacred lands and other sacred places. I have to paint all that I am seeing. The things we are doing 50–100 years from now they are going to have an impact, long lasting effects. We are going to host an After the Salmon Summit, that's what we have to do.

"How you live and conduct your life is a part of the solution. Only when men start to respect women is it going to happen." She has an intergenerational hope, a hope for the time ahead, and a sense of sureness that she will see it. "I want to see a landbase back, a living band of people. I won't settle for anything else in my lifetime. You can't make compromises anymore. You can't settle for less."

Innu Women and NATO:
The Occupation of Nitassinan

Appeared in CULTURAL SURVIVAL QUARTERLY, *April 30, 1990.*

Militarism is a form of colonization that takes away from our lives. That future is without hope for us. But, we will fight for our rights. I believe in nonviolence and civil disobedience. I am ready to go to jail, to take blows or die for our cause, because I believe in the struggle for the freedom of my people. I don't want your sympathy, I want your support, your strong and collective support against the oppression of your government. What we need is your resistance." Penote Ben Michel made this plea at a 31 January 1987 conference in Montreal on militarism in Labrador/Nitassinan.

Northwest River, Labrador—a place called *Nitassinan*, or "our land," by the Innu people who have lived there for some 9,000 years, and a place known as Goose Bay to the Canadian Armed Forces and, more recently, NATO (North Atlantic Treaty Organization)—is the site of one of the most enduring and widely recognized struggles against militarism on the North American continent. This is the struggle of the Innu people against the expansion of the military base, from the present 8,000 flights a year to more than 40,000 flights in a low-level flight training center. The Innu people—and recently a Newfoundland court decision—maintain that this is their land, and they intend to protect it. The Canadian government, in a bid for the billion-dollar international NATO facilities, sees Goose Bay as a money-making military venture.

The war money and the peace of the land are what bring Rose Gregoire, Innu mother of four; her sister, Elizabeth Penashue; and her friend, Francesca Snow to speak throughout the country in defense of their rights. Armed simply with their own words, the daring resolve of this "small, mother-led band of peace warriors," as Toronto's *NOW* magazine calls them, is truly a formidable force. Says Snow, "We are not afraid of anything, even if I get shot. We will struggle all the way, no matter what happens."

In fact these women and their families have led a resilient occupation at the Goose Bay military base. A string of occupations and demonstrations, as well as the peaceful taking by storm of the base's runways, represents the most significant challenge yet to low-level flights and other war exercises being carried out in the Innu homeland. At one point in the early spring of 1989, these women served 19 days in a provincial jail for occupying the military runway. They were acquitted when the Newfoundland court determined that they sincerely believed they were occupying their own land and hence could not be trespassing. Even then, these women, eight other Innu women, and seven other Innu men did their time, refusing to sign the conditions that would have led to their release. By the summer of 1989, more than 250 arrests had taken place. As the Innu gear up their resistance to the new NATO proposal, more arrests are on the horizon.

THE MILITARY BUILDUP

The Goose Bay military base was built in 1941 as an outlying station linking North America and Europe during World War II. In 1952, the U.S. Air Force signed a 20-year lease to use the base; before the lease expired, the Americans were lending their installations to the British Royal Air Force and its Vulcan bombers. By the mid-1970s, the problem had expanded geometrically. With resistance in European countries to low-flying military flights over densely populated areas, a number of countries began looking greedily toward the Canadian north for new testing zones. By the 1980s, more than 4,000 training flights were being carried out over the 100,000 km² area. By 1989, there were 8,000 low-level flights a year between April and November—30 to 50 a day.

THE WORST IS YET TO COME

In 1980, NATO's military committee sponsored a feasibility study for the construction of a fighter plane training center in Goose Bay. Not to be outdone, Canadian Minister of Defense John Crosby announced in 1985 that the government would spend $93 million to modernize the base, and encouraged new countries to join the war games in the sky. Six countries—Belgium, Great Britain, West Germany, Holland, the United States, and Canada—are now using the skies of Nitassinan more intensely than ever. All of this to put in a bid for the NATO training base—a dubious honor that would result in around 100,000 low-level flights a year (250 "outings" a day), not to mention two to six bombing ranges and realistic replicas of landing strips, hangars, surface-to-air missiles, refineries, industrial plants, and other "enemy" targets.

In the summer of 1989, the Innu learned that an "in principle" decision to go ahead with the full-scale NATO tactical weapons training center had been made. The decision will be announced in December, according to Innu spokespersons. "That means that we have seven months to save our homeland," said Rose Gregoire. "I need to make it entirely clear that if the NATO base is established, Nitassinan will be turned into a war zone and our nation will be utterly destroyed."

"BUZZING" IN THE NORTH

Buzzing is the term local people use to describe the low-level flights. Jet bombers currently use 38,000 square miles of northern Quebec and Labrador to fly at lower altitudes than are allowed almost anywhere else in the world. West Germany permits no flights below 250 feet; such levels are considered to be too dangerous over populated areas. The Canadian Department of

National Defense (DND) and NATO apparently think that Nitassinan is uninhabited; the 15,000 Innu who live there know otherwise.

The low-level flights create terrifying, ear-splitting booms that shatter the otherwise unbroken peace of the north woods. It's said that the natural reflex to throw one's self down upon the ground and lie there for several minutes dumbfounded and shaking from every limb is basically unavoidable. This is a war on the senses. Significant studies have shown that buzzing has devastating effects on the hearing, nervous system, and metabolism of most species living within the northern ecosystem.

The impact on humans is what we can feel. The impact on the caribou herds, the beaver, the fish, the geese, and all the animals on which the Innu rely is what the Innu are fighting. The Innu are totally dependent upon the fragile northern ecosystem. The George River caribou herd, the largest migratory mammal herd in North America (estimated at more than half a million animals), shares this ecosystem with the Innu. The Innu are desperately concerned about the impact of the military on the herd. They say the animals are suffering. "The herd has stopped growing," says biologist Stu Luttich, who has studied the herd for over 15 years. "Mortality rates are increasing and the birth rate is declining." Caribou weakened by stress are easy prey for bears and wolves. The buzzing is creating stress in the herd. That constant stress is also what the Innu are fighting.

"The militarization, that's what you have to fight," says Francesca Snow. "They will destroy the land, they will destroy the animals, and they will destroy your life." When the animals are destroyed, the people are forced off the land, into wage work and into welfare, and the very soul of the community is destroyed. Father Alexis Jouveneau, a priest who has lived with the Innu for many years, says that the people must be allowed to continue their way of life on the land. Jouveneau issued a warning to the

Canadian government: "You are destroying not only their lifestyle, you are destroying their whole life so that you may proceed with military exercises. At that point, you might as well build a psychiatric clinic right here, and it will soon be overfilled." If the military goes ahead, says Innu elder Antione Malec, "You will not see us cry. We will not cry. But our hearts will bleed."

"What's going to happen this year," Rose Gregoire says, "is that about five families will be just outside the restricted zone near the range. They are going to walk up to the range and put up a tent to keep it lightly inhabited during the day. They'll be out in the woods hunting, and if the military helicopters come they're going to hide in the woods. If people are living in the bombing range, they are going to come and take them to jail. They don't want that to happen. The people are not going to stop now. They are going to continue. They are going to resist."

Indigenous Women Activists
Form Network

Appeared in LISTEN REAL LOUD, *April 30, 1986.*

More than 200 Native women organizers from North America and the Pacific came together to form an Indigenous Women's Network at a gathering in Yelm, Washington last August, hosted by the Northwest Indian Women's Circle. The event afforded a precious opportunity to share experiences, ideas and visions among the participants, most of whom work in isolated rural/reservation communities, and brought a renewed sense of support and empowerment.

Each day included several Talking Circles, with facilitators and resource people guiding discussions on topics ranging from "Avoiding Burnout" to "The Squaw Syndrome" to "Setting Up a Legal Defense Team." The focus of the gathering as a whole built in concentric circles, moving from the woman as an individual, to the family, to the community, and finally to our nations. Thus the first day included one Talking Circle on "Defining and Defending Our Physical, Mental, and Emotional Well-Being" and another on "The Impact of Sexism and Racism on Native Women." Each day the circle expanded to cover a larger area, with the final sessions addressing the topics of land rights, economic and fiscal planning for reservation communities, and litigation.

This approach reflected the belief that our communities need a wholistic healing, from the internalized oppression of women and men to the disruption of the natural and treaty law systems that protect our peoples and our land. Whatever issues we are working on, we are whole human beings, full of the celebration of life, the pain of oppression and struggle, the love we feel for each other, and the fear of failing our future generations.

The gathering itself also reflected this wholistic view. More than an event in itself, it was planned as a catalyst for furthering the process of networking among Native women and combatting our sense of isolation. For all of us, the gathering was part of the evolution of our communities themselves and cannot be separated from that process.

SPEAKING UP

Many women came together through the gathering who would not have had the opportunity to see each other under other circumstances. We heard from role models in our communities, women who often would not be the ones speaking up at other "meetings." We listened, for instance, to Susanna Oneui, a representative of the New Caledonian Liberation Movement, who told us how this south Pacific people are currently fighting to reclaim their land from France and from French settlers who remain on the islands.

Tallulah Pinkham, an elder from the Nisqually Nation, talked about traditional values in our lives, how we have lost touch with them and how we are moving back toward them. Roberta Blackgoat and Violet Ashkie, both members of the Big Mountain community fighting relocation described how some young people were returning to the land and the traditions that others were moving away from. This continuity of the generations, they explained, is essential in holding onto the land and the values of the land.

Other women discussed efforts to rebuild our traditional economic systems. Rebecca Adamson spoke about her nationwide efforts to help various Indian nations regain control over the reservation economy and build enterprises to increase the economic power of their communities. Elizabeth Garrett of the Rosebud Reservation described her work with traditional agricultural methods and rammed earth housing. A rammed earth house costing $15,000, she explained, can provide the same shelter as a frame house costing $55,000–$70,000. Moreover, it is designed for extended families, unlike housing provided by the federal Department of Housing and Urban Development (HUD), which can accommodate only nuclear families. And rammed earth houses will last 200 to 300 years, in contrast to the 20- to 25-year life of HUD structures.

Women spoke on land struggles from all kinds of perspectives. Researcher Margaret Brigham talked about using research as a tool for developing strategies, to increase the information that Indian communities use in making decisions. "Decision making," she pointed out, "usually ends up in the hands of non-Indians due to the control of the written word." Women from Hawaii talked about the taking of Hawaiian land in the context of the increasing militarization of the islands.

Many women also shared their experiences in overcoming obstacles to organizing, through building a community's understanding of an issue and addressing people's fears of taking action or the belief that we don't have any power to change things.

SETTING OUR OWN AGENDA

The vision of an Indigenous Women's Network has emerged from the experiences of many Native women. Through working in our communities, we have come to see the need to encourage other women, to network, and to share ideas and skills. As organizers from many different areas, we might see each other only at meetings or conferences sponsored by non-Indians. We needed the strength and inspiration that could be gained from coming together to set our own agenda, instead of finding a few scattered moments at someone else's meeting.

In a statement of purpose for the Network, we said, "For many years we have worked within our communities as grassroots women activists. We have fought for sovereignty, land, human and civil rights. We have worked to change out educational and health environment and institutions for the betterment of our people. As indigenous women we have personally struggled against overpowering forces. Indian women are abused, mistreated, battered, sterilized, and are victims of institutional racism and poverty in double doses, as women and as Native Americans. Indian women by the thousands are weeping at night in despair at the conditions of our families and communities. We are compelled to address the problems that confront us. We have united to share with one another our skills and to support each other for the basic survival of our people. Our underlying framework is to work within the visions of our elders, as we apply indigenous values to resolve contemporary problems."

A planning circle of nine women—all from different communities, working on different issues with different constituencies—worked for a year to organize the gathering. As the year moved on, more and more women became interested in the meeting and the role of the Network in our communities.

In some communities, a concern surfaced that we were organizing a "women's liberation" movement that would separate us out from the men; some people said that instead of making divisions we should be trying to keep our communities together. In the planning circle, we talked through this issue all along, because all the women involved were interested in healing and uniting our communities, not dividing them.

We brought out continuously that the Network and the gathering were work "within the vision of our elders." None of us felt that we were doing something totally new that was simply adopted from the women's movement. We believed that what we were doing was a natural part of the growth of our communities. Indian women have always been encouraged to work together in sisterhood societies and other women's circles. For us, the Network reflects this tradition, particularly because it is an informal group of women. To those who brought up the issue of divisiveness repeatedly, some of us would say, "trust us a little—we are from the community, after all, and women don't just get together to gossip." The support we received from our communities and our families was indispensable to the ultimate success of the gathering.

WHERE ARE WE GOING?

As a catalyst, the gathering created an environment to support networking and sharing among women. We believed that after the gathering took place, the participants could decide how to take it from there. One kind of follow-up will be a slide show on Native women's projects and the gathering itself. Also planned are a resource directory and radio programs featuring some of the people at the gathering.

All of these projects will give a deeper and richer understanding than is possible in this report, which reflects only one person's perspective.

Other Native women—particularly a delegation of 20 women from the Haisla and other nations, in what is now known as British Columbia—are now planning a gathering for May 1986. There will undoubtedly be others. The Indigenous Women's Network has no formal organization or membership or strict goals. We have just started this circle and there is plenty of room to join it. Those of us who have joined already feel inspired by each other and the incredible experience we have shared.

Politics and the Presidency

The Case for Hemp

Appeared in INDIAN COUNTRY TODAY, *September 19, 2001.*

The federal government should grant a waiver to Native Nations who seek to legalize the production of industrial hemp. The August raid on the Pine Ridge hemp crop on the White Plume Tiosape land, illustrates a shameful era in the Drug Enforcement Agency. Over the long term, the DEA's policies and actions set back the economic, environmental, and public health needs of not only Native America, but also the broader American community. Many Native nations, including the Oglala Lakota, Navajo, and Saginaw Chippewa, to name a few, have expressed an interest in industrial hemp production. Natives are not the only ones interested in the benefits of industrial hemp; over a dozen state legislatures are discussing industrial hemp production. Now would be the time for the Bush administration to move forward in supporting what will be the crop of the future.

Consider the irony of this situation. Pine Ridge reservation in South Dakota has been deemed by statisticians as the economically poorest area in the United States. The average median income on the reservation is $2,600 per year, which is one-fifth of the national average. The unemployment rate is at 84%, and some 69% of all residents are below the poverty line. Hundreds of tribal members are homeless, and most live in overcrowded and substandard housing. Jobs are far away. Many residents have to travel 120 miles round trip to work in Rapid City, and even then most jobs are minimum wage.

Now consider the alternatives: Native America could cash in on the $100-million-plus hemp food industry. Add that to the 2 million pounds of hemp fiber imported in 1999, not including a pretty substantial market for already produced hemp clothing (imported from countries like China, Hungary, Poland and Romania). Then, there is the growing interest in hemp both as a fiber source for paper and a possible source for building materials. Hemp can be transformed into everything from insulation to something like the "hempcrete" building already constructed at Slim Buttes on Pine Ridge.

In a letter to U.S. Attorney for South Dakota, Michelle Tapken, Oglala Tribal President John Yellowbird Steele reiterated the irony of the situation. "The Controlled Substance Act of 1970 did not divest the Lakota people of our reserved right to plant and harvest whatever crops we deem beneficial to our reservation, nor did the Act abrogate Congresses ratification of the reserved rights. . . . Therefore, we regard the enforcement of our hemp ordinance and prosecution of our marijuana laws tribal matters to be handled by our Oglala Sioux Tribal Public Safety Law Enforcement. . . ."

Steele continued, "We ask for your government's compassion as we try to ease the pain of our poverty through hemp manufacturing." Steele goes on to note that during "World War II, your government signed contracts with members of the Pine Ridge Reservation to grow industrial hemp for your war effort. In other words, when your government needed the benefits of growing hemp to aid your war effort, and encouraged its growth on the reservation, we supported your government by doing so. Now my nation needs to grow industrial hemp to aid our efforts at becoming more self-sufficient. We would appreciate your support in our endeavors. . . ."

This is not a new crop. For at least 12,000 years, hemp has been grown for fiber and food. Many of the U.S. founding fathers grew hemp, including both George Washington and Thomas Jefferson. Benjamin Franklin owned a mill that made hemp paper, and Jefferson drafted the Declaration of Independence on hemp paper.

Although industrial hemp is taxonomically classified under the same name as marijuana, *Cannabis sativa*, industrial hemp has less than 1% THC, the primary psychoactive ingredient in marijuana. As it turns out, however, you wouldn't want to smoke industrial hemp: It would take about a bale to get you high, and then you'd pass out anyway. Industrial hemp is to marijuana what nonalcoholic beer is to beer. They are related, but that is about it.

Hemp's versatility, and the fact that almost the entire plant can be used, has made it a thriving crop throughout the world. Hemp seeds are the richest known source of polyunsaturated essential fatty acids, and are high in some essential amino acids, including gamma linoleic acid (a very rare nutrient also found in mother's milk). Hemp fiber is considered useful for many products, ranging from car parts, to rope, to alternatives to gasoline. The energy production potential itself should excite the combustion-happy Bush administration.

Even the forest products industry sees hemp as an excellent option for the future. Kimberly Clark has a mill in France that produces hemp paper, where it is preferred for bibles, both based on its longevity and on its ability to retain its whiteness. The crop also has environmental benefits with regards to paper production. Hemp has a low lignin content, allowing it to be pulped using less chemicals, especially chlorine bleach, a leading cause of dioxin contamination in the environment.

One large paper company with a Fox River, Wisconsin mill has suggested that if hemp could be grown in Wisconsin, they would use it for up to 45% of their feedstock at their mill within five years. Another huge paper company plans on moving up to 90% of its world feedstock to non-forest sources within ten years, and sees hemp as a major component of that plan. The reality is if the company can't grow hemp in the U.S., it will grow it elsewhere.

Present U.S. Department of Agriculture projections soft peddle the market for hemp and its viability. The Department suggests that the present market is, "a small, thin market," and that a few large farms could produce the amount of annually imported hemp fiber. The USDA, however, does note that hemp production, in eastern North Dakota, for instance, would yield (according to 1998 estimates) around $74 on the average per acre in net returns, as compared to an average of $38 for corn or 86 cents an acre for sunflowers. USDA estimates as to hemp's viability, however, fail to consider the growing worldwide demands for alternatives to wood fiber, in everything from the paper industries to building industries. And indeed, there are industrial hemp supporters inside the USDA. Jeff Gain, Board Chair of the USDA's Alternative Agricultural Research and Commercialization Corporation, says, "We must have diversity, and crops like hemp that grow without pesticides." Other organizations are optimistic and hopeful. The Institute for Local Self Reliance reported that 1999 hemp yields averaged 800 pounds per acre (roughly four times as much fiber as wood per acre), and had gross earnings of $308 to $410 per acre, as compared to $103 to $137 per acre for wheat and canola.

It is perhaps those figures that have driven a multitude of interests to seek alternatives. March 23, 2001, marked the third anniversary of a petition signed by over 200 organizations asking the Drug Enforcement Agency to decriminalize industrial hemp production in the U.S.

Decriminalizing industrial hemp is the way of the future. The sovereign status of Native Nations raises questions about the application of DEA regulations in the face of tribal ordinances. The need for alternative economies in Indian country supports the need for change. As DEA officials chopped away at the White Plume hemp crop, Alex White Plume "told the plants to be brave and strong and come back again next year." Let us hope they do.

Reflections on the Republic of Dubya

Summer 2001

The first 100 days of the Bush Administration have been an unbelievable nightmare. It appears we will not awaken any time soon. The actions President Clinton took in the closing hours of his presidency (the last frenzy of "good deeds"—actions he should have taken earlier, certainly before his nefarious pardons), and much of their subsequent undoing, was an ominous indicator of what was to come.

Then it began, almost like a set of CIA acts in the making: a trumped up energy crisis in California (one major contributor was a nuclear power plant that malfunctioned in California just at the apex of demand), promises of blackouts and big price tags at the gas station to come, rollbacks in arsenic in the drinking water, cuts in children's programs, and a few military crises—a Chinese plane, a Japanese sub, Iraq, etc., etc.

Then came the business of isolating and making of a pariah of John Kerry and, perhaps to a lesser degree, Jesse Jackson, two progressive leaders in this country who may—or may not—have brought the karma on themselves. In both situations, it certainly has been convenient timing for Bush. Now, of course, we have the massive and amazingly horrific energy plan—a sort of icing on the cake—and not nearly enough of an outcry.

George W. Bush is definitely the worse of two evils, to use the vernacular of the Green Party. Few of us thought it possible for him to be in office today, and we are still stunned. Those of us who worked hard to register and organize thousands of voters—including those from the largest party in America: the more than 50% of the American electorate who don't vote—are pretty exasperated. *It's hard to tell people to vote when their votes don't seem to count.* Those of us who argued for democracy—the need to diversify the political landscape in this country—join with many others in immense concern for our present crisis. In the end, of course, Dubya is the President—although how exactly he got there is something we may never know to the fullest detail. His getting there has unfurled a political crises in almost every community in this country—except, of course, the Republic of Dubya.

What vote got Dubya elected? Was it the three million votes for the Greens, including those 97,000 some odd votes in Florida that put him in? Was it perhaps, in part, Al Gore's own shortcomings that cost him votes? Was it a few misguided Floridians who put him in? Was it his brother, Jeb Bush, who kept a promise to the family by insuring that Dubya got elected, or at least that George did not lose in his brother's own state? Or was it just the Supreme Court, who appointed him? I am sure it was the combination of all of the above, and I, myself, was a part of it. I am hopeful there are some lessons to be learned.

Let us not forget that Al Gore won the election. Al Gore won the popular vote, receiving more votes than any other presidential candidate in history. George Bush got in, pretty much on a technicality, by winning the Florida vote by a few hundred votes and consequently winning the electoral college. Then, he got that nod from the High Court. This is not subject to debate. But, as we know, it isn't quite that simple.

Consider, for example, that Pulitzer Prize–winning investigative journalist John Lantigua uncovered what has turned out to be a well-set strategy to disenfranchise hundreds of thousands of Florida voters, primarily black and Democratic. That strategy most likely had a major impact on the Florida election. As Lantigua found, " . . . the reality is that state's election officials and hired data crunchers used a sophisticated system to target thousands of voters, many of whom were purged from the voter rolls without reason. Thousands more saw their votes thrown out as a result of error-prone voting machines and poorly designed ballots. . . ." In all, some 200,000 Floridians were either not permitted to vote in the November 7 election, on questionable or possibly illegal grounds, or saw their ballots discarded, the result of "error." A large and disproportionate number of those who were disenfranchised were black.

The Florida vote was a mess, and most likely occurred with widespread violations of the law. The U.S. Commission on Civil Rights is expected to release a final report this summer on their assessment of what happened. The commission, in a preliminary assessment issued this spring, noted that the Voting Rights Act of 1965 was aimed at subtle, as well as obvious, state regulations and practices that could deny citizens the right to vote because of their race. The Commission said it found evidence of "prohibited discrimination" in Florida's polling process.

Lantigua won a 1999 Pulitzer Prize for his investigative reporting on Florida voter fraud. In his recent story, (*The Nation*, April 30, 2001) he talked about Jeb Bush's long-term strategy. "During a debate in Tampa on Bush's first unsuccessful run for governor, Bush was asked by a journalist what he would do for Florida's black community, if elected. ' Probably nothing,' he said, explaining that he was interested primarily in 'equality of opportunity' for all." While Bush avoided such statements in future debates and press appearances, the African American community did not forget, and when he won in 1998, he received only 10% of the black vote. All of these factors, plus a rise in general activism in the African American community meant that by election day 2000, 300,000 more blacks voted than four years before.

As Lantigua notes, "but while black Floridians were registering in unprecedented numbers, state officials were busy removing other blacks from the voting rolls." A series of new laws, under Jeb's leadership have disenfranchised some 17 percent of Florida's black voting age males. Additionally, "Florida leads the nation in the rate at which juveniles are charged with felonies, meaning those youths lose the right to vote before they are ever able to exercise it." Elsewhere, "purge lists," as they are called, "target black voters in extremely disproportionate numbers. . . .

[In] Tampa, where only 15 percent of the voters are black, 54 percent of the names on the purge list were African Americans." Not surprisingly, the NAACP filed suit against Florida Secretary of State Katherine Harris, charging the state with violating the Fourteenth Amendment and the 1965 Voting Rights Act and demanding changes to the electoral system within the state.

And, finally, the notorious inferior ballots. As Lantigua reports, "In four of the counties in the state with the largest black populations—Miami-Dade, Broward, Palm Beach and Duval, punch card systems (chad, half a chad, partial chad, hanging chad) are used. Some 100,000 votes were discarded in those counties—more than half of the state discards. And eighteen out of the nineteen precincts in the state with the highest rate of discards have black majorities." In total, 70 percent of Florida's African American population was forced to use the punch-card system.

Remember all the discussions about voting and campaign finance reform and the like by the Democrats—heck, even Republicans—Greens and the smithereens of the Reform Party? I'm not sure where that went, but it seems like a good place to go. This summer a movement is being launched in Florida called Democracy Summer. It is catalyzed by college students who are interested in electoral reform, campaign finance reform, and probably just getting their vote to count. What an idea. Looks like they are having a meeting in Florida the week of June 17th to move into the issues of electoral reform.

On the other end of the spectrum is all the excellent voter registration work done this past year by the Native community, the Black community, and the environmental community. The most amazing stories, from what I can figure, are in Montana and Washington State. In Montana, organizers at Native Action and a host of other groups like the Montana Indian Democrats, the Salish/Kootenai, and Blackfeet Nations got out and organized a phenomenal campaign to register Indians to vote, and then get them to the polls. "Indian voters apparently turned out in droves," wrote the *Great Falls Tribune*, calling it the largest turnout in Montana history. The results were also historic: six Indians elected to the legislature—five representatives and one senator. All un-precedented. The Montana voting demographics were also a bit unusual. All the blocks of land with Native communities were Democratic; the rest of the state, heavily Republican; then a few Greens, mostly in Missoula and the cities. But Bush took the state, big time.

As well, one should point out that the Greens were successful in breaking down ballot access barriers in a number of states, increasing the potential for participation by independent par-ties. In total, the Greens were on the ballot in 43 states, but only after challenging unfair barriers to ballot access, including through the use of eight lawsuits charging discriminatory prac-tices. Those actions will benefit lots of folks. Remember that in 40.1% of state legislative districts in 2000, down from 41.1% in 1998, either Democrats or Republicans failed to run candidates. This means that the number of uncontested races were pretty much astounding and full of potential for most of the folks who are barely represented in government—for instance, the Native community.

Interestingly enough, once in the presidential campaign, I was approached by an esteemed and prominent Native leader who suggested that I consider backing out of the campaign in order to insure Gore a victory. One of the major issues the leader pointed to was the Supreme Court and, of course, the 108 federal judge-ships that may end up with Bush appointees. The suggestion: ask for a few Native Federal Judgeships as a concession. The ques-tions I asked was *where was Al Gore in offering federal judgeships to Native people? Why must we concede to secure a deal? Why doesn't he offer them to court the Native vote in the first place?* Al Gore might have even got a few more Montana votes had he more openly courted the Native community there, not to mention the other big Native states. But that's water under the bridge. One lesson we all may learn from Montana and elsewhere in Indian country (the Florida Seminoles and Miccosukees are rumored by and large to vote Republican) is that the Native vote should not be taken for granted—and the trust of Native people needs to be earned.

Another interesting political lesson was the defeat of the nefarious Slade Gorton in Washington State. In the final breaths of election night, Maria Cantwell won the election, but by a very small margin. Her victory can in part be attributed to both the Get Out the Indian Vote work and the Get out the Green in Washington State, which, together, pulled from the ranks of non-voters at least a few thousand votes.

So here we are into the first full year of the Republic of Dubya. The cutbacks (in social services, for example) will have immense effects on many communities, whether Native, African American, or just poor and politically powerless. The environmental degradation will affect us all. The Bush Energy Plan will seek to crush the Gwich'in of the Arctic National Wildlife Refuge, undo every protection the Northern Cheyenne and other Native people of Montana have held in place for their water, oil, methane gas and coal resources. And it will seek to move nuclear waste—90,000 or so shipments of it—across this country, on railroads and highways, to Western Shoshone territory or Goshute territory. In the process, Bush's plan will open up and subsidize more and more nuclear power plants, an industry both incredibly lethal and incredibly uneconomic. The continued train of free trade, absent any reins on the great corporate interests like the nation of EXXON and the others, is projected to continue, *much as it did under the previous Clinton administration.*

Where is the opposition? *Chi Miigwech* to Senator Jeffords, for at least a glimmer of hope in this time of political darkness. As for creating political pariahs and immobilizing the opposition, like John Kerry, there are still some unanswered questions. My position is that the character attack on Kerry was a standard military maneuver: weaken the opposition. Yes, he did the wrong thing in Vietnam—and so, of course, did many others, most importantly those in government. But why did this incident come out now, when it occurred so long ago and so many have been aware of it for years? For that matter, if we are going to start stripping medals, let's go all the way back to the Wounded Knee Massacre, and take back those medals awarded for killing Native women and children. Thirty some were rumored to have been awarded and, thus far, only a few have been returned, voluntarily by the families, but absent any military formalities. Let's start reconciling all of it; if we want to start with the Vietnam War, just keep on going. That would be fair—bring it on.

Here we are now. The Republic of Dubya is in high form. And all of this is pretty much rotten for Native people, not to mention the rest of the folks. So, what the heck do we do? There are no easy answers. I do know that during the saga of the last Bush, the rise in community advocacy by the larger political movement was pretty astounding—folks got organized, because there were some major things to oppose. During the Clinton administration, on the other hand, there was a major decline in citizen activism. People thought things were going to be pretty good, so they got complacent. Then came a few interventions that cost a lot of money: the drug war in Colombia (protecting some really special interests like Occidental Petroleum and Al Gore), the militarization of Mexico ($52 million in guns and all), etc. These were companioned by community- and family-weakening proposals like welfare reform. Then, the tip of sovereignty bashing—the World Trade Organization went through enough tear gas and riots for all. Finally, the last amazing insult of January—the presidential pardons. Or, *if you have enough money you can get anything.*

And now it's mid summer 2001. *Inaaske*, it's time. *Ji misawaabandaaming.* Time to make a positive future: in our communities, in our voting rights, in our work to protect our Mother Earth and future generations. *So, I pledge myself to raise my voice, raise my vote, raise every ounce of strength I have to keep up our struggle—and to continue it all—demand that votes get counted, struggle for a set of systems that work, and work to protect Mother Earth.*

Too Much Roundup:
The Plan Colombia Vote

Summer 2001

Too much Roundup is not a good thing. We all know that, this week in Congress, new funding for Plan Colombia (a.k.a. the Andean Regional Initiative) will hit the floor for debate. The centerpiece of that plan is continued aerial spraying of Roundup Ultra over hundreds of thousands of acres of Colombia and expanded military aid to the region. It is, in my opinion, a gross misappropriation of federal funds.

This past year, Congress approved $1.3 billion to fund Plan Colombia, a plan whose goal in part is the elimination of coca bushes, which are seen as key to stemming the tide of drug trafficking in the U.S. The Bush Administration has proposed an expansion of this program, known as the Andean Regional Initiative, and is asking for $882 million to continue support for the work in Colombia, and expand it to the greater Andean region. The Colombian government has been spraying herbicides on drug fields for decades, but escalated the program with U.S. support in December 2000. Since that time, close to 40,000 hectares of land (or around 180,000 acres) in southern Colombia have been sprayed.

The spraying has not destroyed the majority of the coca bushes. Pesticide drift is inevitable with any aerial spraying and is exacerbated under Plan Colombia since planes fly higher than normal to avoid armed attack. The herbicides are consequently spread far beyond the targeted coca fields and into fields of food crops, other natural vegetation and waterways of the fragile ecosystem of the Amazon basin. While both the Colombian and U.S. governments have maintained that there have been few problems with the spraying, this is not the reality on the ground. Food crops on small family farms have been destroyed, children from local schools are showing signs of serious skin lesions that heal over but continually reappear, and animals and fish have died by the tens of thousands.

Elsa Nivía, a Colombian agronomist and director of Pesticide Action Network Colombia, responds to the federal government's claims that Roundup Ultra is safe and no more poisonous than aspirin or table salt. Early this year, she reported that in the first two months of this year local authorities reported that 4,289 humans suffered skin or gastric disorders, and that the chemicals killed 178,377 animals including cattle, horses, pigs, dogs, ducks, hens and fish.

Sort of a nasty tally, I'd say. Not content to sit at home and read about it, Minnesota Senator Paul Wellstone went down to Colombia this spring, inquiring about Plan Colombia. As the story goes, Wellstone was assured that the aerial spraying was safe and innocuous, yet, mistakenly, somehow, when the planes sprayed elsewhere, the aerial drift drenched the Senator.

In short, the whole question of how much Roundup to supply sets in motion a flashback to Vietnam and the Agent Orange Syndrome. Really, enough is likely enough.

Then there is the second facet of Plan Colombia, which is increasingly reminding me of Vietnam. Although there are not officially American soldiers in Colombia, there are about 500 U.S. "trainers" in Colombia, mostly private military contractors, who are working with both the Colombian military, and quite often the Colombian paramilitary. (According to sources at Amazon Watch, a public interest research group, nineteen out of twenty-one Colombian military brigades have direct links to the paramilitary groups in the country.) Each year, the U.S. is getting more deeply involved in the country, and one might ask who are the largest beneficiaries of this involvement? For instance, around $700–800 million of the last "aid" package to Colombia ended up in the pocket of Huey, and other helicopter companies, who are not doing too badly as the country gets more and more militarized. Additionally, increasing amounts of U.S. military infrastructure is going to provide security and support for facilities and pipelines of Occidental Petroleum, whose (widely opposed) pipeline has been bombed—no kidding—110 times in the past six months, gushing a whopping 2.2 million gallons of oil onto Colombian soil.

The price of all this militarization is increasingly high—too high for any of us. According to Amnesty International's Annual Report 2001 on Colombia, in the year 2000 "more than 4,000 people were victims of political killings, over 300 disappeared, and an estimated 300,000 people were internally displaced. At least 1,500 people were kidnapped by armed opposition groups and paramilitary organizations; mass kidnaps of civilians continued." Sadly, if approved, over 70 percent of U.S. assistance to Colombia would be directed toward the military and police. I actually don't think the Colombians need any more guns.

I must confess some personal interest in this story. First of all, one of my closest friends, Ingrid Washinawatok-El Issa, was kidnapped and shot in Colombia in 1998, a victim of the political violence, and a bullet I essentially paid for with my tax dollars. Second, I have two sons and remember all too well the body tolls from Vietnam. I am absolutely sure that I don't want to see that era again. There are alternatives. Spend that money on drug treatment programs in the U.S. Spend that money on investing and financing small farmers in Colombia to switch to legal crops. Support humanitarian aid and a clean up of the oil spills left by American companies in the region. Consider amendments like that from Massachusetts Representative James McGovern, which urges a cut in the military budget for Colombia and a transfer of some of this money to TB prevention, child survival and maternal health. Our tax dollars can be better spent.

Buying the Presidential Debates

October 2000

The presidential and vice presidential debates have become a set of immense corporate contributions to the Republican and Democratic parties. Intended to be a forum for discussion of the issues at stake in this country, the debates have become almost a charade, a parody, in the least an illustration of the spoiling of a democratic process. The corporate sponsorship of the debates should be eliminated, the arbitrary and discriminatory exclusions of third party candidates of substance should be removed, and, in short, the League of Women Voters should take back the control over the debates from the now Democratic- and Republican-controlled Federal Debate Commission.

Start with the problem of corporate sponsorship, and its consequences. The first presidential debate at the University of Massachusetts will be seen, in person, by a select few October 3rd. By Sunday, October 1st most of the 350 tickets had been taken by well-heeled corporate sponsors, who had coughed up $100,000 or more in campaign contributions to either George W. Bush or Al Gore's campaign. "Well-heeled corporate sponsors and campaign donors are snaring nearly all of the tickets for Tuesday's presidential debate, shutting out the public . . ." read a front-page story in a Boston paper. That meant that not only did the 1,000 students who had requested tickets get shut out, as did most of the general public, but ironically, the University was closed down for security reasons—so not only could students not attend the debates, but they couldn't attend classes. "They make a big thing about using a public school, but they don't let the public in," said one Massachusetts Congressman. "Open it up or shut it down," that's the call.

To be in the debates, one must fulfill three qualifications: constitutional eligibility, one must be on the ballot in enough states to mathematically have a chance of winning, and one must reach fifteen percent in five national polls. The first two are fair, it would seem. But, what about the third? Why fifteen percent? The only similar threshold the Federal Debate Commission could have utilized in developing the criterion is the percentage of vote for a party to be eligible for matching campaign funds—that threshold is five percent.

Neither Minnesota Governor Jesse Ventura or past Reform Party candidate Ross Perot would have qualified under those rules. Yet Ventura was allowed in the gubernatorial debates in Minnestoa and went on to not only win the governorship, but was able to encourage the highest voter turnout in Minnesota gubernatorial elections: 65%—a far cry from the less than 50% who usually vote in these elections, and a farther cry from the paltry 16% who turned out for the primary.

Ross Perot's story was similar and, along with Jesse Ventura's, was most likely why the rules have been changing, becoming more exclusive for third party candidates than ever before in the history of democracy. After Ross Perot entered the debates in 1992, largely at the behest of both the Republican and Democratic party leadership who figured that Perot would take votes away from either, he came away with some 18.9 % of the votes— in spite of being called a "spoiler." That 18.9% is not much to sneeze at, considering that President Bush and later President Clinton both boasted their people's "mandate," scarfing in less than 33% of the votes—and that was those who turned out, who today represent less than half the American electorate.

Ralph Nader has infinitely more political experience than either of the major party candidates. He has authored, and proposed, more national legislation than either Al Gore or George Bush Jr. in a career spanning over 40 years. Those bills have secured highway safety and consumer safety—like seatbelts and airbags—workplace safety, cleaner air, cleaner water, and freedom of information from our government officials, just to start. Nader, as well, represents not an extremist position in America, but in fact, more of the mainstream. Take for instance the issues of trade. The hotly contested World Trade Organization and the demonstrations over the past year against the WTO represent not a minority of the people, but in fact, broader sentiments. For example, only 10% of the Americans, by most polls, consider themselves free traders, while some 37% consider themselves protectionists, and 50% fairtraders. Gore and Bush are both staunch free traders. Pat Buchanan would be considered a protectionist, and Nader would be considered a fairtrader, yet, neither candidate will be allowed into the debates to discuss these issues, and in fact, the topic might not be discussed at all.

America is the single most difficult democracy in the world in which to participate. And, fewer and fewer people do. The reality is that the largest party in America is neither the Democrats nor the Republicans—the largest party is the non-voters.

Today, over half the potential electorate—people who could vote—don't. This is the largest political party. To those who are outside the folds of the Democratic and Republican parties, it is incredibly difficult to participate in this democracy. To get on the ballot of all 50 states, a presidential candidate must now get 750,000 signatures. Those figures make it the most difficult of any democracy. In 1924, a U.S. presidential candidate only needed a tenth as many signatures, yet in subsequent elections—largely elections in which third party candidates, whether to the right or left, had strong showings—the ante went up.

The League of Women Voters, a non-profit, non-partisan group dedicated to voter education, was the right home for the debate commission. Their work was usurped by the Commission on Presidential Debates, created by former Republican national Committee Chairman Frank Fahrenkopf, Jr. and former Democratic National Committee Chairman Paul Kirk, with a board comprised entirely of Republicans and Democrats. The league, in 1987, deemed third party candidate John Anderson worth debating by the same criteria applied now, and the Democrats and the Republicans protested. The two parties decided that the Commission on Presidential Debates would sponsor the first debate and the League of Women voters would sponsor the second and third. Then the two parties and their candidates made new rules, including allowing candidates to review the moderator's script and barring follow up questions. The candidates also wanted the audience to be comprised primarily of their supporters, not the general public. The major party candidates and their commission kept on pushing new rules, did not allow the League of Women Voters a part in the rule-setting process, and the League of Women Voters finally withdrew from the process.

Today, we have a sham which remains. We have a campaign system skewed towards those with millions. From the campaign contributions and war chests of Al Gore and George Bush Jr., both of whom have come under heavy fire for the ethics of their contributions (i.e., nights in the Lincoln Room, Buddhist temples, or friends of daddy). Add to this the insult of the only public forum for the debates—their activities now underwritten by corporations like 3Com, Anheuser-Busch, US Airways, Century Foundation, AT&T—and you come to understand that corporations now-a-days not only underwrite the campaigns, the debates and the lobbyists, but by implication, the democratic process itself. It is now owned/financed by the corporations.

The funding of the Debate Commission is now subject of a lawsuit by Nader arguing that the corporate underwriting of the debate commission constitutes illegal corporate contributions to the parties. The Nader lawsuit joins with John Hagelin's lawsuit (Natural Law Party) and Pat Buchanan's complaints that the Federal Election Commission is too closed.

Almost 65% of the Americans polled believe Ralph Nader should be allowed to debate. Not only would the debates be more interesting, but it would be a signal that the process might open up to a real democracy. Nader is the only candidate who had campaigned in all 50 states, including Alaska where he is running at a respectable 17%.

In the greatest democracy in the world, we have a problem. Slipping voter turnout, increased exclusion in the electoral process, and the absence of an open forum in which to discuss the future options for the country. We can do better. We are a country with immense diversity as well as potential, all of which are best realized through a political and governance process which allows for participation and meaningful dialogue, not excludes it. Campaign finance reform that both Senator John McCain on the right, and Senator Russ Fiengold on the left advocate for is a must, including a reform of how the debates continue. Voter participation must be increased through decreasing obstacles to registration, and allowing more voices to be heard in the whole electoral process.

Winona LaDuke, Green Party Vice Presidential Candidate: Position on Makah Whaling

Written in response to the controversy surrounding LaDuke's position on various environmental issues, August 2000.

The Makah Nation, situated at Neah Bay, in what is now known as Washington State, has thousands of years of tradition as ocean harvesters, including the harvesting of fish, seals, and whales. When U.S. Territorial Governor Isaac Stevens arrived at Neah Bay in December of 1855, he entered into treaty negotiations for three days with Makah leaders. The Makah made it clear to him that while they were prepared to cede their lands to the U.S., they wanted a guarantee of their traditional rights on the ocean, and specifically the right to take whales. The treaty provides that the Makah ceded most of the land in the Olympic Peninsula to the United States in exchange for "the right of taking fish and of whaling or sealing at usual and accustomed grounds and stations. . . ."

The Neah Bay Treaty of 1855, ratified by the U.S. Congress, is the law of the land under the Constitution and has been upheld in the federal courts and the U.S. Supreme Court. That treaty to the Makah is as "powerful and meaningful a document as the U.S. Constitution is to other Americans, it is what our forefathers bequeathed to us." As a Vice Presidential candidate of the United States, I believe that the U.S. should abide by international law, and honor treaties. The treaty with the Makah is the only treaty between a Native Nation and the U.S. government which explicitly guarantees a right to whale.

Indigenous peoples on a worldwide scale are increasingly impacted by wanton industrialization, and its impacts on ecosystems, animal populations, culture, and the ability of peoples to sustain themselves with dignity. The United Nations has increasingly become concerned about the losses of cultural diversity and human lives in the world, and have designated, for instance, decades of Indigenous peoples and working groups on the issues of Indigenous peoples. Prior to this, however, the International Whaling Commission, after appeals by member nations as well as Indigenous Nations, has specifically allocated whale harvest quotas to Indigenous peoples for the past decades, recognizing the nutritional and specific spiritual needs of these communities to continue their harvests. The International Whaling Commission, at its last meeting, continued this practice, approving a combined 620 gray whale quota for Russian and U.S. aboriginals to be taken over a five-year period. The Makah quota is 20 whales landed over five years (1998–2002), with no more than 33 strikes. This Makah quota did not increase the IWC allocation, but, instead, was removed, according to both the Makah Whaling Commission and the Northwest Indian Fisheries Commission from the Chukotki (Indigenous people from Russia, whose annual take is 165 whales). In short, the Makah allocation in no way increased the subsistence allocations internationally for the harvest of gray whales.

The Makah had taken a 70-year fast from what is one of their most important spiritual and subsistence foods, since the industrialized whale harvest had devastated whale populations in the eastern Pacific herd. The decline in subsistence harvest of whales, like other traditional foods also decimated by industrial fishing and harvesting, has had detrimental impacts on Native communities like the Makah—many of which today have diabetes rates averaging 40% in adults and related nutritional problems associated with the forced rapid transformation of indigenous diets from traditional foods to processed foods. The impacts of these devastating health effects cannot be understated in Native communities, whose public health services have been entirely underfunded (in comparison to vast expenditures on the military and other non-human needs allocations in the federal budget). Native health statistics and funding nationally fall far below even the most dire conditions in the general population. Whale meat, like other ocean-mammal meat, has oils and nutritional sources that are absorbed into the system directly, and are considered essential to the recovery of the health of the Makah people and other traditional Native peoples who are ocean harvesters.

The Makah assumed that when the International Whaling Commission, combined with the U.S. government, estimated that the health of the eastern Pacific gray whale herd was well established, with at least 22,000 members, and the animal was considered "recovered" and delisted from the Endangered Species Act in 1994, it was safe to resume their traditional harvest. That harvest, while guaranteed in the treaty, is considered a sacred right and responsibility of the Makah people. The U.S. government supported the Makah Nation's request for aboriginal subsistence whaling, and sought an IWC approved quota.

The Makah whale hunt's resurrection was supported by a referendum vote in the Makah people, in which 85% of those voting favored whaling. Provisions for the whaling included both the use of traditional harpoons (adapted with the best technologies), and the use of a .50 caliber rifle, which is considered the most humane and expedient method of killing the animal. The Makah consulted with Dr. Allen Ingling, a veterinarian at the University of Maryland, along with the National Marine Mammal Laboratory, in the determination of the most humane way of harvesting a whale, and utilized this practice simultaneous to their traditional harvesting practice. The community also undertook the hunt with the understanding inside the village, and with the National Marine Fisheries Service (NOAA), that there would be no commercial sale of whale meat. The tribe further committed this in a written agreement with NOAA, reinforced by 50CFR part 2300 which states, "No person may sell, or offer for sale, whale products from whales taken in an aboriginal subsistence hunt, except that authentic articles of native handcraft may be sold or offered for sale."

The Makah whale harvest was successful in the taking of one whale in 1999. That was in spite of organized and aggressive interference by the Sea Shepard Society, in coordination with some additional interests. The actions of the Sea Shepard Society additionally cost the United States Coast Guard up to perhaps $5 million in expenditures to protect the Makah exercise of their legal rights. The whale taken is presumed to be from the eastern Pacific whale herd, the harvest taking place in May of 1999, just after the formal allocation of the permit from NOAA to the Makah Whaling Commission, and the subsequent allocation of the whaling permit by the Makah Whaling Commission.

Based on the above information, the Vice Presidential Candidate of the Green Party supports and will enforce the law of the United States in honoring its treaties and in the protection of the Makah right to continue their harvest of gray whales. At the same time as the Makah exercised their treaty right, I have great concerns as to the continued industrialized whaling practices by Norway and Japan, and the sudden increase in whale mortality. I would propose measures to seek mitigation of both these problems.

The International Whaling Commission introduced a moratorium on commercial whaling in 1986. However, Japan and Norway exploited "loopholes" in the moratorium in order to continue their whaling practices. Norway hunts whales commercially off its own coasts, and Japan is pressing the IWC to allow it to do the same. In 1998, Norway hunted down some 624 whales. Using a pretext of "scientific whaling" Japan killed 389 whales in the Southern Ocean, within the borders of the Southern Whale Sanctuary in 1999. The wholesale value of the 1,700 tonnes of whale meat caught by the Japanese in the Antarctic was about 3 billion yen, the retail value about three times that.

I support a moratorium on commercial whaling. I also support the expansion of whale sanctuaries including the development, initially of a South Pacific Whale Sanctuary, as supported by Australia and New Zealand, and a South Atlantic Whale Sanctuary as proposed by Brazil at the International Whaling Commission. I also support a Global Whale Sanctuary and the abolition of commercial whaling.

In terms of possible whale destruction by the U.S. Navy, I would call for a cessation of the SURTASS LFAS Program (Surveillance Towed Array Sonar System utilizing Low Frequency Active Sonar). This program is a continuation of the militarization of the ocean and represents not only an excessive cost to taxpayers in a post-cold war era, in which the U.S. military budgetary expenditures dwarf those of any other "potential enemies" by at least ten fold, but also represents a clear threat to whale, dolphin and other ocean species.

The proposed military acoustic program would be a network of very high powered sound generators placed in various places around the oceans—some stationary, others towed behind ships. The sound generators can blast 250 decibels of noise, which is 100,000 to one million times greater than the loudest whale, and perhaps a billion times louder than the subtle acoustical signals of other sea creatures. These sounds are the loudest sounds ever generated by humans, with the possible exception of the noise at nuclear Ground Zero. After almost every known Navy test, whales and dolphins show up on beaches for "mysterious reasons," some with bleeding eyes, damaged and infected cochlea, and other unusual tissue damage—and these are only the creatures we know about. The Navy has thus far maintained that the strandings are only "anecdotal," unconnected to its testing, and refuses the study the matter further. Based on extensive strandings in the Canary Islands (1985, 1988, 1989), the Atlantic Coast (1987), Northern California (1995, 1997), British Columbia, Hawaii, U.S. Virgin Islands, and the Bahamas, I advocate for a complete cessation of this program, and a study of the anecdotal data. I would advocate for this based on a precautionary principle, in that we are not sure of the long-term impact, but are quite aware of the present anecdotal evidence.

Furthermore, in related issues, an increase of whale beachings and whale autopsies report increases in health problems among the whales, starvation, and other causes of whale mortalities— an estimated 300 whales died in the past year. These mortalities are, according to federal studies, related largely to ecosystem decline, contamination, overharvesting of species, and perhaps global warming. The continued overharvesting of fish species in industrialized fishing poses a great threat to our ecosystems, and our economies. The allocation of ITQs (individual transferable quotas) is based on false ecological premises of maximum sustainable harvests, and has been part of the process through which the UN today estimates that nearly every commercial species surveyed is fully exploited, over exploited or depleted. Catches have gone from 3 million tonnes in 1900 to 86 million tonnes in 1989, largely driven by the introduction of factory trawlers. By 1991, 50 vessels of the fleet comprised only 2.5 percent of all boats in the groundfish fisheries off Alaska that year, yet landed 1.4 million metric tonnes of catch, nearly three quarters of the total. Additionally, almost 70% of that which is caught is tossed back dead into the ocean as "bycatch," considered waste, but is a total waste of life to all those fish. As well, one third of all fish caught by the factory trawlers is reduced to fish meal, to produce for hogs and chickens, and represents a total loss of protein potential for the world's peoples, many of whom live on the brink of starvation.

The overharvesting and devastation of our oceans indicated by industrialized fishing destroys all of this life, offsets potential income for family fishers, and is a whole part of the mismanagement of the world's oceans. I support conservation measures, including no-fishing zones in order to restore fish stocks in the world. All of these measures represent the necessary steps for the future of our communities, our relatives, and our planet.

Winona LaDuke's Acceptance Speech for the Green Party's Nomination for Vice President of the United States of America

Delivered on July 22, 2000.

I am here to announce today that it is with great honor that I am joining with Ralph Nader and the Green Party in a national effort in this presidential campaign. I will be his vice presidential running mate.

As Mr. Nader has previously stated, we intend to stand with others around this country as the catalyst for the creation of a new model of electoral politics, not to run any campaign. This will be a campaign for democracy waged by private citizens who choose to become public citizens.

I am not inclined toward electoral politics. Yet I am impacted by public policy. I am interested in reframing the debates on the issues of this society—the distribution of power and wealth, the abuse of power and the rights of the natural world, the environment and the need to consider an amendment to the U.S. Constitution in which all decisions made today will be considered in light of their impact on the seventh generation from now. That is, I believe, what sustainability is all about. These are vital subjects, which are all too often neglected by the rhetoric of major party candidates and the media.

I believe that decision making should not be the exclusive right of the privileged. That those who are affected by policy—

not those who by default often stand above it—should be heard in the debate. It is the absence of this voice which, unfortunately, has come to characterize American public policy and the American political system.

As most of you probably know I live and work on the White Earth reservation in northern Minnesota, the largest reservation in the state in terms of population and land base. And as most of you know—in terms of recent political and legal struggles—the site of a great deal of citizen activism and change in recent months. That is how I view myself, as a citizen activist. Yet I find that as small and rural as is my area of the northwoods, as small as my pond may be, the decisions made in Washington still affect me. And it is that fact, that decisions made by others—people who have never seen my face, never seen our lakes, never tasted our wild rice or heard the cry of a child in Ponsford—have come to impact me and my community. I am here to say that all people have the right and responsibility to determine their destiny and I do not relinquish this right to PACs, to lobbyists, and to decision makers who are far away.

When you live in one of the poorest sections of the country and in the state of Minnesota, you are able to understand, perhaps better, the impact of public policy. It is indeed my contention that there is no real quality of life in America until there is quality of life in the poorest regions of this America.

For instance over half of the American Indians on my reservation live in poverty. This represents five times the state average. Of particular concern is that nearly two thirds of the children on my reservation live in poverty. Also 90 percent of the children in female-headed households live in impoverished conditions. Median family income on my reservation is just slightly above half the state average for median income. Per capita income is at the same level. Unemployment on the reservation is at 49 percent according to recent BIA statistics. And nearly one third of all Indians on the reservation have not attained a high school diploma. Finally it is absolutely critical to note that approximately 50 percent of the population on the reservation is under 25 years of age, indicating that these problems will need to be addressed over the long term.

What does that mean in the larger picture? Let me give you some examples.

Welfare reform legislation

This is the nation leading the world in terms of number of people in poverty. There are some 9 million children in this country in poverty. Welfare reform eliminates the safety net for those children. Now let me tell you about some real people. Native Americans are the poorest people in the country. Four out of 10 of the poorest counties in the nation are on Indian reservations. This is the same as White Earth. My daughter's entire third grade class, with few exceptions, is below the poverty level. The only choice those parents have with any hope—with 45 percent unemployment—is to work at the casino for about six bucks an hour. With two parents working and paying childcare expenses makes them ostensibly the working poor. Not much different than being in poverty. So my friends, a family of seven who live in a two bedroom trailer down the road from me—a fifteen-year-old trailer—on AFDC have few options under the new welfare reform plan. I will not stand by mute as the safety net is taken away from those children and that third grade class.

Environmental policy

This is a long list. WTI Incinerator is a hazardous incinerator in East Liverpool, Ohio, located less than 1,000 feet from a school. It was visited by Al Gore in 1992 where he pledged if elected, it would not open. It did.

Endangered species. Bill Clinton said in 1992 that he would not allow a weakening of the Endangered Species Act, yet he signed an appropriations bill in 1994 that prohibits any funds to be used to uplist or list any species under the endangered species act. This put a freeze on any action on over 1,000 species that are waiting to be listed under the act.

Our forests. The salvage rider. Clinton vetoed the first version of this, then signed it the second time when it was attached to an appropriations bill for the Oklahoma City bombing victims, later claiming that he never thought the timber industry could use it to get around the laws. In total salvage available for future harvest in the northern Rockies alone is equivalent to 237,000 logging trucks full of trees. Nationally, 900,000 logging trucks full of trees. Allowable cuts are now acceptable under headings like "winter injury," "poor vigor," "old age," and "to realize forest productivity"—broad and subjective terminology. This situation is of course mimicked in the Superior National Forest.

What is my experience in this? I come from a forest culture. Our creation stories are about those forests, our ancestors are buried there, our food, our medicinal plants, our relatives, live in those forests. We call them forests, but they are viewed by Potlatch, Blandin, and Champion as board feet of timber.

Now let me ask you a question. How is it that when the people of the White Earth reservation ask the federal government for the return of the Tamarac National Wildlife Refuge or to manage the Tamarac National Wildlife Refuge—lands taken illegally from our people—we are refused or put off? Yet these same lands are basically given to Potlatch and Champion. Why is it that the state and other officials refer to last year's wind shear on my reservation that took down over 200,000 acres of trees as a natural disaster? Yet Potlatch expands present mills and they will be cutting a square mile of Minnesota's northwoods daily—the equivalent of an eight-foot pile of logs piled across both the north and south bound lanes of Interstate 35 from Minneapolis to Duluth—and that is referred to as economic growth.

Who's going to be there when all those trees are gone? Who will be there when there are no forests except for a monoculture poppel and tree farms? You can't eat money.

How about Indian policy? Lots of promises and no action. Two free lunches, some Kodak moments, and immense budget cuts. Indian policy has come far in America, there's no question. Until almost the end of the nineteenth century, Indians were dealt with by the Department of War. Since then Indian people have been in the Department of Interior; we are the only humans in the Department of Interior treated as a natural resource. This is a problem in budget cuts. Literally we are fighting with ducks over appropriations. Is that changing? Right now in the international arena the U.S. State Department is opposing the classification of indigenous peoples as "peoples"under international law. Peoples have rights under international law and those rights are not the sole and exclusive jurisdiction of member states. We are arguing that we have fundamental rights to self-determination, to language, land, territory, natural resources, and our children. And the U.S. State Department is opposing our human rights.

Now a question you may ask me is: Can a person who lives in the northwoods of Minnesota have thoughts big enough for national policy debate or international policy? I would argue yes. In fact I would question the inverse. Can men of privilege—who do not feel the impact of policies on forests, children, or their ability to breastfeed their children—actually have the compassion to make public policy that is reflective of the interests of others? At this point, I think not.

I have seen my neighbors, small farmers in northern Minnesota, go under while corporate agriculture subsidies in the sunbelt mount. I have seen dairy cows with x's on their foreheads for the dairy termination program leave on cattle cars never to return, and I have been at too many farm auctions to feel that things are good on the farm. I know the difference between water quality on a small dairy farm and that on a 3,000 or 10,000-acre hog farm. As former Texas Agriculture Secretary Jim Hightower says: "Sometimes there's just too many pigs in the creek."

I have looked into the eyes of Tzotzil women in Chiapas, Mexico, whose eyes are all that show. Women whose faces are covered in the tropics with ski masks because if the Mexican military or paramilitary see them they will be killed if they are known. I've seen the U.S. military-supplied armored personnel carriers on small dirt roads in Chiapas and recognized the absence of human rights and dignity that is central to NAFTA. And

I also recognize the impact of $250 million in U.S. military aid and trade to a country like Mexico—a country with no known enemies.

American foreign policy is reflective of American economic policy, and at best, both presently and historically, it makes refugees. That is the major reason we have the challenge of immigration. I congratulate Paul Wellstone on his principled stand on NAFTA, Colin Peterson's opposition to NAFTA, and ask one more time for Senator Rod Grams's office to return my calls. And while Dan Quayle could not spell potato, I can. O-P-I-N-II-G. That's Ojibwe for potato. And that language is one of 187 endangered indigenous languages which do not benefit from English—only legislation.

As a human, I understand these issues; and as a woman, I ask why it is that I should be more concerned about the sugar content of breakfast cereal than the amount of mercury in my son's tissue from eating fish from Minnesota lakes.

In conclusion, until American domestic and foreign policy addresses quality of life issues for the poorest people in the country, we cannot say that there is quality of life. Until all of us are treated as peoples—with full human rights—we cannot tout a human rights record. Until policy decisions are made that do not benefit solely the 1 percent of the population that has more wealth than the bottom 90 percent of the population, I do not think that we can collectively say that we are talking about real economic and social benefits. And finally, until we have an environmental, economic, and social policy that is based on the consideration of the impact on the seventh generation from now, we will still be living in a society that is based on conquest; not one that is based on survival. I consider myself a patriot—not to a flag—to a land.

And in that spirit I am pleased to join with other citizen activists, with Cam Gordon, with Lee Ann Tall Bear, with Ralph Nader and the Green Party to make this truly an inclusive and substantive dialogue on the future of this America.

Miigwech, Mi'iw.

A Seventh Generation Amendment

Appeared in OJIBWE NEWS, *October 4, 1996.*

The framers of the U.S. Constitution envisioned life, liberty, and the pursuit of happiness in that document, but had little idea of what was to come. Since that time we've seen the landscape of the continent change dramatically—culturally, politically, ecologically, and economically. Today, the social and technological foundation of the society has, in fact, outstripped the law itself. It's time to amend the Constitution to preserve "the commons" for all of us. It's time for a Common Property, or Seventh Generation, Amendment to the U.S. Constitution.

The preamble to the U.S. Constitution declares as one of its purposes, to "secure the blessings of liberty, to ourselves and our posterity." Should not those blessings include air fit to breathe, water decent enough to drink, and land which is as beautiful for our descendants as it was for our ancestors?

American public policy has come to reflect short-term interests, fiscal years, "deficit reduction" programs, and is increasingly absent of any intergenerational perspective. That long-term perspective is crucial to our well-being and a valuable role for democratic government. As a consequence, or by default, that which is collectively ours—oceans, air, rivers, water, forests, public lands—is often pilfered or degraded by a private interest. The Exxon Valdez oil spill disaster is one example of the destruction of common property by private interests. An accident, however, and we hope the exception. The rule, however, is chilling.

Consider the challenge of industrial fishing. Seafood conglomerate Tyson's and its factory trawlers work inside the U.S. 200-

mile limit of the north Pacific Ocean. Tyson's nets plunder the ocean with an "economic efficiency" that leaves little. One net can hold up to six jumbo jets in its grasp, and such fleets now dominate the industry. With 38,000 registered commercial fishing vessels on the seas, it's ironic that only 60 boats catch 21% of total U.S. catch. More ironic is the waste. Factory trawlers annually waste 580 million pounds of fish in the north Pacific alone. Tossed dead-as-a-doornail back into the ocean.

In the past decade, we've seen the collapse of the Atlantic haddock stocks, salmon stocks, and soon pollock stocks, all largely a result of "overfishing" and factory trawling. That collapse puts thousands of people out of work (in Canada) and costs U.S. taxpayers millions in economic aid. The impact lasts decades, if the fish recover at all.

The question might be asked: "What right exactly does the factory trawling industry have to cause the collapse of an entire species of fish—our fish?"

Here's another example—Dow Chemical, Monsanto, Dupont and dioxin. Dioxin is a true child of the 20th century. Its chemical family was created in a laboratory by Herbert Dow (Dow Chemical) in the 1900s and later became that household savior, chlorine bleach. Subsequent offspring have included most pesticides, solvents and plastics. And dioxin now appears through our economy and food chain. The Environmental Protection Agency (EPA) has known of the serious health consequences of dioxin since the early 1970s, but has taken limited action largely a result of lobbying by groups like the Chlorine Council, the industry's advocacy group. However, after the results of a huge EPA study, commenced in 1992, were released this year, the problems are worse than anticipated.

Nearly everyone in the country is already carrying what is called a "body burden of dioxin" 500 times greater than the "acceptable risk" level for carcinogens. Dioxin can be considered a sort of environment hormone that ravages the endocrine system, distorting cell growth. In men, dioxin elevates testosterone levels, reduces sperm count, and leads to increased rates of diabetes. In the last 50 years, sperm counts have declined by more than 50 percent, while testicular cancer has tripled.

In women, dioxin seems to prompt endometriosis, a painful uterine disorder that now afflicts five million women a year. Dioxin exposure has also been linked to breast cancer, a disease that has more than doubled since 1960. Pregnant women are especially vulnerable, since the daily level of dioxin intake is enough to cause long-term damage to fetuses, giving rise to birth defects, disrupted sexual development, and damage to the immune systems.

If you live in the Great Lakes region, your body burden of dioxin may be two to three times greater than that of someone living on the West Coast. Both weather patterns and clustering of Chemical plants produce this additional exposure. Dioxin is a fat-soluble chemical, meaning it bioaccumulates up the food chain. For example, fish from Lake Michigan show levels of dioxin more than 100,000 times higher than the surrounding water, plants, and sediment. However, two thirds of the average American's exposure to dioxin comes from milk, cheese, and beef, a result of cows eating contaminated food crops.

Now what's the problem? Environmental laws of today are outstripped by the poisons in our air, water, and land and the cumulative impacts. We are frequently facing a "catch up" situation at best, and most frequently no cumulative or long-term policy protection. We don't even know what the combined impact of a complicated chemical soup is on our bodies, ecosystem nor least the impact on future generations. Public policy is lagging behind our ability to destroy ourselves.

We need a Seventh Generation Amendment to insure the blessings of liberty to ourselves and our posterity. Today, the Fifth Amendment (we hope) preserves our rights to private property, and the protection of that property. Now the U.S. legal system needs to establish a clear distinction between private property and common property, and both must be defended vigorously. If private property has found safe haven in the Fifth Amendment, where is common property equally protected?

Common property resources are those that are not or cannot, by their nature, be owned by an individual or a corporation, but are held by all people in common. These "blessings of liberty" envisioned in the Constitution should be used or enjoyed only in ways that do not impair the rights of others—including future generations—to use or enjoy them. This philosophy is perhaps best reflected in the Iroquois Confederacy's philosophy—that we must consider the impact of a decision made today on the impact on the seventh generation from now.

The rights of the people to use and enjoy air, water, and sunlight are essential to life, liberty, and the pursuit of happiness. These most basic human rights have been impaired by those who discharge toxic substances into the air or water, thereby taking life, liberty, and the ability to pursue happiness. These rights are also damaged by those who cause a crash of our fish or destroy our oceans. Such "taking" must be recognized as a fundamental wrong in our system of laws, just as a taking of private property is a fundamental wrong.

As a result, we should consider a Seventh Generation Amendment or Common Property amendment to the U.S. Constitution stating, "the right of citizens of the United States to use and enjoy air, water, sunlight, and other renewable resources determined by the Congress to be common property shall not be impaired, not shall such use impair their availability for the use of future generations. . . ."

It's hard to imagine those who framed the U.S. Constitution could have imagined the U.S. at the millennium. It's harder yet to imagine what we'll pass on, if we don't think of the seventh generation from now.

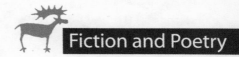

Fiction and Poetry

Coming Home

From LAST STANDING WOMAN *(Voyageur Press, 1997).*

BI-AZHI-GIIWEWAG
COMING HOME
SUMMER 2000

The ancestors were loud and getting louder. Moose Hanford could hear the ancestors even over the music from his tape deck and the roar of the road beneath the wheels as his ex-UPS delivery van hummed down the interstate through southern Illinois. There were forty-five ancestors in the back of the van. Resting. Now on their way home. Sometimes he could hear them sing, other times they were crying out. Now they seemed to just rattle.

The tape of Little Otter singing intertribals accompanied Moose on his journey. When Little Otter's drum stopped between songs, the sounds from the ancestors also ceased for a moment, but the rattling continued. Moose realized this noise was coming from his van. He turned off the casette player and listened closely to the mechanical cacophony.

The van was an old UPS delivery van that had been virtually donated to Moose by the UPS driver who had had the misfortune of having White Earth on his route. The van had been well used by the time Moose had gotten his hands on it, and now it counted two hundred thousand miles more on the odometer before that too broke. Moose sifted through his mind, discarding various squeaks, rattles, and creaks that he had grown accustomed to in his van and focused his mind on a possible source for this new ailment.

He moved the van into the right lane and continued listening intently. He inadvertently drove over a pothole and the rattle became a scraping sound accompanied by the full-bore roar of the engine. Only one thing made that music: an exhaust system gone bad.

Moose quickly scanned the horizon for a place to pull over. *The last thing I need*, he told himself, *is for a cop to stop me, see I'm a skin, and give me a ticket for driving without an exhaust—and start asking me questions.* He sighted a rest stop a few miles ahead. He glanced in his sideview mirror to change lanes and to see if he had left any important parts of his van behind. He drummed his fingers on the door, slowed the van to thirty-five and set his sights on the rest stop, tiptoeing his van the last two miles.

Moose pulled the van into the rest area and killed the engine. He grabbed his pack of cigarettes from the dash, opened the door, and stepped down. He lifted his pony tail off his back and shook the back of his shirt for ventilation. *A bush Indian was not meant to travel the southland during the summer. It must be eighty-five degrees with no wind. Too warm for an Ojibwe.* He stopped for a moment and scanned the scene. The rest stop was vacant.

Moose lit a cigarette and walked toward the back of the van. With some effort, he bent over and examined the muffler, reaching his hand toward it. "Shit! It's hot," he inadvertently yelled. Sure enough, the hanging clips had broken and most of the exhaust system was dangling precariously from one remaining anchor. He realized duct tape would not fix this one.

There was a lot of responsibility in this journey and it weighed heavily on Moose. People around White Earth joked that Moose must have been Mole Clan on account of his uncanny knack at finding things in the ground. The only problem was that there wasn't a Mole Clan on White Earth, and so his Marten Clan tendencies would have to account. Moose had discovered the grave diggings in the first place. Then, with Elaine and Danielle Wabun's help, they had come up with an amazing inventory of the people and belongings missing from the reservation through the years.

Where they were now was anybody's guess, but they bet the Smithsonian Institution, Peabody Museum at Harvard, Minnesota Historical Society, and the University of Minnesota were the first places to look. The list of missing persons and their belongings ran to fifty type-written pages comprising approximately two hundred and fifty ancestors.

With some digging of her own, Elaine traced the work of a Smithsonian researcher, one Dr. Ales Hrdlicka, who had made several "scholarly" forays to White Earth in the 1910s. He had dug up the remains of forty-five White Earth ancestors, labeled them, packed them away in wooden crates, and shipped them one thousand miles away to Washington so they could be measured, cataloged, and studied. And there they remained.

The White Earth Government, with the agreement of the *Midewiwin* Society, had drafted several polite letters to the Smithsonian. The *aanikoobijigan*, the ancestors, were to come home, the religious leaders wrote, as were all of the traditional objects of the *Anishinaabeg*, particularly those from White Earth. Finally, after years of wrangling, they succeeded in winning an agreement from the Smithsonian that the remains of some of the ancestors could be repatriated. Moose's journey was the first mission to bring back the ancestors, and it was not surprising that there were some technical difficulties.

The Smithsonian's was known to be the largest collection with more than thirty-two thousand remains in one location, not to mention a million or so "artifacts" that were held in various boxes, drawers, and warehouses at the museum. The Smithsonian's White Earth collection was a result of the physical and social anthropologists they had enthusiastically dispatched over the years.

The Peabody at Harvard had a similar number of "specimens," and over the past few years had also begun to return remains and objects to Indian tribes nationally, and to a lesser extent, internationally. The Maoris and Tasmanians had been picked over particularly badly, and they had waged an aggressive campaign for the return of their objects that had been underway for almost twenty-five years.

Smaller public collections at state historical societies and universities were also under pressure, and both the Minnesota Historical Society and the University of Minnesota had joined with the various reservations to form local historical societies and museums so they had somewhere to return artifacts.

The curator at the Smithsonian had been courteous, even helpful. The Smithsonian, it seemed, had become a repository for all bastions of colonial and military expansion. In an era when collecting the heads of Indian men was a common practice of the military and anthropologists, the Smithsonian, over the years, had received the booty of ornithologists, generals, and anthropologists—men who literally lifted the human remains off burial scaffolds to send east for scientific journals and presentations.

From Denver, Alanis Nordstrom, with her penchant for research, had volunteered to painstakingly review the anthropologists' and Indian agents' records for White Earth and, after a few trips to Washington with more of her ubiquitous frequent flyer coupons, had matched to the best of her ability people, documents, and sacred items. Under a new law, funerary objects, human remains, and objects of cultural patrimony were required to be made available to their people.

Moose and George Agawaateshkan took the trip to Washington. The Great White Father's closets were full. The Smithsonian's Office of Repatriation had twenty full-time staff members, all busy trying to sort out whose femur belonged with whose skull and where they might have come from. It was a complex task in the face of tens of thousands of cases.

Moose and George followed the lanky Smithsonian anthropologist through the maze of rooms in the immense building, the doors clanging shut in one airtight and fireproof section after another. The man with a clipboard led them on and on, through the rooms, while the air seemed increasingly more precious and less available. Thousands of green boxes lined shelves built from floor to ceiling and contained bones, birds squished behind glass, reptiles, insects, and dinosaur parts. Moose and George walked through rooms where ancestors languished in small boxes the size and length of a femur, the largest bone in a human skeleton.

At first it was a hum, somewhere in the back of Moose's mind. Slowly, death chants, lullabies, love songs, and war songs became a composite of music, chants in his mind and ears, as their voices crescendoed. An immense graveyard of the unwilling dead, out of order. He broke into a cold sweat, beads dribbled down his face and back, as he followed the anthropologist and George Agawaateshkan through the vault.

George was singleminded and hummed a song to himself, and in that way he kept the music of the others at bay. Moose's eyes scanned the names written on the boxes: Inuit, Kiowa, Pawnee, Oklahoma, New Mexico, Florida, Florida, Florida. George, however, stared straight ahead, until the anthropologist stopped. The boxes read "Minnesota, White Earth Ojibwe." The Smithsonian man looked at his clipboard and flipped through the inventory list, running his fingers over the numbers in the aisle. George and Moose watched quietly.

"These are all of them," the anthropologist finally announced. "You can look them over if you want, and we'll bring them out for you tomorrow."

George nodded. *"Miigwech,"* he whispered, "thank you."

"I'll leave you now," the anthropologist said, looking at his watch. "Should I come back in an hour?"

"OK. Good."

It was in this vast warehouse of the collected remains of people from around the world that George Agawaateshkan, with shaking voice and trembling hands, made an initial inventory of the White Earth ancestors and those contents of their graves the Smithsonian would return to them. Moose gently moved the bones as George carefully placed medicine bags, clan markers, moccasins, and other articles of clothing in with the old people. Then George wrote it down as best as he could in his notebook, listing from what village or site the bones had originated, names if possible, and any other notes.

The men worked a full two days with the forty-five ancestors, and when they were done, they placed each femur-sized green box into a larger box for shipping. Finished, they went to a local Piscataway native man's sweat lodge, cried tears that were lost amid their sweat, and prayed to get the smell of death off their bodies before they headed home. Moose was designated to drive the ancestors home.

George flew back to attend to lengthy preparations at home. He was to arrange for a reburial ceremony as well as to determine what articles might go into the White Earth museum.

The museum was located in the old St. Benedict's Mission in the community college complex. The museum housed memorabilia from White Earth history, some ceremonial objects, copies of birchbark scrolls, and other aspects of the cultural traditions of the White Earth *Anishinaabeg*. Most of the religious objects, however, had been removed from the exhibits and were either in use or in "safekeeping" with various families. The pipes had previously been displayed in the museum in the border town of Detroit Lakes. Now all the pipes that belonged on White Earth were back in the correct place, and as best as people were able, were presently in use in the different ceremonies in the villages.

The same was true of the *Midewiwin* water drums and the big drums, both of which were in use in the villages and not on display or stored away in a backroom in the museum. Most of these drums had been stored for fifty or so odd years since the day they were taken by the priests or Indian agents. In later times, museum curators might have preserved the drums for observation, but not for use. The drums were now repaired by each of the families in charge of the twelve drums returned to White Earth.

The White Earth museum now played a different role: The displays and collections chronicled popular culture. For instance, the museum displayed the old fur press that the Northwest Company had used in trading with the Indians almost a century ago. The press had compressed furs so the trader could cheat Indians.

Also on display were the black hats and some gambling sticks from an old moccasin game at White Earth.

The museum had a beaded outfit worn by Bugonaygeeshig when he traveled with a delegation of White Earth chiefs to Washington to negotiate for better treatment. Bugonaygeeshig's outfit was on display alongside Selam Big Bear's ribbon shirt and blue jeans, which he had worn to Washington to testify against the taking of the land in the White Earth Settlement Act in the 1980s, almost one hundred years later. The truth was, it was easier to get the ornately beaded outfit of the old headman than it was to get those jeans and the shirt. Moose had persuaded Selam's wife, Georgette, to make Selam a new, even fancier ribbon shirt, and the museum budgeted for a new pair of Levis to replace the old ones.

There was also a display of shoes, illustrating traditional shoes and social shoes from different generations. When Georgette had suggested this to the White Earth Historical Society, people had laughed and said she had a "foot fetish." But after they saw the collection, everyone admitted that it was pretty damn interesting, all the kinds of shoes Indians had worn in one hundred and fifty years or so. Those were the kinds of things the Indians wanted in their own museum, and they were not necessarily the kind of things the white people liked to look at. These things made the people of White Earth feel a part of their history, not as though their *aanikoobijiganag* were "objects" to look at and "things" to take apart.

So George Agawaateshkan had flown home, leaving Moose with the responsibility of bringing the ancestors home. Moose had meticulously prepared his old UPS van for this trip. The van was fitted with shelves that were ideal to carry the ancestors. He had wrapped the wooden boxes in wool blankets and then strapped them onto the shelves so they were safe and secure. He slept in the cab when he stopped; he wasn't going to leave the ancestors on their own now. On one hand, he had to make sure that nothing else happened to them. On the other hand, it was out of respect for them. Someday, when he himself walked down the pathway of the souls and met with the ancestors again, he wanted to at least be able to say that he tried to make their long journey home comfortable.

Moose took another puff on his cigarette and then focused his mind on repairing the van. His tool set was onboard, as his van was prone to odd noises, parts unceremoniously left behind on the road, and breakdowns. But what he needed now was a long piece of strong wire to rig up an exhaust system repair. He checked behind the seat of the van. Nothing. He put his cigarette out and slowly started walking around the van, looking at the ground, his eyes scanning his surroundings for any bit of wire or, ideally, a clothes hanger. Again nothing; the rest area was unusually clean. He started walking toward the restrooms, figuring the garbage can might yield some useful bits in the least. As he crossed the parking lot, Moose looked up at the sound of an approaching vehicle.

As if by some mysterious radar that attracts hippies to Indians, an aging Volkswagen van pulled into the rest stop. Moose watched the van drive slowly by. It was painted brilliant purple from front bumper to tailpipe with rainbow mandalas on the side windows, American flags as curtains, *Free Leonard Peltier* and *Garcia Lives* stickers on the rear bumper alongside the Colorado license plate. Rock 'n' roll drifted out the open windows like a trail of marijuana smoke. Moose observed the entrance of the Deadhead out of the corner of his eye as he began to dig through a garbage can. The van stopped, and Moose continued to scavenge, now acutely aware of being observed. He shrugged and picked up a stick to aid his search through the garbage. No hanger. He turned his back on the van and went to check the men's room. Nothing. With one eye on the van, he gingerly opened the door to the women's room and checked inside. No luck.

Moose exited the women's room and began walking slowly back toward his van just as a big hairy guy with a paunch covered by a tie-dyed T-shirt stepped out of the van. His reddish hair stuck out in all directions, absent of any wind. The man stretched his arms and wiggled his hips slightly to loosen up, most of his body continuing to move in several directions simultaneously even when he was standing still. His arms still outstretched, he looked to be poised for flight. Moose cringed and stopped in his tracks, still weighing the limits of his options.

With his radar lock on, the Deadhead moved toward Moose with a familiarity only Deadheads have for complete strangers. "How's it going, bro?" the Deadhead hailed him.

Moose winced and calculated quickly in his mind just how badly he needed that coat hanger. Besides, this guy did not look like someone who had hung up his clothes in quite a spell.

"Well," Moose said, "my tailpipe is falling off but besides that, I'm OK."

"Hmmm. . . . Where you from?" The Deadhead was obviously less concerned about the present than the overall story.

"White Earth," Moose said. "Minnesota."

"Long way from home, eh?"

"Yup."

A pause.

"That'd be Ojibwe, right?"

"Yup." Moose was feeling cheap with his information.

Another pause as the Deadhead looked over Moose's ailing van from afar. Moose popped the question:

"You wouldn't happen to have any wire, like, say a coat hanger, would you?" He was both hopeful and skeptical.

"Let me take a look," the man offered. "By the way, my name's Mike," he said, offering a soul-brother's handshake to Moose.

"Moose," Moose said.

Mike dug into his van with a vigor that belied his paunchy build. He seemed hopeful that he could help an Indian. Tie-dyed clothes were thrown in all directions and boxes of cassettes were dumped out. Finally, Mike blurted out from the depths of his van, "Hey, I've got it!" With a hard pull, a length of speaker wire came free in his hands. Mike appeared out the door, pregnant with the pleasure that he was valuable to his Indian brother.

"But your tunes . . ." Moose began.

"Worry not, bro. I've got six speakers set up in my van. I can live with only five."

Moose smiled and thanked him, turning now to the task of fixing his exhaust system. He walked back to his van with Mike following hopefully behind, wishing for a small morsel of Moose's affections. Moose laid down on the pavement and worked himself under his van to survey the damage. The scent of patchouli oil told him Mike had joined him under the vehicle.

"What you got in the van, buddy?" Mike said as they worked side by side to lift the exhaust pipes back into place. "If you don't mind my asking, that is."

Moose had anticipated this question and now weighed his answers. Potatoes or bones were his two choices. He sensed Mike's earnestness and gave in.

"Bones," Moose said, grunting as he wrapped the speaker wire around a muffler.

Mike's face lit up, privy to new information.

"How's that?" he asked.

"The bones of our ancestors," Moose explained.

"Wow!" the Deadhead responded. "Where did you get them?"

"We're going home from Washington. They were at a museum out there, and we want them back." Moose generously offered the information to his ally.

Just then, another car pulled into the rest area and parked close to Moose's van—too close. A door opened and shut. Moose and Mike could hear the sound of footsteps on the pavement coming closer. They looked out from under the van to see two black, shiny boots.

"Uh oh," Mike said.

Moose held his breath.

The boots bent as their owner leaned down. Moose and Mike looked upside-down into the face of a highway patrolman. They could see themselves reflected in his mirror sunglasses, two grime-covered men on their backs with uncomfortable looks on their faces.

"What's going on here, boys?" said the patrolman in that expressionless drawl officers of the law have perfected.

Moose looked over at Mike, and Mike looked back at Moose. "I'll explain," Mike whispered to Moose, and then repeated it louder to the patrolman as he lumbered out from underneath the van.

Moose could hear them talking but could not understand anything they said from his listening post. Presently he heard the trunk of the patrol car open and then shut. *The cop's arrested him and thrown him in the trunk*, Moose worried to himself, concerned for a moment, wondering if he should intervene for his new ally.

Suddenly there was the high-pitched sound of squeaky wheels, and the next thing Moose knew, the patrolman was next to him under the van, with Mike sliding in on the other side. The officer had removed his hat and sunglasses and in his gloved hands he now carried pliers and a wirecutter. He was laying on a mechanic's dolly that he must have retrieved from the trunk.

"I've been reading up on this whole issue of repatriation," the patrolman said. "Let me see if I can lend a hand here."

As Mike held the exhaust pipe aloft, the officer ran the speaker wire around it and over part of the chassis frame. Moose felt like a fifth wheel.

"Got any duct tape?" the patrolman asked.

"Yeah, sure," Moose said, somewhat confused at how he had been so quickly marginalized. He dragged himself out from under the van.

As he retrieved the duct tape from his toolbox, a fake-wood-sided station wagon with Pennsylvania license plates pulled into the rest area and parked on the other side of the van. All five doors swung open at once and a man, woman, four children, and a golden retriever came spilling out. The man stretched, the woman yawned, and the children and dogs raced for the restrooms.

"Howdy," the man said in his best frontier accent when he saw Moose. He looked around at Moose's van, the highway patrol car, and the brilliant purple VW van. "What's all the excitement about?"

"Well, my van's exhaust broke, and we're fixing it . . ." Moose began, only to be interrupted by the patrolman who was suddenly standing beside him, wiping his sweating forehead with the back of one his gloves.

"He's carrying an important load," the officer authoritatively told the family. "He's bringing back remains of his ancestors to be reburied."

The man and woman looked surprised, then the woman asked Moose, "They're probably from the Smithsonian, I'll bet?" The man looked questioningly at his wife as she explained, "I heard all about this on public radio."

Moose looked at them both quizzically, "Yeah, they are."

"Is there anything we can do to help?" the man offered.

"No, sir," the officer said. "We're just finishing it up. Exhaust system's as good as some wire and duct tape can make it."

They all stood for a moment not knowing what to say next. Then the woman chimed in: "Well, have you all eaten?" She pulled a wicker picnic basket from the back of the station wagon and began handing out sandwiches primly wrapped in waxed paper. "That one's tunafish," she told Moose as she thrust the sandwich into his hands. He wanted to tell her he was not hungry, but he suddenly realized he had not eaten all morning.

Before Moose knew what had happened, he was sitting at a picnic bench with a red-checked tablecloth eating sandwiches with Mike the Deadhead, the patrolman, and the Walker family from Harrisburg, Pennsylvania, who were on their way to see the Grand Canyon. The officer and Mrs. Walker were discussing repatriation while Mike ate tunafish sandwiches with glee. The Walker children had just returned from under the van where they were inspecting the repairs. Exhaust grime now accompanied the Kool-Aid mustaches on their faces.

290 The Winona LaDuke Reader

"Well," Moose finally said. "I need to get going."

"Yes, you better," said the patrolman, nodding.

"*Miigwech* to you all," Moose said.

The whole picnic table responded with a chorus of *miigwech*, and Mike told Moose to look him up if he was ever in Colorado.

The big Indian extended his hand and walked toward his van. He jumped into the driver's seat and started it up. Everything sounded good. He looked into his sideview mirror to see the people at the picnic table waving to him, and he stuck his hand out the window in return. He wheeled the van out onto the turnpike and north toward Champaign to take the ancestors home through Wisconsin. *That should be some smooth traveling,* he said to himself. *Besides, that's Ojibwe country so the old people will like that.*

Once he was out on the road and up to speed, it seemed to Moose as though he heard a lot of noise from the back of the van again. Noise, and even some singing. This time he realized that the new rattles were the old people, not the van. Once again, the ancestors were loud and getting louder.

That was why he decided to move his tape player into the back of the van. Moose had a good boombox cassette player and an excellent collection of music. On this trip he had tossed aside most of his country western and rock music and opted for his more traditional collection. This seemed to work out just fine with the old people.

He played grass dance songs part of the way back, and then started in with some special tapes he had made of "traveling songs" from Big Drum ceremonies. That's what he put in now, a nice tape of traveling songs from Leech Lake. *That should keep those old people happy,* he thought as he turned up the tape player in the back of the van. Then he shifted into high gear and headed home.

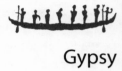

Gypsy

From THE CLOUDS THREW THIS LIGHT,
edited by Phillip Foss, 1983.

Gypsy children
stand on a cold streetcorner
selling flowers
for
American Indian Children

I laugh
buy a flower
stolen from the
Waldorf-Astoria
Which reservation are you from?

The White Flower reservation
in California
or
Oklahoma, was it?

Gypsy children
disappear

Tinker families
chased town to town
camp next to
toxic dumps

Tinker Children
play in terror
chased by
Irish boys

Tinker children
disappear

A circle of
Minnie-Winnie
Winnebago Motor Homes

Disappear

Gypsy man smiles at me
New York subway
New York people

disappear
disappear.

Takelma

From THE CLOUDS THREW THIS LIGHT, *edited by Phillip Foss,*
1983.

Josh's feet were so worked that
each toe fought separately
The soles were a fortress,
treaded with
the stuff they make callouses of.

We ambled over boulders, brush, and
the lava remains of Mt. Mazama,
As I gingerly missed thorns and spikes
you ran ahead undaunted.

With your freckled pale face, and
expanding haircut
my dark skin and knotty hair
we lived an unrestricted freedom.

At my parents wedding
we screamed in delight
at
the manicured lawn and sidewalk
while
our bows and arrows were flying.

Returning to the mountain,
we rolled naked in the mud,
and in our nakedness
expertly ambushed your parents visitors.

You wiped the blackberries off your face
but I never got the mud off my feet.

I flew between cultures as fast
as the jeep moved,
But you stayed on the mountain,
till they made you come down.

The militaresque school threw you between
padlock, locker, and hallway
time, bells, and buses—
Sargenti would have shot you if he could,
but he did better.

Slowly, slowly, he eroded your mind,
and in the confusion of
time, bells, and padlocks of a few months,
you ended up behind bars.

I kept going to the mountain,
but somehow
you were kept wandering behind
bars, halls, and locks.

And now,
I sleep 3000 miles away
between two cultures
and at an Institute of Technology

You too sleep away
in two places in your mind
and
at the state mental institution.

How are your feet now, my brother?
I will tend to my feeble callouses
until
those cushioned hospital slippers
are
cut away
and your rebellious toes move
undaunted.

Song for Moab, Utah

From BLOOD OF THE LAND, *by Rex Weyler, 1982.*

In the beginning, the Earth Mother was alone
Longing for company
She invited friends

The Ant people
carefully worked their way through her hair
Softly touching her skin
They loved her with each gift
each moment

The ant people too
were in want of company,
metakwease—relations
The people were invited to the surface
the skin of the earth.

Quiet people,
they asked the Earth Mother for water
Never taking, only gathering
They prayed for food
Never taking, only gathering
They prayed for life
Never taking, only gathering
They cared for Eachother.

The Earth
the ants
the people
And the Creation grew.
Their marks on the earth
dissipated over the generations of
wind, rain, and power.
Their baskets and sacred pottery
remained
A legacy for remembering.

This was the beginning of our eternity
only the beginning
They were the Anasazi, the old ones
The ancestors.

The Diné came to live on this sacred place
here in this place
here in this place
Living carefully, they gathered,
they prayed.

The Spaniards only sought
the riches of the land
Not to possess it for eternity
Only to possess the riches
These they took
and they left
left their cross
burned into the Earth
burned into the skins
of the
Diné, Keresan, Tewa.

They left their fathers and brothers
to continue collecting
the Booty of the land.

The Spaniards were soon sent home
twice
Once by the red
and then by the white.
The Mericanos won,
they said
and they were called
"the Mericanos."

In the new alchemy
the Mericanos found uses for
the black golds—coals and oils.

The people told to starve or move
to work
or starve
became the oil workers.

Standard Oil
killed their food—livestock, sheep and
green relatives—*metakwease*
killed their coworkers at
Ludlow
very close to them
and brought them wage work.

It was called the capitalist system
but this system was
for some
and not
for others.

In the 1940s a new sort of
capitalism
came to the Diné
came to the Land.

They were sent to Moab, Utah
an internment center
a "Jap Camp"
a relocation center
for Japanese
non-patriotic Japanese Americans
that is.

On the reservation
in old Bureau of Indian Affairs buildings
the Japanese people were
confined
in isolation
isolation centers.
And together they
lived in
those isolation centers
like a special flower—
yellow surrounded by red
all
carefully monitored by
those federales.

And all the while
those Indians (as they were called)
were sent over
to fight those
wars
against those people
thousands of

those Indians
fighting
those Japs
over there.

Then in what they called
the Final Ceremony
the Black Magicians
came together
in their new religion they
brought atoms out of
those sacred rocks
prayer rocks of the
Diné, Keresan, and Tewa people.
Those sacred rocks
who they said
boiled up the slaughter
of those Japs
those people
who lived elsewhere
but who also
lived here.

And it was still Moab, Utah
when those Mericanos
with all that power—
who had allowed those
gentle farmers and ranchers
the Mormons
to settle like
their special story said—
did that to them.

The Mericano Defense Department
dropped their bombs
made of that sacred Earth
on those people
near Moab.

And the Earth screamed
and the wind screamed
and the people of the
creation
lived with those radiation poisons
and screamed
in the night.

Moab,
that place with all those
uranium mines, uranium mills
That nuclear fallout
those voices in the wind
the voices of the Japanese
interred forever
embalmed in those mesas
the voices of the wageworkers of
the new alchemy
making their fast money
in the night.

The old people
and the shadows of
the Anasazi
who will not go away
who will remain
who cry in the night
those sacred songs
in the night.

Only the ants remain
to tell all the stories
they stay
never changing their paths
never changing their houses
never changing their lives
never changing their prayers.

And the Earth never moved
offended, pained
She was still in need of
company and prayers.

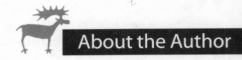

About the Author

About the Author

Winona LaDuke is an internationally respected Native American and environmental activist. She began speaking about these issues at an early age, addressing the United Nations at age eighteen, and continues to devote herself to Native and environmental concerns, as well as political and women's issues.

The Harvard-educated activist is the founding director of the White Earth Land Recovery Project, the co-chair of the Indigenous Women's Network, and the program director of Honor the Earth. In 1994, *Time* magazine called her one of America's fifty most promising leaders under forty years of age, and in 1997, she was named a *Ms.* magazine Woman of the Year.

In addition to numerous articles, LaDuke is the author of the novel *Last Standing Woman* (Voyageur Press, 1997) and the non-fiction work *All Our Relations* (South End Press, 1999). She also served as Ralph Nader's vice-presidential candidate on the Green Party ticket in the 1996 and 2000 presidential elections.

An enrolled member of the Mississippi band of Anishinaabe, LaDuke lives with her family on the White Earth Reservation in northern Minnesota.

Ralph Nader is a consumer advocate, lawyer, and author. He is the founder of numerous public interest groups including Citizen Works, Public Citizen, the Public Interest Research Groups (PIRGs), the Project for Corporate Responsibility, and the Center for Study of Responsive Law. Nader also served as the Green Party presidential candidate in 1996 and 2000.